THE DEAD SEA SCROLLS:
Rule of the Community

Photographic Multi-Language Edition

THE DEAD SEA SCROLLS:
Rule of the Community

Photographic Multi-Language Edition

Edited by
JAMES H. CHARLESWORTH

with
HENRY W. L. RIETZ

assisted by
MICHAEL T. DAVIS AND BRENT A. STRAWN

In cooperation with the Israel Museum, Jerusalem,
the Shrine of the Book, and
the D. Samuel and Jeane H. Gottesman
Center for Biblical Manuscripts

Published by
AMERICAN INTERFAITH INSTITUTE/WORLD ALLIANCE
IRVIN J. BOROWSKY, CHAIRMAN
Philadelphia

AMERICAN INTERFAITH INSTITUTE/WORLD ALLIANCE
321 Chestnut Street
Philadelphia, PA 19106-2779

THE CONTINUUM PUBLISHING COMPANY
370 Lexington Avenue
New York, NY 10017

This transcription and English translation in this work is based on the critical edition of the *Rule of the Community* published by J.C.B. Mohr (Paul Siebeck) and Westminster John Knox Press in 1994. That work contains the texts and translations of not only 1QS but also of all the texts of this Qumran document found in Caves IV and V. The present volume appears with the permission of J.C.B. Mohr (Paul Siebeck) in Tübingen, Germany.

Library of Congress
Catalog Card Number 95-83546
ISBN 0-8264-0911-3

Printed and Bound in the United States of America

The publishers appreciate the cordial cooperation of the Israel Museum and the Shrine of the Book and the permission to publish the photographs of 1QS taken from *The Dead Sea Scrolls* published by Kodansha, Ltd., Tokyo.

CONTENTS

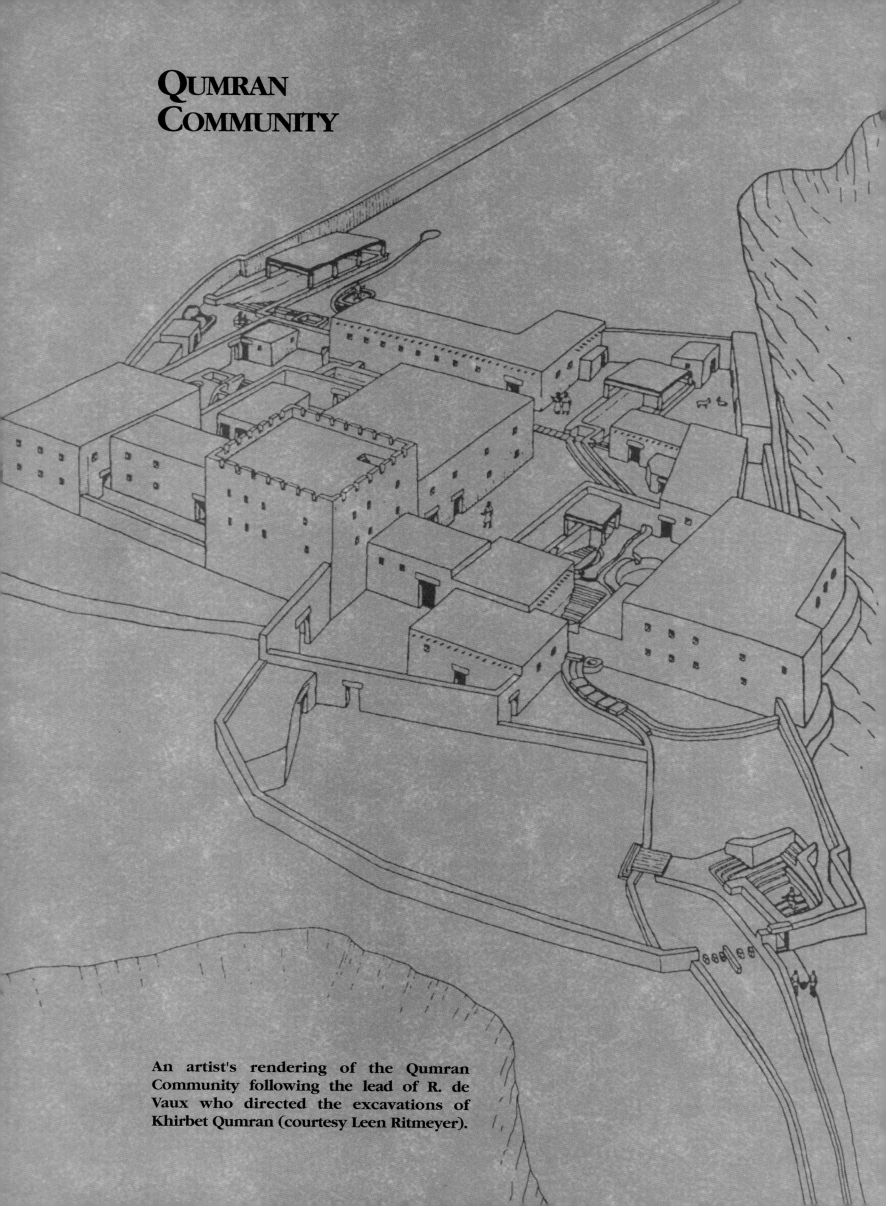

QUMRAN COMMUNITY

An artist's rendering of the Qumran Community following the lead of R. de Vaux who directed the excavations of Khirbet Qumran (courtesy Leen Ritmeyer).

PREFACE

The American Interfaith Institute is pleased to publish one of the most significant of the Dead Sea Scrolls, the *Rule of the Community*.

Since the discovery of these valuable documents, scholars have recognized the profound effect of the Scrolls on understanding Jewish and Christian origins. The Scrolls provide, for the first time, a direct window into the literary, religious, social and cultural milieu of the formative period that preceded and helped shape early Rabbinic Judaism and Christianity. The texts illuminate a world of religious experiences and ideas that influenced Hillel, Jesus, Gamaliel and other profound thinkers of the first century. Consequently, much can be learned of the common background of Christianity and Rabbinic Judaism through careful study of this precious library.

The Scrolls do not undermine Christian faith nor do they disparage some aspects of Jewish beliefs, despite outrageous claims popularized in the media. As a result of the Scrolls' discovery, even the most insulated readers now realize that the study of Early Christianity is linked to the study of Early Judaism. Like twins, both were struggling with similar issues as they began to mature.

The American Interfaith Institute organizes both scholarly studies and practical, educational initiatives within a framework of symposia, publishing and the distribution of teaching materials. With the publication of this important volume, the Institute continues to focus on the core elements that provide scholars and interested laypeople with historical research for reflection and perception. Clearly, an accurate reconstruction of our shared history will help dispel the illusion that Jews and Christians are alien to one another.

The *Rule of the Community* is published in cooperation with the Israel Museum and the Shrine of the Book, incorporating state of the art photography and transcription of the original Hebrew text. To make the Scroll more accessible to the world community, Institute scholars have prepared translations in English, German, Spanish, French and Italian, along with modern Hebrew.

Clearly, a deeper understanding of the Qumran Community and the Dead Sea Scrolls will help us identify and acknowledge our common origins as Jews and Christians.

IRVIN J. BOROWSKY, *FOUNDER / CHAIRMAN*
American Interfaith Institute
World Alliance of Interfaith Organizations

Scriptorium in which the *Rule of the Community* was probably composed and copied. Ink wells and a table were found on the floor of this room.

Introduction
and History

Qumran Cave I

(The first cave discovered in which Qumranite Jews concealed their library before the conquest by Roman soldiers in 68 C.E.)

In this cave a copy of the document known as the *Rule of the Community* was hidden by the Qumran Essenes before their Community was burned by Roman soldiers in the spring of 68 C.E. The document, along with other scrolls, lay hidden until an Arab shepherd boy found the cave and the scrolls in the late winter of 1947. The hole at the top right is the opening through which the Arab shepherd threw the stone, which careened off earthen jars. The lower holes were made in this century by Arabs and finally archaeologists who found fragments of scrolls in the debris.

What are the Dead Sea Scrolls?

The Dead Sea Scrolls come to us from an ancient Jewish library that contained hundreds of documents. These documents predate 68 C.E. when the Romans conquered the area in and around Jericho. The owners of these scrolls, the Qumranites, were all Jews. Most of them were of priestly descent. Many died at the hands of Roman soldiers or fled in numerous directions, perhaps southward towards Masada or westward towards Jerusalem. The Romans burned the buildings in which some of the Dead Sea Scrolls had been written and read. These ruins have now been excavated and lie exposed for scholars and interested persons to visit. Within this ancient Jewish library were found copies of every book in the Hebrew Bible (the so-called "*Old Testament*"), with the possible exception of *Esther*, some of the writings known as the Apocrypha and Pseudepigrapha of the Old Testament, and — most importantly — numerous documents previously unknown. These new treasures of once lost ancient writings include collections of rules which sometimes discuss the origin of evil, psalms and even hymnbooks, commentaries on sacred scriptures, scripturally inspired compositions, and other related works.

Cumulatively the Dead Sea Scrolls, especially the previously unknown compositions, have revolutionized our understanding of Judaism before the destruction of the Temple in 70 C.E. They have also revealed not only pellucidly but also palpably that *Christianity began as a sect within Judaism.*

When were the Scrolls found and who discovered them in the caves?

In late 1946 or early 1947 during the last months of the British Mandate in Palestine, three cousins who were Taʿâmireh Bedouin were leading their flocks of sheep and goats on a plateau just west of the Dead Sea. One of them, Jumʿa Muhammed Khalil, found a cave in the side of a rocky, gently sloping cliff to the west of the plateau. Ostensibly he threw a rock through a small opening in the cave, and heard it clatter off what sounded to him like large earthen jars. A few days later, early in the morning while the others slept, Muhammed Ahmed el-Hamed — it is rumored — slipped away from his cousins. He climbed the cliff, raised himself up to the cave opening and, because he was smaller than the others, slipped through the narrow hole.

According to this Bedouin, who is also called ed-Dîb ("the wolf"), he spied ten large earthen jars. None contained immediately recognizable treasures, like gold, silver, or precious gems. He contended that only one jar preserved something interesting: cloth bundles and a leather roll. Eventually these unperceived treasures were transported to a place near Bethlehem. Allegedly, some hung for weeks in a bag attached to a tent pole.

The discoveries subsequently wound up in Bethlehem in a cobbler's shop in the vicinity of Manger Square. The cobbler, Kando (Khalil Eskander Shahin), won the confidence of the Bedouin. He promised he would give them the major portion (two thirds) of the profits from the sale of these old leather scrolls.

The contents of these foul-smelling lumps eventually, after much debate, were identified. They are now called the *Rule of the Community* (1QS), the *Habakkuk Pesher* (or Commentary; 1QpHab) the *Genesis Apocryphon* (1QapGen), and a copy of the book of *Isaiah* (1QIsaᵃ). The first three scrolls preserved documents that were completely unknown to scholars; not one of

Qumran Cave I from inside.

Inside Cave I, looking through the small opening through which the Arab shepherd threw a stone, which hit earthen jars left by the Qumran Essenes two thousand years ago. He — Jum'a Muhammed Khalil of the Ta'âmireh tribe of Bedouin — apparently thought the cave was inhabited by jinn, desert demons; hence he fled, according to his own story. Later Muhammed ed-Dîb returned and crawled through the tiny opening. He found leather scrolls hidden in clay jars. These were the first of the Dead Sea Scrolls discovered. Probably some scrolls, or at least fragments of them, were lost by the clandestined digging by the Bedouins.

them was mentioned in the history of literature and none was quoted by the scholars of the Early Church or by the rabbinic sages. The scroll of *Isaiah* is also invaluable; it is over a thousand years older than the manuscripts that were used to establish the critical text of the Hebrew Bible, the so-called "*Old Testament.*" The first scholars to examine it were astounded to discover that its text is virtually identical to the earliest medieval Hebrew copies of *Isaiah*.

Through avenues of intrigue and danger, Kando and a Syrian Orthodox Christian attempted to have the scrolls appraised and sell them. The four scrolls were eventually acquired by the latter, Archbishop Athanasius Yeshue Samuel, who was the Syrian Orthodox Metropolitan of Saint Mark's Monastery in the Old City of Jerusalem (see his *Treasure of Qumran*).

While this sale was taking place, three more scrolls were brought to Kando. They also had been found in Cave I, but had been buried beneath nearly two thousand years of collapsed ceiling, rock, desert sand, and accumulated waste. These additional scrolls were eventually obtained by the famous scholar Eliezer L. Sukenik of the Hebrew University. These are the *War Scroll* (1QM), the *Thanksgiving Hymns* (1QH), and another copy of *Isaiah* (1QIsaᵇ). In his diary Sukenik mentions how he returned from Bethlehem, which in 1947 was in "Arab territory," to Jerusalem with these scrolls tucked inconspicuously under his arm "like a bundle of market produce." Around midnight, his preoccupation with these ancient leather scrolls was interrupted when his son, Mati, ran into his study with the news that the United Nations had just voted to give the Jews a homeland (see Y. Yadin with J. H. Charlesworth, *The Message of the Scrolls*).

Professor Sukenik recorded in his diary that he saw "the other scrolls" — that is the four large scrolls— "towards the end of January 1948." He reported that he studied these scrolls in his office and then returned them, arranging for a meeting "the following week." Because the war of 1948 canceled any possible meetings, and because Sukenik died in 1953, he never saw the scrolls again. He feared that "the Jewish people have lost a precious heritage." In a turn of events as intriguing as a mystery novel, his son, Yigael Yadin, bought these scrolls in 1954 from Archbishop Samuel, who had brought them to the United States and offered them for sale through an advertisement in *The Wall Street Journal* (see Yadin's comments in *The Message of the Scrolls*).

The seven scrolls witness both to an ancient tale and a modern story. These scrolls (or portions of them) are now on public display (sometimes in facsimiles) in the Shrine of the Book in Jerusalem.

Did the shepherds find the remains of a Jewish library?

Certainly. The scrolls found in the eleven caves near Qumran can be organized into five major categories:

1. **Biblical Texts**. Fragments of every document in the Hebrew Bible (the so-called "*Old Testament*") with the possible exception of *Esther* have been found among the scrolls.

2. **Texts of the Old Testament Apocrypha and Pseudepigraha**. These discoveries include fragments of *Tobit,* the *Letter of Jeremiah,* additions to *Daniel, Susannah, Jubilees,* the *Books of Enoch* (*1 Enoch*), and perhaps the earliest versions of the *Testaments of the Twelve Patriarchs.* These works were not composed at Qumran; but the last three are closely related to Qumran terms and ideas.

Qumran Cave I from inside.

The *Rule of the Community* was hidden along with six other ancient leather scrolls in this cave. This cave, on the northwestern shore of the Dead Sea, the lowest place on earth, was the first discovered. Eleven Qumran Caves containing manuscripts have been discovered; in these the most important document for an understanding of the life and rules of the Qumran Community is the *Rule of the Community*, which is known now from copies in Caves I, IV, and V. In all 12 copies have been found; the only full copy is that featured in this book. It dates from approximately 75 to 100 B.C.E.

3. **Qumran-Edited Documents**. These are scrolls which may have originated elsewhere, but probably received definitive editing at Qumran. Among such documents are the *Damascus Document* and the *Temple Scroll.*

4. **Non-Qumran Documents**. These scrolls probably originated elsewhere and apparently were not altered at Qumran. Among these scrolls are the *Qumran Pseudepigraphic Psalms* (4Q380 and 4Q381), the *Prayer of Joseph* (4Q371-373), and *Pseudo-Ezekiel* (4Q385-388, 391). The *Copper Scroll* (3Q15) is unique. Because it postdates 68 C. E. and is in grammatically poor Hebrew, it was probably neither known to the Qumranites nor composed by them.

5. **Scrolls Composed at Qumran**. Some documents were certainly composed at Qumran. What is most important from this ancient library for scholars trying to understand Judaism before 70 C.E.? The answer is rather easy. What is most precious from the horde are the writings that were completely unknown until the discovery of the desert caves in which the scrolls were placed or hidden. Among such writings are the following works probably composed at Qumran:

Rule of the Community (1QS, 4QS, 5QS),   *Rule of the Congregation* (1QSa),

Blessings (1QSb),   *War Scroll* (1QM, 4QM),

Thanksgiving Hymns (1QH),   *Pesharim* (esp. 1QpHab, 4QpNah, 4QpPs68,4QpIsa^{a-e}),

Angelic Liturgy (4Q400-407, 11Q17),   *Qumran Mosaic Pseudepigrapha* (1Q22, 1Q29, 4Q376)

Horoscopes (4Q186),   *Calendrical Documents* (4Q320-330),

More Precepts of the Torah (4Q394-399).

The rich diversity of these Jewish compositions is significant. It justifies describing the Dead Sea Scrolls as the remains of a Jewish library. In it were found documents composed throughout ancient Palestine, including Galilee, Jerusalem, and — of course — Qumran.

The Jewish Community of the Dead Sea Scrolls

Who wrote and hid the Dead Sea Scrolls?

The authors of all the Dead Sea Scrolls were Jews. Those who composed the sectarian documents referred to themselves as "the Sons of Zadok," "the Poor," members of "the Way," and "the Sons of Light." All others (including, especially, the priests presiding over the Jerusalem Temple cult) were considered "the Sons of Darkness." Qumranites conceived of themselves as "the Holy Ones," who lived in "the House of Holiness," because "the Holy Spirit" dwelt with them (and no longer resided in — or hovered over — the Temple). They were priests who left — or, better, were driven from — the Temple in Jerusalem. They claimed to trace their lineage back to Zadok, the high priest of Kings David and Solomon, and even to Aaron, the brother of Moses and the first Israelite priest who officiated in the Tabernacle in the wilderness.

Qumran Cave II from inside.

In Cave II about 33 biblical and non-biblical scrolls were recovered. Cave I, however, yielded fragments of at least 70 scrolls, found on the floor of the cave. Only seven "full" scrolls made their way to scholars and eventually to the Shrine of the Book in Jerusalem. They are now called the *Rule of the Community*, the *Thanksgiving Hymns*, the *Genesis Aprocryphon*, the *War Scroll*, the *Great Isaiah Scroll*, a second *Isaiah Scroll*, and the *Habakkuk Pesher*. These are virtually intact scrolls; besides Cave I only Cave XI has preserved full scrolls. In the other caves only fragments of scrolls have been recovered. Cave VIII may have once contained many scrolls, because numerous leather fasteners for them were found; but the cave collapsed many centuries ago, leaving the remains of only five scrolls.

A fragment from the floor of Cave I.

This is one of the fragments that has not yet been identified, although "going," and "Belial" (the name of Satan in the Dead Sea Scrolls) appear obvious (see the *Rule of the Community* 1.18, 1.24, 2.5, 2.19).

The members of the sect saw themselves as a faithful remnant pitted against the forces of evil and forced to endure persecution until vindicated by God. Many of their ideas, their rigorous lifestyle, and their place of habitation signal that they are similar to, if not identical with, the Essenes described by the ancient historians. Most scholars rightly conclude that the sectarians, the Qumranites, are to be identified with the Essenes described by Josephus, Pliny, and Philo.

What can be known about the history of the Community?

The Dead Sea Scrolls belonged to a Jewish religious community that lived in caves or modest dwellings in the Judaean Desert at the northwest area of the Dead Sea near a site known by the Arabic name Khirbet Qumran. The Qumranites, or the Qumran Essenes, most likely occupied the site near Qumran from the middle of the second century B.C.E. until 68 C.E., when it was destroyed by Roman soldiers. The Community was originally composed of priests who had either abandoned or were expelled from the Temple in Jerusalem. They were led by someone they called "the Righteous Teacher."

In the early decades of the first century B.C.E. more Jews apparently joined the Qumranites, because the compound was extensively expanded during this period. Some scholars think the latter may have included Pharisees or precursors of the Pharisees.

Who was the Righteous Teacher?

The Righteous Teacher was a priest, probably of Zadokite lineage. He may have once served as a high priest in the Jerusalem Temple. He led a group of priests from Jerusalem to Qumran around 150 B.C.E. Subsequently, he was persecuted by someone who is known in the scrolls as "the Wicked Priest," probably the reigning high priest in Jerusalem.

It is conceivable that the Righteous Teacher composed some portions of the *Rule of the Community*, some of the *Thanksgiving Hymns*, and possibly the legal (halakic) epistle known as *More Precepts of the Torah* (4QMMT).

The Sensational Nature of the Dead Sea Scrolls

Has the Vatican suppressed publication of the Dead Sea Scrolls because they are a threat to Christian Faith?

Absolutely not! Charges that the Dead Sea Scrolls remain unpublished because they will disprove the Christian faith are unfounded. Roman Catholics, Protestants, and Jews have been working to edit the unpublished material. Moreover, all extensive scrolls have already been published. Still awaiting publication are thousands of isolated fragments, many of which belong to previously unknown documents. The fragments are sometimes smaller than a fingernail. The task of reconstructing literary works out of these fragments that have been mixed together is tedious and painstaking; then, the reconstructed document must be comprehended, interpreted, and prepared for publication.

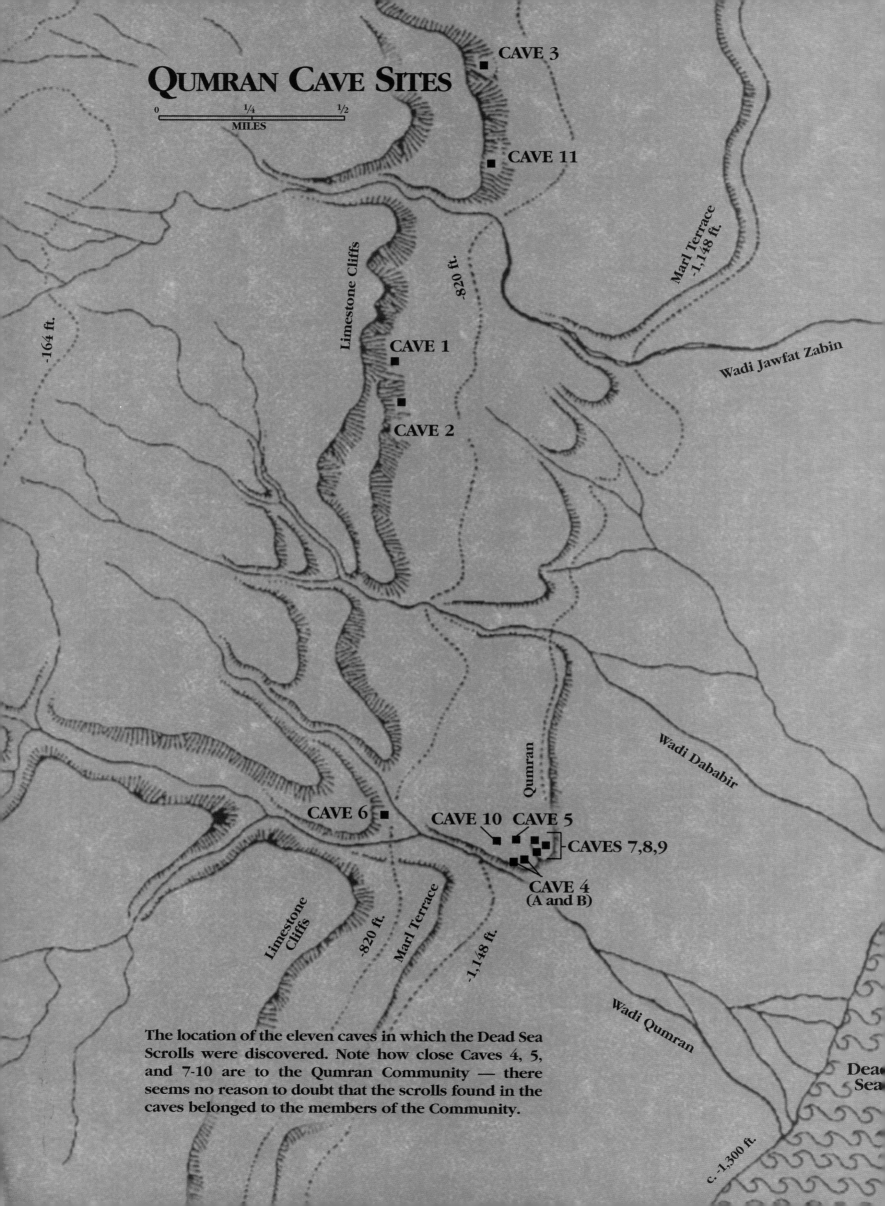

QUMRAN CAVE SITES

0   1/4   1/2
MILES

CAVE 3

CAVE 11

Marl Terrace -1,148 ft.

Wadi Jawfat Zabin

Limestone Cliffs

-820 ft.

-164 ft.

CAVE 1

CAVE 2

Qumran

Wadi Dababir

CAVE 6

CAVE 10   CAVE 5

CAVES 7,8,9

CAVE 4
(A and B)

Limestone Cliffs

-820 ft.

Marl Terrace

-1,148 ft.

Wadi Qumran

Dead Sea

c. -1,300 ft.

The location of the eleven caves in which the Dead Sea
Scrolls were discovered. Note how close Caves 4, 5,
and 7-10 are to the Qumran Community — there
seems no reason to doubt that the scrolls found in the
caves belonged to the members of the Community.

The task of preparing these fragments for publication in a coherent and responsible form is more daunting than if one were asked to assemble (at the same time) 600 jigsaw puzzles, of which many of the pieces had been mixed together, and vast numbers of sections completely lost. I have worked on some of the unpublished fragments, and none of the fragments known to me and others who work on them can be judged in any way to threaten, let alone disprove, the hallmarks of Judaism or Christianity. The proof of this claim, like the ones to which it reacts, can only be convincingly demonstrated by publishing all the fragments. And that is the purpose of the Princeton Theological Seminary Dead Sea Scrolls Project.

Are all the Dead Sea Scrolls now being prepared for publication?

Yes. In 1985 the Princeton Theological Seminary Dead Sea Scrolls Project was launched to meet the need for an improved and critical edition of all the Dead Sea Scrolls that are not simply copies of books in the Hebrew Bible. The sub-editors include Roman Catholics, Protestants, and Jews from the United States, Canada, Great Britain, Germany, and Israel. The PTS DSS Project is publishing both critical texts and English translations in ten volumes. When the volumes are opened, the Hebrew, Aramaic, or Greek will be seen on the left page, and the translation (with notes) on the right page. One-volume works in English, German, Modern Hebrew, and other languages are also presently being prepared so that those who do not have need of expensive text-translation volumes can purchase a relatively inexpensive collection.

The *Rule of the Community*, from Elisha Qimron's reading of the text in 1QS, along with all copies of this document (or compositions that evolved somehow towards it and even after it) from Caves IV and V, are published in the first volume of the PTS DSS Project.[1]

The Enduring Significance of the Dead Sea Scrolls for Jews and Christians

Are the Dead Sea Scrolls essential for understanding Early Judaism?

Obviously. The scrolls have opened scholars' eyes to the sociological and intellectual diversity within Early Judaism (Judaism before the compilation of the Mishnah around 200 C.E.).

The Qumran Covenanters were not an insignificant group of Jews living in isolation in the Judaean desert. They were a conservative wing of a large and influential group of learned men in Early Judaism. This group was probably the sect called the Essenes; it had at least two sub-groups. According to Josephus one of the groups married. Many specialists wisely concur that the *Rule of the Community* defines the life of celibate Essenes living at Qumran, and the *Damascus Document* qualifies the less strict group of Essenes living elsewhere in ancient Palestine.

[1]See J. H. Charlesworth, with F. M. Cross, J. Milgrom, E. Qimron, L. H. Schiffman, L. T. Stuckenbruck, and R. E. Whitaker, *The Dead Sea Scrolls: Hebrew, Aramaic, and Greek Texts with English Translations; The Rule of the Community and Related Documents*, Volume 1 (Tübingen: J.C.B. Mohr [Paul Siebeck] and Louisville: Westminster/ John Knox Press, 1994).

Qumran Caves, with Cave IV in the center.

Looking from the marl terrace on which the Qumran ruins are located. In Cave IV were recovered fragments of hundreds of scrolls. It was one of the major locations, in which the Qumranites stored their manuscripts. The Qumran Community was abandoned by the Qumranites in the spring of 68 when Roman soldiers, moving from Galilee to Jerusalem, destroyed sites in and around Jericho. Fortunately for us, the Qumranites never returned to recover their scrolls.

Khirbet Qumran.

A view looking eastward form a cave towards the ruins of Qumran (to the left center) and then on towards the Dead Sea.

Philo and Josephus reported that the Essenes living in Palestine numbered more than four thousand. Since less than two hundred people could congregate at Qumran at any given time, the vast majority lived elsewhere. As we learn from Philo and Josephus, the Essenes dwelt in many villages in ancient Palestine.

These scrolls, unlike many of the Jewish Pseudepigrapha, were neither transmitted nor preserved by Christians. The documents are primary Jewish sources that were never edited by Christian scribes. They provide us with invaluable first-hand information regarding a wide range of issues and topics current in Early Judaism. Most important among these are the qualifications for continuing in covenant with God (or, entering into the "new covenant" with God), the reflections on the nature of the human and the character of God, the explanations for evil in the world and the development of the light-darkness paradigm, the presence and influence of good and evil angels, the concept of the Holy Ones on earth and in heaven, the development of the concept of the Holy Spirit, the descriptions of the heavens above and the next age, the delineations of the beginning and culmination of the day (week, month, and year), calendrical and cosmological elaborations of the creation, the necessity for purification and praise, and the impossibility of earning forgiveness, which is seen as a divine gift to those who faithfully approach God. Most of these ideas and concepts are found in the previously unknown rule book (the *Rule of the Community*) and hymnbook (the *Thanksgiving Hymns*) of the Qumranites.

Have they revolutionized the perception of Christian Origins?

Indubitably. Christianity originated as one of many groups within Early Judaism. Jesus and his earliest followers were Jews. As the scrolls transform our understanding of Early Judaism, they also inform us of the religious traditions and perspectives, as well as the culture, inherited by Jesus and his earliest followers.

As Jews, Jesus and the authors of the Dead Sea Scrolls were similar in many ways. Foremost, they believed in the existence of only one God, who is loving and purifies the "poor" from their sinfulness. Both Jesus and the Essenes knew of the power of the Evil One, calling him either Satan or Belial; yet, they affirmed monotheism through the belief in one — and only one — creator (*Mark* 12:29; 1QS 3).

The Torah embodied God's will. Jesus and the Essenes endeavored to live in absolute devotion to God's will. They inherited the same guiding source for thought and deed; it was the Hebrew Scriptures (the so-called "*Old Testament*"). Jesus and the authors of the Dead Sea Scrolls also shared other, more particular similarities. Among the scriptures, Jesus and the Essenes may conceivably have had special fondness for the same books, namely, *Deuteronomy, Isaiah*, and especially the Davidic *Psalms*. These preferences may, but do not necessarily, indicate some relation between Jesus and the Essenes; nevertheless, it is interesting to ponder why Jesus and the Essenes seem to have shared a fondness for the same books of scripture.

Jesus and the Essenes followed a similar means to interpret the scriptures. They read them under the guidance of the Holy Spirit (that is, pneumatically), and affirmed that God's promises were being fulfilled in their midst. Both were "eschatologically" oriented; that is, they believed that the present belonged to the beginning of the new age (see *Mark* 9:1; 1QH 8). Apparently Jesus and the Essenes saw their actions as constituting a new covenant (*Mark* 14:24, *Matthew*

Qumran, looking eastward towards the Dead Sea.

This large room is where the Qumranites gathered for meetings of "the Many," which is the term for the full assembly. This and other terms appear in the *Rule of the Community.*

26:28, *Luke* 22:20). The Qumran Essenes stressed the importance of "the new covenant" (see esp. CD 6.19; 8.21=19.33b-34a; 20.12); to enter the Qumran Community was "to pass over into the covenant" (see esp. 1QS 1.16, 18, 20, 24; 2.10).

One of the most dramatic advances provided by the Dead Sea Scrolls concerns our understanding of the *Gospel of John*. Before the discovery of the Dead Sea Scrolls, it was conceivable that the *Gospel of John* was a late-second-century composition inspired by Greek philosophy. Near the beginning of this century New Testament specialists published books to defend this conclusion. Today, a growing scholarly consensus finds the *Gospel of John* to be a late first-century composition. More surprising still, most experts on the *Gospel of John* conclude that it is the most Jewish of the Gospels. Concepts and phrases, even specific terms, that were once seen as proof of Greek philosophical influence are now found in the Dead Sea Scrolls. These pre-70 Palestinian Jewish writings have been *a* - if not *the* - major force in this paradigmatic shift in the winds of Johannine scholarship.

The major impact of the Dead Sea Scrolls on our understanding of the *Gospel of John* relates to the conceptual world and theology reflected in the *Gospel of John*, especially the dualism that pervades it. For example, in *John* 12:35 Jesus says:

> The *light* is with you for a little longer. *Walk* while you have *the light*, lest *the darkness* overtake you; *he who walks in the darkness does not know* where he goes. [Italics highlight technical terms also found in the *Rule of the Community*].

In this verse we clearly see the dualism of light versus darkness. In the very next verse (12:36) Jesus exhorts his listeners to become "Sons of Light": "Believe in the light, that you may become Sons of Light." Many experts on Early Judaism and Christian Origins have published research that demonstrates (convincingly in my opinion) that the appearance of the technical term "Sons of Light" is almost always an indication of Essene thought or influence. The term is found almost exclusively in pre-70 Jewish writings composed by the Essenes or influenced by them. It was specifically defined and developed in the *Rule of the Community*, columns 3 and 4; this section of the document was most likely memorized by initiates who spent over two years studying and learning Essene thought so as to pass the entrance examinations. It is also now evident that the thoughts and terms in these two columns directly influenced the author of the *Gospel of John*. Some experts on the *Gospel of John* even conclude that its author was an Essene who became a Christian and lived in the Johannine Community (see J. Ashton, *Understanding the Fourth Gospel*). Let me attempt to illustrate these insights.

The dualism appearing in the *Gospel of John* was conceptualized and developed in the Dead Sea Scrolls, especially in the *Rule of the Community*.

Note the appearance of the technical term "the Sons of Light":

> The Master [*maśkîl*] shall instruct and teach all the Sons of Light... (1QS 3.13). [As in *John*, light is conceptually contrasted with darkness].

Note this striking passage which refers to the end of time:

> He created the human for the dominion of the world, and designed for him two spirits in which to walk until the appointed time for his visita-

Closed room with plastered benches on which
the members of the Council of the Community
(see 1QS 7.22-8.11) may have sat in secret and
sequestered deliberation. The Scriptorium is on
the left.

tion, namely the spirits of truth and deceit. In a spring of light emanates the nature of truth and from a well of darkness emerges the nature of deceit. In the hand of the Prince of Lights (is) the dominion of all the Sons of Righteousness; in the ways of light they walk. But in the hand of the Angel of Darkness (is) the dominion of the Sons of Deceit; and in the ways of darkness they walk (1QS 3.17-21).

In the *Rule of the Community* a cosmic dualism is developed; it is characterized by two powerful forces (both are angels). This dualism is expressed in terms of a *light-darkness paradigm*, with humans as the center of the struggle and divided into two lots: the Sons of Light or the Sons of Darkness. This dualism influenced the compositions or redactions of numerous compositions among the Dead Sea Scrolls. One is known as the *War Scroll* (1QM). This work depicts an eschatological battle between the Sons of Light and the Sons of Darkness.

In one of the most famous passages in the *Gospel of John*, we find this same dualism:

And this is the judgment, that the light has come into the world, and people loved darkness rather than the light, because their deeds were evil. For all who do evil hate the light, and do not come to the light, so that their deeds may not be exposed. But the one who does the truth comes to the light, that it may be clearly seen that his deeds have been accomplished through God (*John* 3:19-21).

Nowhere in ancient religious traditions do we find the dualism of light and darkness developed so thoroughly as in the *Rule of the Community* and the *Gospel of John*. The light-darkness imagery is also found in some other traditions (e.g., the Hermetica, Mandeanism, and Neo-Platonism), but the unique *paradigm* is found only in Essene and Johannine writings.

While virtually all scholars agree that the author of the *Gospel of John* was influenced either directly or indirectly by the Dead Sea Scrolls sect, there is no consensus on how this influence made its way into this Gospel. After thirty years of thinking on this issue, I am convinced that the most probable scenario is the following: Not all the Qumranites died in the Roman attack on their settlement in the wilderness in 68 C.E. Some were still alive when the *Gospel of John* was being written. Some of them, as is now widely acknowledged, no doubt became Christians. I am persuaded that some Essenes became Christians and lived in the Johannine Community, which is often portrayed in modern scholarship as a "School."

Do these new insights disclose a shared history and tradition between Judaism and Christianity?

Unquestionably. Scholars used to refer to the Judaism of Jesus' time as "Late Judaism" (and some still unfortunately perpetuate the term). This can be a pejorative term which indicates that Judaism was dying out. Now, thanks to new archaeological discoveries in and around Jerusalem and Galilee — and especially the recovery of the Dead Sea Scrolls — we have palpable evidence that Judaism was one of the most creative cultures prior to 70 C.E. and the destruction of the Temple by the Romans. In fact, I am convinced that the time of Hillel and Jesus — and earlier of the Righteous Teacher — was one in which insightful and symbolic theological perceptions and expressions were diverse and abundant. I have become persuaded that during the time between Alexander the Great's conquests of the area in the late fourth century B.C.E. to 70 C.E. Judaism developed into one of the most advanced ideological cultures in the history of human thought.

This Jewish world was stimulated by contacts with Persia, Syria, Greece, Rome, and Egypt. This vibrant culture enabled the rise of such poetic and religious geniuses as the Righteous Teacher, Hillel, and Jesus. The latter was thoroughly Jewish, indeed he was a very devout Jew. He ascended to Jerusalem for the required Passover pilgrimage and proclaimed that the Temple is "a house of prayer for all nations" (*Mark* 11:17). Jesus was, of course, quoting from *Isaiah* 56:7,

> For My House shall be called
> A house of prayer for all peoples.[2]

Jesus, his fellow Jews like the Righteous Teacher and Hillel, and his Jewish followers shared the same sacred traditions (the Hebrew scriptures, especially *Isaiah* and the *Psalms* [perhaps more than one of Jesus' followers also cherished some ideas preserved in the Dead Sea Scrolls and the so-called Pseudepigrapha]), the same nation, the same geographical area (ancient Palestine), and the same time period in the history of Judaism (c. 150 B.C.E. to 70 C.E.).

What is the Rule of the Community?

The *Rule of the Community* is the name of a document found in Qumran Caves I, IV, and V. It contains the rules of the Community in which many of the Dead Sea Scrolls were composed or copied. The document is a collection of rules for the celebration of the Covenant with God and for admission, promotion, demotion, and expulsion from the Community. Hence, it is one of the most important documents for ascertaining the history and theologies of this Community. It also contains a strikingly brilliant explanation for the presence of evil in the universe and within the human. Originally the Community probably consisted of priests only, and was thus exclusively for males. The rules and various sections of the *Rule of the Community* evolved during the early period of the Community, taking shape in the copy known as 1QS sometime after 100 B.C.E. (see the enclosed photographs). Thus, it is understandable why the rules sometimes tend to be contradictory and are intermittently redundant. Prospective members of the Community were examined by these rules, and most likely memorized sections of this document (esp. 3.13-4.26). The contents of the *Rule of the Community* can be divided into eight sections:

1) The Preamble (1.1-15). The *Rule of the Community* begins with an explanation of how an initiate (a Son of Light) is to enter the Community and cross

[2]TANAKH: *A New Translation of the Holy Scriptures According to the Traditional Hebrew Text* (Philadelphia: The Jewish Publication Society, 1985 [5746]).

over into God's covenant. He is to seek God totally, unreservedly, and to obey all the commandments revealed through Moses.

2) Entering the Covenant Community (1.16-2.18). This section emphasizes that when one enters the Community, by crossing over into God's covenant using the guidelines preserved in the *Rule of the Community*, he must never turn back because of the power of the Angel of Darkness (Belial) in this world and over him. The priests and Levites, shall praise God for those who enter the covenant; the latter shall curse all the men controlled by Belial.

3) Renewal Ceremony, Denunciations, Atonement (2.19-3.12). The rank order of those who celebrate the yearly renewal of the covenant shall be the priests, the Levites, and then all the people. One is cleansed from impurities by the Holy Spirit. This section stresses the rigid hierarchy in the Community.

4) Qumran's Fundamental Dualism (3.13-4.26). The author of this work, or at least one of its oldest sections (3.13-4.14), was a genius. He may have been the Righteous Teacher who founded the Community. The author informs the "Master" to teach all the Sons of Light the following: There is one God, the God of Knowledge, who is the God of Israel. The dominion of the cosmos is divided between two angels, the Angel of Light (or Prince of Lights) and the Angel of Darkness. Humanity is also bifurcated into two predestined groups: the Sons of Light and the Sons of Darkness. Evil is caused by the Angel of Darkness who controls the Sons of Darkness and even the Sons of Light, presumably through the darkness in them (see 4Q186). The Sons of Darkness will be punished and finally destroyed in the end of time, whereas the Sons of Light will receive pleasures, blessings, and everlasting life.

5) Rules for Life in the Community (5.1-6.23). This section, which is called "the rule for the men of the Community," instructs those who have separated themselves from deceit to become a Community by following the lead of the Sons of Zadok (these are descendants of Zadok, David's high priest). They shall dedicate all that they have to found a community of truth for Israel. The members of the Community are to be distinctly separate from all others, including other Jews. The men of the Community are forbidden to discuss any law or judgment with others, and must not accept anything from them "without payment." Each member of the Community is to be examined by the Sons of Aaron (the priestly descendants of Moses' brother, and probably another name for the Sons of Zadok) regarding "his insight and his works in the Torah." During a yearly evaluation members of the Community are raised or lowered in rank.

6) Rules for Punishment (6.24-7.25). This section mentions a vast number of causes for punishment of members by the leadership in the Community. The most severe punishment is banishment (for blaspheming [pronouncing God's ineffable name], slandering the Many [the full group], or undermining the authority of the Community). These rules reflect the past problems in the Community; hence, members are punished for sleeping or spitting during a meeting. Where ten men are present one must study Torah day and night. The hierarchy in this section is again rigid and yet noticeably different: first the priests, then the elders, and finally the rest of all the people. It takes at least two years to become a member of the Community, and at that time all property is given to the Community.

7) Rules for the Holy Congregation (8.1-10.8). The Council of the Community is to consist of twelve laymen and three priests. This Council is God's eternal plant, the House of Holiness consisting of Israel, and a most holy assembly for Aaron. It is to atone for the land and to decide judgment. The members of the Community have followed God's word to Isaiah; they have departed into the wilderness to prepare the Way of the Lord. Banishment from the Council of the Community will be for any one who transgresses Torah deliberately or even negligently (but not inadvertently). God's favor is obtained not through sacrifices but through the offerings of the lips (praise). The Sons of Aaron alone are in charge of judgment and property. A member of the Community must not argue with others (the men of the pit), because the meaning of Torah is to be kept secret. All members are to praise God at the rising and setting of the sun, at the beginning of months, seasons, Jubilees, and on holy days. The author explains how he will praise God with "the offering of the lips."

8) Hymn of Praise (10.9-11.22). The *Rule of the Community* ends with a hymn of praise to the glory of God. The author is joyful and full of praise for the light which has shined into his heart. He confesses his sinfulness, and praises God for his mercies, and acknowledges that God alone can and will atone for all his iniquities.

This series of publications of the Dead Sea Scrolls is intended not only to serve scholarship, it is also directed to those who are interested in Jewish traditions and writings that have been formative in the origins of Judaism and Christianity. Let us share the dream of the Righteous Teacher, Hillel, and Jesus: may God's will be done on earth as it is in heaven. Let us not only share this dream but also help to transform prejudices and perceptions so that our grandchildren will not face what our grandparents suffered. And so I end with a prayer which unites all of us who are human beings, not only Jews and Christians: "Our Father, let your name be hallowed ... may your will be done on earth."

JAMES H. CHARLESWORTH
Princeton Theological Seminary

Color Photographs of 1QS
with Transcriptions

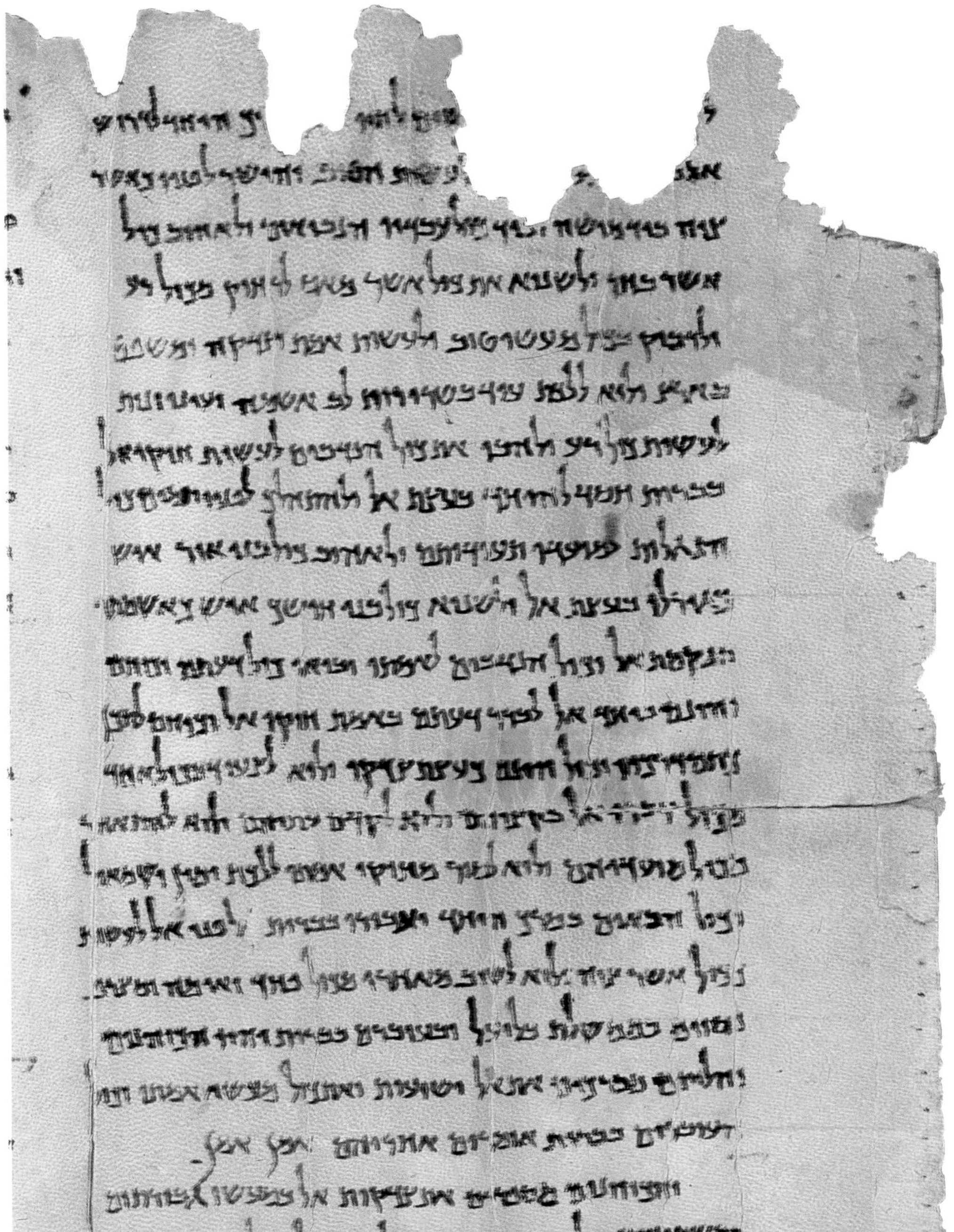

1	ל[				]שים ¹ולחיו [ספר סר]כ היחד¹ לדרוש

2	אל ב[כול לב ובכול נפש]לעשות הטוב והישר לפניו כאשר

3	צוה ביד מושה וביד כול עבדיו הנביאים ולאהוב כול

4	אשר בחר ולשנוא את כול אשר מאס לרחוק מכול רע

5	ולדבוק בכול מעשי טוב ולעשות אמת וצדקה ומשפט

6	בארץ ולוא ללכת עוד בשרירות לב אשמה ועיני זנות

7	לעשות כול רע ולהבי את כול הנדבים לעשות חוקי אל

8	בברית חסד להיחד בעצת אל ולהתהלך לפניו תמים כול

9	הנגלות למועדי תעודותם ולאהוב כול בני אור איש

10	כגורלו בעצת אל ולשנוא כול בני חושך איש כאשמתו

11	בנקמת אל וכול הנדבים לאמתו יביאו כול דעתם וכוחם

12	והונם ביחד אל לברר דעתם באמת חוקי אל וכוחם לתכן

13	כתם דרכיו וכול הונם כעצת צדקו ולוא לצעוד בכול אחד

14	מכול דברי אל בקציהם ולוא לקדם עתיהם ולוא להתאחר

15	מכול מועדיהם ולוא לסור מחוקי אמתו ללכת ימין ושמאול

16	וכול הבאים בסרכ היחד יעבורו בברית (א)לפני אל לעשות

17	ככול אשר צוה ולוא לשוב מאחרו מכול פחד ואימה ומצרף

18	נסוים בממשלת בליעל ובעוברם בברית יהיו הכוהנים

19	והלויים מברכים את אל ישועות ואת כול מעשי אמתו וכול

20	העוברים בברית אומרים אחריהם אמן אמן

21	והכוהנים			מספרים את צדקות אל במעשי גבורתום

22	ומשמיעים כול חסדי רחמים על ישראל והלויים מספרים

23	את עוונות בני ישראל וכול פשעי אשמתם וחטאתם בממשלת

24	בליעל [וכו]ל העוברים בברית מודים אחריהם לאמור נעוינו

25	[פ]שענו [חט]אנו הרשענו אנו [וא]בותינו מלפנינו ב(ה)לכתנו

26	[			] אמת וצדי[ק]ק אל ישראל ומ[שפטו שפטו בנו ובאבותי[נו]

ורפ הארץ וכל עלו... על עולה נע מעולם ועד עולם והכנודולוכ מברכים אתאציל
אנשראורל אל הארולצוח תברם כול דרכי ואומרים יברכצה בצול
פורב ויאמרי צוד מול רע וראי לבצה בשבל חיים ויחנצה טאצת עולמים
ורשא פנו חסו אלוכה לשלום עולמים   וחלוים מקללים אתצול אנשר
אתצל בליעל ועני ואמרו אירד אתוד בצם מעשי רשע אשמתויה ותצוה
אל ועוח כוצו צול עקבצו נקם וחפוצי אחוריצה בלוהרי צול משלמי
אתצולמים ארור אתה לאין ראשית בארשך מעשיצה וועום אתה
כאפלת אש עולמים לוא ראו נוצרה אל כפי ראצתה ולוא דסלח לצפר עוונצ
רשא פני אפו לנקמתצה לוא והודלצוה שלום בפיוצל אתאוד אבות
דצול העוברים בראת אמרים אאחר הברצים והמשולים אמן אמן
ווהצפר והדולצים יחלוום ואצרך אור באלחה לצו לעובר
ותבא בביית ומצשול וצעשון עומו ושים לבנו לדעאת בן וחוד
בשוצשה את אבדף הברות הוותוחברך בלבבו לאמרי שלום דהצלה
צרא בשרירותני לב ונולך ונכבסה דנומן יעצעא את צנו חיוד לאין
סלחאור אבול רעות נצשפסו ובצרה בלצאת עולמין וצצסו בצ צול
צלות הברעת חות וצצרונוצ אל לראצה וצצרת מתוצצל בנו אור כהצמוא
מאחדדאאל בצלולני ומצשוד עונו וחן עוצלה בתוצ אדורד עולמים
וצול כאתו הברות ועו ואצנין אחריוהם אמן אמן
צביד ועשר שוח בצשוד צול חמו ומצשלת צלועל החצוהשם ובוור
בר שצנו כדרך לצודוורהם וזה אאוד וזה אלוים ועבתף אאחרוהצ
וצול חעם   מעבורך בשלושות בצרצ וזד אאר וזה לאלתם ואצת
וצלב שוח רע שרית לצעת צול אוש ושראל אוש פת מצפאי כותב אל
לצעת עולתברה ולוא ושפל אשמצבר בצבצצ ולוא דרום מצקום צורלו
צוא החצו וחוד טראת אאת ועצוח טוב ואתצת מצאצ מאאשלת צדק
שלדשותוד בצצת קוש בונו מוצ וצול הפום לבוא
לצעת בשרירות לבו לוא   אאצ אמצו צוא אעוד

1   ורחמי חסדו גמל עלינו מעולם ועד עולם   והכוהנים מברכים את כול

2   אנשי גורל אל ההולכים תמים בכול דרכיו ואומרים יברככה בכול

3   טוב וישמורכה מכול רע ויאר לבכה בשכל חיים ויחונכה בדעת עולמים

4   וישא פני חסדיו לכה לשלום עולמים   והלויים מקללים את כול אנשי

5   גורל בליעל וענו ואמרו ארור אתה בכול מעשי רשע אשמתכה יתנכה

6   אל זעוה ביד כול נוקמי נקם ויפקוד אחריכה כלה ביד כול משלמי

7   גמולים ארור אתה לאין רחמים כחושך מעשיכה וזעום אתה

8   באפלת אש עולמים לוא יחונכה אל בקוראכה ולוא יסלח לכפר ¹עווניך¹

9   ישא פני אפו לנקמתכה ולוא יהיה לכה שלום בפי כול אוחזי אבות

10 וכול העוברים בברית אומרים אחר המברכים והמקללים אמן אמן

11 והוסיפו הכוהנים והלויים ואמרו ארור בגלולי לבו לעבור

12 הבא בברית הזות ומכשול עוונו ישים לפניו להסוג בו והיה

13 בשומעו את דברי הברית הזות יתברך בלבבו לאמור שלום יהי לי

14 כיא בשרירות לבי אלך ונספתה רוחו הצמאה עם הרווה לאין

15 סליחה אף אל וקנאת משפטיו יבערו בו לכלת עולמים ודבקו בו כול

16 אלות הברית הזות ויבדילהו אל לרעה ונכרת מתוך כול בני אור בהסוגו

17 מאחרי אל בגלוליו ומכשול עוונו יתן גורלו בתוך ארורי עולמים

18 וכול באי הברית יענו ואמרו אחריהם אמן אמן

19 ככה יעשו שנה בשנה כול יומי ממשלת בליעל הכוהנים יעבורו

20 ברשונה בסרך לפי רוחותם זה אחר זה והלויים יעבורו אחריהם

21 וכול העם ( )יעבורו בשלישית בסרך זה אחר זה לאלפים ומאות

22 וחמשים ועשרות לדעת כול איש ישראל איש בית מעמדו ביחד אל

23 לעצת עולמים ולוא ישפל איש מבית מעמדו ולוא ירום ממקום גורלו

24 כיא הכול יהיו ביחד אמת וענות טוב ואהבת חסד ומחשבת צדק

25 איש לרעהו בעצת קודש ובני סוד עולמים וכול המואס לבוא

26 [בברית אל] ללכת בשרירות לבו לו[א   יח]ד אמתו כיא געלה

¹ 4QS MS B: עוונכה.

אשר במעירו רעת משפטו צדק לוא חוק לעשוב ביד ועם ישרים לוא תתאשב
ואעתו ובטחתו וחרות לוא יבואו בעצת ראיצ ציא ציאן במאן רשע מעורשי ולאורם
בשועתו ולוא יצדק במתר שרירות לבו ונושך ובוס לעדבו אוד בעון תעומם
לוא יתאשב לוא ועצה בצטריונ ולוא וטוהר במו ועד ולוא יתקדש במוש וברות
ונהרות ולוא יטוהר בצלמי ראיצ טבא טבא יהוה ציל יומי ברואמו במעשסו
אל לטוחו וביוחר הראיצ בראיצ עצחר ציא כרוא עצת ציא כרוא עלת אמת אל ואיצו איש עיוטריציו
עוונתו לעבום ובודוד מעור ודחוות ובוצוה קצושת לואצ באעצעון ומוחין מציל
עוונתו ובוצוה ואשר יעעה תצוותצ מטתו ועצעות בצשר לצוח ואקר אל ומוחך
בטצר לצחות בצעראיצה להצתקדש ואורצי צבו ואוצו וודצין עצעון לוחלצת תביונ
בצול ציאיצו אל צאשר עוח לצרוצצר תעורצתו ולוא למור ובחון וצמאורל ואוגן
לצעוג על אאוצ מצול ולביור אע חי צצע צצטורר בוהוצ לבו אל ומחוולו לצרות
ורוצו עולמים
לעשויל לעדבן וללמצ את ציול צבו אוך צתוליאות צול צבו אעש
לצול שעע רוחותם באותותם למעשותם בעעורותם לפקורת עעעותונ עם
קצצ שלומם מאל חיעעות צול חוה ונחיוה ולפמ דחוזת הצן צול מושבתצי
ובאחרתם לצעצורתם צמוטשבת צבורצ ומלאצ מעולתם ואגן לורשעות עראצ
משפטו ציול וחראאד וצלצם בציל הבעצוחט ותואד צצא אעש לממשלת
תבל וישם לו שתו רוחות לחתולהצב עד מועצ בקורוצו הנעו רוחות
האצות ואימל במען אוך תולצוות דראאת וממקוך דראאת והשצ תולצות העול
בוץ שר אודים ממשלת צולבו צדיצ באצדו אוך תחולצו ובצו מלאצ
הושצ צול ממשלת בעו על ובצדיצי ונשצ ותאלצו ובמלאצ הושצ תעות
ציולבו צדיצ וצול המשאתם ועונורות ואשמתם ונשאו מעשראתצ בממשל
לפיצו אל עצצצר וצול עעוודם ונעצר ועצותם צרצתם בממשלת משטמתו
ובלרוחות גורלו להצשיל בצו אוך וצאל ושראל ואל עולאצ עמתו עור לצול
בנו אור ואואצ פרא רוחות אעג ומעשצ עלוותצ וספצצול מעשו
טן צול עבוצצ ועל אצצורה ורשאצ אות אהב אל לציל

1   נפשו ביסורי דעת משפטי צדק לוא חזק למשוב חיו ועם ישרים לוא יתחשב

2   ודעתו וכוחו והונו לוא יבואו בעצת יחד כיא בסאון רשע מחרשו וגׄוׄלים¹

3   בשובתו ולוא יצדק במתור שרירות לבו וחושך יביט לדרכי אור בעין תמימים

4   לוא יתחשב לוא יזכה בכפורים ולוא יטהר במי נדה ולוא יתקדש בימים

5   ונהרות ולוא יטהר בכול מי ²רחצ טמא² טמא יהיה כול יומי מאסו במשפטי

6   אל לבלתי התיסר ביחד עצתו כיא ברוח עצת אמת אל דרכי איש יכופרו כול

7   עוונותו להביט באור החיים וברוח קדושה ליחד באמתו יטהר מכול

8   ³עוונותו וברוח יושר וענוה³ תכופר חטתו ובענות נפשו לכול חוקי אל יטהר

9   בשרו להזות במי נדה ולהתקדש במי דוכי ויהכין פעמיו ⁴להלכת⁴ תמים

10   בכול דרכי אל כאשר צוה למועדי תעודתיו ולוא לסור ימין ושמאול ואין

11   לצעוד על אחד מכול דבריו אז ירצה בכפורי ניחוח לפני אל והיתה לו לברית

12   יחד עולמים

13   למשכיל להבין וללמד את כול בני אור בתולדות כול בני איש

14   לכול מיני רוחותם באותותם למעשיהם בדורותם ולפקודת נגועיהם עם

15   קצי שלומם מאל הדעות כול הויה ונהייה ולפני היותם הכין כול ⁵מחשבתם⁵

16   ובהיותם לתעודותם כמחשבת כבודו ימלאו פעולתם ואין להשנות בידו

17   משפטי כול והואה יכלכלם בכול חפציהם והואה ברא אנוש לממשלת

18   תבל וישם לו שתי רוחות להתהלך בם עד מועד פקודתו הנה רוחות

19   האמת והעול במעון אור תולדות האמת וממקור חושך תולדות העול

20   ביד שר אורים ממשלת כול בני צדק בדרכי אור יתהלכו וביד מלאך

21   חושך כול ממשלת בני עול ובדרכי חושך יתהלכו ובמלאך חושך תעות

22   כול בני צדק וכול חטאתם ועוונותם ואשמתם ופשעי מעשיהם בממשלתו

23   לפי רזי אל עד קצו וכול נגועיהם ומועדי צרותם בממשלת משטמתו

24   וכול רוחי גורלו להכשיל בני אור ואל ישראל ומלאך אמתו עזר לכול

25   בני אור והואה ברא רוחות אור וחושך ועליהון יסד כול מעשה

26   ל[   ]הן כול עבודה ועל דרכיהן ⁶[כול   ]ודה⁶ אחת אהב אל לכול

---

¹ 4QS MS C: וגא]לי[ם. ² 4QS MS H: [רחיצה טמ]א. ³ 4QS MS A: עוונותו וברוח ישר וענו]ה. ⁴ 4QS MS A: להלכ. ⁵ Perhaps מהשבתם wrongly corrected by changing ה to ח. ⁶ It has been speculated that within the gap in the leather of 1QS was a repetition of the phrase ועל דרכיהן כול עבודה. But this is inconsistent with both the length of the gap and the traces of the letters that have remained.

1   [מו]עדי עולמים ובכול עלילותיה ירצה לעד אחת תעב יסודה¹ וכול דרכיה שנא לנצח

2   ואלה דרכיהן בתבל להאיר בלבב איש ולישר לפניו כול דרכי צדק אמת ולפחד לבבו במשפטי

3   אל ורוח ענוה וארך אפים ורוב רחמים וטוב עולמים ושכל ובינה וחכמת גבורה מאמנת בכול

4   מעשי אל ונשענת ברוב חסדו ורוח דעת בכול מחשבת מעשה וקנאת משפטי צדק ומחשבת

5   קודש ביצר סמוך ורוב חסדים על כול בני אמת וטהרת כבוד מתעב כול גלולי נדה והצנע לכת

6   בערמת כול וחבא לאמת רזי דעת   אלה סודי רוח לבני אמת תבל ופקודת כול הולכי בה למרפא

7   ורוב שלום באורך ימים ופרות זרע עם כול ברכות עד ושמחת עולמים בחיי נצח וכליל כבוד

8   עם מדת הדר באור עולמים

9   ולרוח עולה רחוב נפש ושפול ידים בעבודת ²צדק רשע ושקר גוה ורום לבב כחש ורמיה אכזרי

10   ורוב חנף קצור אפים ורוב אולת וקנאת זדון מעשי תועבה ברוח זנות ודרכי נדה בעבודת טמאה

11   ולשון גדופים עורון עינים וכבוד אוזן קושי עורף וכובוד לב ללכת בכול דרכי חושך וערמת רוע ופקודת

12   כול הולכי בה לרוב נגועים ביד כול מלאכי חבל לשחת עולמים באף עברת אל נקמה לזעות נצח וחרפת

13   עד עם כלמת כלה באש מחשכים וכול קציהם לדורותם באבל יגון ורעת מרורים בהויות חושך עד

14   כלותם לאין שרית ופליטה למו

15   באלה תולדות כול בני איש ובמפלגיהן ינחלו כול צבאותם לדורותם ובדרכיהן יתהלכו וכול פעולת

16   מעשיהם במפלגיהן לפי נחלת איש בין רוב למועט לכול קצי עולמים כיא אל שמן בד בבד עד קץ

17   אחרון ויתן איבת עולם בין מפלגות ‸תועבת אמת עלילות עולה ותועבת עולה כול דרכי אמת וקנאת

18   ריב על כול משפטיהן כיא לוא יחד יתהלכו ואל ברזי שכלו ובחכמת כבודו נתן קץ להיות עולה ובמועד

19   פקודה ישמידנה לעד ואז תצא לנצח אמת תבל כיא התגוללה בדרכי רשע בממשלת עולה עד

20   מועד משפט נחרצה ואז יברר אל באמתו כול מעשי גבר ויזקק לו מבני איש להתם כול רוח עולה מתכמי

21   בשרו ולטהרו ברוח קודש מכול עלילות רשעה ויז עליו רוח אמת כמי נדה מכול תועבות שקר והתגולל

22   ברוח נדה להבין ישרים בדעת עליון וחכמת בני שמים להשכיל תמימי דרך כיא בם בחר אל לברית עולמים

23   ולהם כול כבוד אדם ואין עולה והיה לבושת כול מעשי רמיה עד הנה יריבו רוחי אמת ועול בלבב גבר

24   יתהלכו בחכמה ואולת וכפי נחלת איש באמת יצדק וכן ³ישנא³ עולה וכירשתו בגורל עול ירשע בו וכן

25   יתעב אמת כיא בד בבד שמן אל עד קץ נחרצה ועשות חדשה והואה ידע פעולת מעשיהן לכול קצי

26   [מועד]ן וינחילן לבני איש לדעת טוב [ולה]פיל גורלות לכול חי לפי רוחו ב[ה]פקודה

בעבודת צדק‸

¹ ם? and ס are difficult to distinguish in the script of this scroll.   ² 4QS MS C: לב[ב ורום גוה ושקר רשע ידים‸מודה.
³ Possibly originally ישנה, the ה being corrected to א.

[*apparatus criticus* continued from page 41]

ואשר לא יגעו לטהרת אנשי :4QS MS D ;הקודש [ ] ... על כול מעשי הבל כי הבל כול] אשר לוא י[דעו ... מעשיה]ם לנדה לפניו [
[הקד]ש ואל יוכל אתו ב[יחד ואשר לא ישוב א]יש מאנשי היחד על פיהם לכל [תורה] ומשפט ואש[ר לא ... עמו בהון וב]עבודה ואל
יואכל איש מאנשי הקדש [ ] [ל] [ ] ולא ישענו על כ]ל מע]שי ההבל כי הבל כל אשר [לא ידעו את בריתו וכל מנאצ]י דברו להשמיד
For 1QS 5.21- 25. מתבל ומעשיהם לנדה ל]פניו וטמא בכ]ל [הונם ...]ם גוים ושבעות וחרמים ונדרים בפיהם] ... [רשל] [ל] [ל] [
ואת מעשיהם בתורה על פי בני אהרון המתנדבים להקים את בריתו ולפקוד את כל חקיו אשר צוה לעשות על פי :25 cf. 4QS MS D
רוב ישראל המתנדבים לשוב ביחד ולהכתב איש לפני רעה איש בסרך איש לפי שכלו ומעשיו בתורה להשמע הכול איש לרעה איש הקטן לגדול
והיות פוקדים את רוחם ומעשיהם בתורה שנה בשנה ל[ה]עלות איש כפי שכלו ולאחרו כנעותיו להוכיח איש את רעהו ואהבת חסד
26 4QS MS G: לרעהו ... הכול is missing in 29. שכ[ן]לו מעשו בתור[ה]. 27 4QS MS G: ולכת]ב. 28 4QS MS G: לשבת יחד.
4QS MS G. 30 4QS MS D: בעורף [קשה. 31 ואל ידבר איש אל רעהו באף או בתלונה is missing in 4QS MS D. 32 4QS MS D:
ולוא ... is missing in 4QS MS D. ואל ... 33 או בקנאת רשע

1 ¹וזה הסרך לאנשי היחד המתנדבים¹ ²לשוב מכול רע ולהחזיק בכול אשר צוה² ³לרצונו³ ⁴להבדל מעדת

2 אנשי העול להיות ליחד בתורה ובהון ומשובים⁴ ⁵על פי בני צדוק הכוהנים שומרי הברית⁵ ⁶על פי רוב אנשי

3 היחד⁶ ⁷המחזקים בברית על פיהם יצא תכון הגורל⁷ לכול דבר לתורה ולהון ⁸ולמשפט⁸ לעשות אמת יחד ⁹וענוה

4 צדקה ומשפט ואהבת⁹ חסד והצנע לכת בכול דרכיהם אשר לוא ילך איש בשרירות לבו לתעות אחר ¹⁰לבבו

5 ועינוהי ומחשבת יצרו¹⁰ ¹¹ויאם¹¹ ¹²למול ביחד עורלת יצר ועורף קשה¹² ליסד מוסד אמת לישראל ליחד ¹³ברית

6 עולם לכפר¹³ לכול ¹⁴המתנדבים לקודש באהרון ולבית האמת בישראל והנלוים עליהם ליחד¹⁴ ¹⁵ולריב ולמשפט

7 להרשיע כול עוברי חוק ואלה תכון דרכיהם על כול החוקים האלה בהאספם ליחד¹⁵ כול הבא לעצת היחד

8 ¹⁶יבוא בברית אל לעיני כול המתנדבים¹⁶ ¹⁷ויקם על נפשו בשבועת אסר לשוב אל תורת מושה¹⁷ ¹⁸ככול אשר צוה¹⁸ בכול

9 לב ובכול נפש לכול הנגלה ממנו ¹⁹לבני צדוק הכוהנים שומרי הברית ודורשי רצונו¹⁹ ²⁰ולרוב אנשי בריתם²⁰

10 ²¹המתנדבים יחד לאמתו ולהתלך ברצונו ואשר יקים על נפשו²¹ להבדל מכול אנשי העול ²²ההולכים

11 בדרך הרשעה כיא לוא החשבו בבריתו כיא לוא בקשו ולוא דרשהו בחוקוהי לדעת הנסתרות אשר תעו

12 בם²³ לאשמה²³ והנגלות עשו ביד רמה לעלות אף למשפט ולנקום נקם באלות ברית לעשות בם (מ)שפטים

13 גדולים לכלת עולם לאין שרית²² ²⁴אל יבוא במים לגעת בטהרת אנשי הקודש כיא לוא יטהרו

14 כי אם שבו מרעתם כיא טמא בכול עוברי דברו ואשר לוא ייחד עמו בעבודתו ובהו(.)ו פן ישיאנו

15 עוון אשמה כיא ירחק ממנו בכול דבר כיא כן כתוב מכול דבר שקר תרחק ואשר לוא ישוב איש מאנשי

16 היחד על פיהם לכול תורה ומשפט ואשר לוא יוכל מהונם כול ולוא ישתה ולוא יקח מידם כול מאומה

17 אשר לוא במחיר כאשר כתוב חדלו לכם מן האדם אשר נשמה באפו כיא במה נחשב הואה כיא

18 כול אשר לוא נחשבו בבריתו להבדיל אותם ואת כול אשר להם ולוא ישען איש הקודש על כול מעשי

19 הבל כיא הבל כול אשר לוא ידעו את בריתו וכול מנאצי דברו ישמיד מתבל וכול מעשיהם לנדה

20 לפניו וטמא בכול הונ(ו)ם²⁴ וכיא יבוא בברית לעשות ככול החוקים האלה להיחד לעדת קודש ודרשו

21 את רוחום ביחד בין איש לרעהן לפי שכלו ²⁵ומעשיו בתורה על פי בני אהרון המתנדבים ביחד להקים

22 את בריתו ולפקוד את כול חוקיו אשר צוה לעשות ועל פי ר(י)ב ישראל המתנדבים ²⁶לשוב ביחד²⁶ לבריתו

23 ²⁷וכתבם²⁷ בסרך איש לפני רעהו לפי ²⁸שכלו ומעשיו²⁸ להשמע ²⁹הכול איש לרעהו²⁹ הקטן לגדול ולהיות

24 פוקדם את רוחם ומעשיהם שנה בשנה להעלות איש לפי שכלו ותום דרכו ולאחר כנעוותו להוכיח

25 איש את רעהו בא[מ]ת וענוה ואהבת חסד²⁵ לאיש ³⁰אל ידבר אלוהיהי באף או בתלונה³⁰

26 או בעורף [קשה או]³¹ ³²בקנאת]³² רוח רשע]³³ ³³ואל ישנאהו [בעורלת] לבבו כיא ביומ( ) יוכיחנו ולוא³³

1 4QS MS D: להשיב מכל רע ולהחזיק. 2 4QS MS D: מדרש למשכיל על] ; 4QS MS B: [מדרש למשכיל על; מדרש למשכיל על אנשי התורה המתנדבים :4QS MS D ולבדל מעדת אנשי העול ולהיות יחד בתור[ה] ובהון is missing in 4QS MSS B and D. 3 לרצונו :4QS MS D. 4 בכל אשר צוה is missing in 4QS MS D and perhaps in 4QS MS B. 5 על פי ... הברית is missing in 4QS MS D: על ; על פי הרבים 6 4QS MSS B and D: הברית seems to be corrected from אל. 7 הגורל ... המחזקים is missing in 4QS MSS B and D. 8 למשפט is missing in 4QS MS D and possibly B. 9 4QS MS D: יצרו ... לבבו is missing in 4QS MSS B and D. 10 ענוה וצדקה ומשפט ואהבת] 4QS MS D. 11 ויאם in 1QS is most likely an error for כיא אם; both 4QS MSS B and D read כי אם at this point. 12 קשה ... למול is missing in 4QS MSS B and D. 13 ברית ... לכפר is missing in 4QS MSS B and D. 14 4QS MS D: [ם]המתנדב לקדש באהרן ובית אמת לישראל והנלוי. המתנדב לקדש באהרן ובית אמת לישראל והנלוי[ם] 15 ולריב ... ליחד is missing in 4QS MSS B and D. 16 המתנדבים ... יבוא is missing in 4QS MSS B and D. 17 4QS MS D: כאסר לשוב אל תורת משה; 4QS MS B: יקים על נפשו באסר לשוב לא[ת]ורת מש[ה]. 18 ככול ... צוה is missing in 4QS MSS B and D. 19 עצת אנש]י [היחד]; 4QS MS B: עצת אנשי היחד; 4QS MS D: [היחד]. 20 רצונו ... לבני is missing in 4QS MSS B and D. 21 לאשמה ... המתנדבים is a scribal error for לאשמה. 22 שרית ... ההולכים is missing in 4QS MSS B and D. 23 לאשמה is missing in 4QS MSS B and D. 24 For 1QS 5.13-20 cf. 4QS MS B and D. MS B: [לוא יגע לטהרת אנש]י הקודש ואל יוכל אתו [ב]יחד ואשר ל[ר]א[ן] ישוב איש מאנשי היחד על פיהם] לכול תורה ומשפט ואשר לוא °°°° [בהון בעבודה ואל יואכל איש מא[נשי]

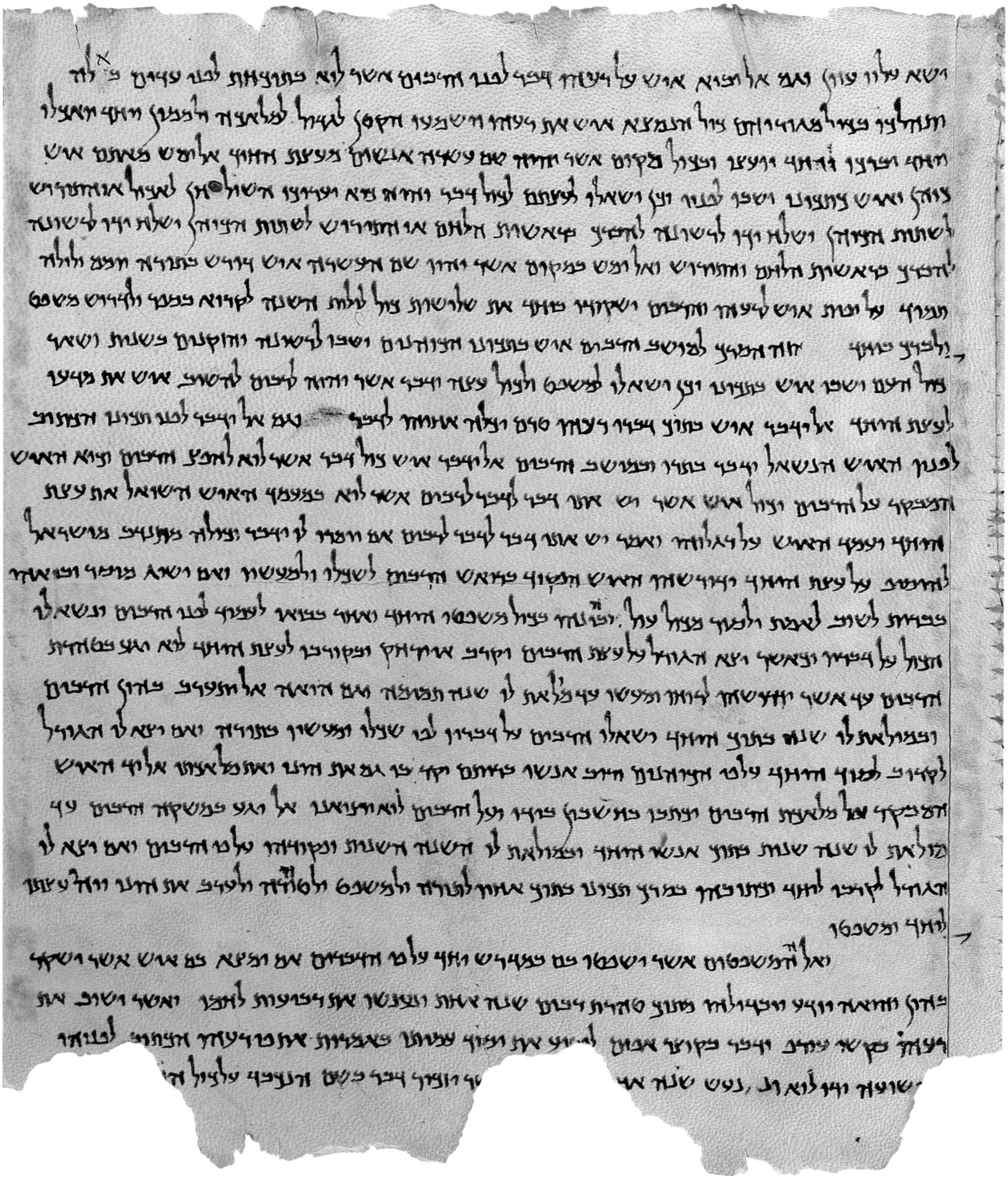

1 ¹יישא עליו עוון¹ ²וגם אל יבא איש על רעהו דבר לפני הרבים אשר לוא בתוכחת ³לפני עדים² ב(א)לה

2 יתהלכו³ בכול מגוריהם כול ⁴הנמצא איש את רעהו⁴ וישמעו הקטן ⁵לגדול למלאכה ולממון ויחד יואכלו

3 ויחד יברכו ויחד יועצו ובכול מקום אשר יהיה שם עשרה אנשים מעצת החיד אל ימש ⁶מאתם איש

4 כוהן⁶ ואיש כתכונו ישבו לפניו וכן ישאלו לעצתם לכול דבר והיה כיא יערוכו השולחן לאכול ⁷או התירוש

5 לשתות הכוהן ישלח ידו לרשונה להברך בראשית הלחם או התירוש לשתות הכוהן ישלח ידו לרשונה

6 להברך בראשית הלחם והתירוש⁷ ואל ימש במקום אשר יהיו שם העשרה איש דורש בתורה יומם ולילה

7 תמיד על יפות איש לרעהו והרבים ישקודו ביחד את שלישית כול לילות השנה לקרוא בספר ולדרוש משפט

8 ולברך ביחד   וזה הסרך למושב הרבים איש בתכונו הכוהנים ישבו לרשונה והזקנים בשנית ושאר

9 כול העם ישבו איש בתכונו וכן ישאלו למשפט ולכול עצה ודבר אשר יהיה לרבים להשיב איש את מדעו

10 לעצת היחד   אל ידבר איש בתוך דברי רעהו טרם יכלה אחיהו לדבר   וגם אל ידבר לפני תכונו הכתוב

11 לפניו האיש הנשאל ידבר בתרו ובמושב הרבים אל ידבר איש כול דבר אשר לוא ⁸להפץ⁸ הרבים וכיא האיש

12 המבקר על הרבים ⁹וכול⁹ איש אשר יש אתו דבר לדבר לרבים אשר לוא במעמד האיש השואל את עצת

13 היחד ועמד האיש על רגלוהי ואמר יש אתי דבר לדבר לרבים אם ¹⁰ידבר לו¹⁰ יומרו לו ¹⁰ידבר וכולה מתנדבי¹⁰ מישראל

14 להוסיף על עצת היחד ידורשהן האיש הפקוד ברואש הרבים לשכלו ולמעשיו ואם ישיג מוסר יביאהו

15 בברית לשוב לאמת ולסור מכול עול (ו)יֹבֹינהוֹ¹¹ בכול משפטי היחד ואחר בבואו לעמוד לפני הרבים ונשאלו

16 הכול על דבריו ¹²וכאשר יצא הגורל על עצת הרבים יקרב או ירחק¹² ובקורבו לעצת היחד לוא יגע בטהרת

17 הרבים עד אשר ידרושהו לרוחו ומעשו עד מֹלאת לו שנה תמימה וגם הואה אל יתערב בהון הרבים

18 ובמולאת לו ¹³שנה בתוך היחד ישאלו¹³ הרבים על דבריו לפי שכלו ומעשיו בתורה ואם יצא לו הגורל

19 לקרוב לסוד היחד על פי הכוהנים ורוב אנשי בריתם יקר(י)בו גם את הונו ואת מלאכתו אל יד האיש

20 המבקר על מלאכת הרבים וכתבו בחשבון בידו ועל הרבים לוא יוציאנו אל יגע במשקה הרבים עד

21 מולאת לו שנה שנית בתוך אנשי היחד ובמולאת לו השנה השנית יפקודהו על פי הרבים ואם יצא לו

22 הגורל לקרבו ליחד יכתובהו בסרך תכונו בתוך אחיו לתורה ולמשפט ולטוֹהרה ולערב את הונו ויהֹ עצתו

23 ליחד ומשפטו

24 ואל הֹמשפטים ¹⁴אשר ישפטו¹⁴ בם במדרש יחד על פי הדברים אם ימצא בם איש אשר ישקר

25 בהון והואה יודע ויבדילהו מתוך טהרת רבים שנה אחת ונענשו את רביעית לחמו   ואשר ישוב את

26 רעהו בקשי עורף ודבר בקוצר אפים לפרוע את יסוד עמיתו באמרות את פי רעהו הכתוב לפנוהי

27 [והו]שיעה ידו לוא ונ(א)נעש שנה אח[ת ומובדל וא]שר יזכיר דבר בשם הנכבד על כול ה[ן]

---

¹ עוון ... ישא is missing in 4QS MS D. ² 4QS MS D: וגם אל יבא איש על רעהו דבר לרבים אשר לא בהוכח לפני ע[דים. ³ 4QS MS D: ובאלה יתהלכו ולה[לון; 4QS MS I: [ובאלה יתהלכ]כו. ⁴ 4QS MS D: הנמצא את רעהו. ⁵ 4QS MS D: לגדול למלאכה ולה[לון. ⁶ 4QS MS D: מ[אתם כו]הן. ⁷ 1QS 6.4-6 is disrupted by a lengthy dittography apparently due to homioarchon. This begins at the end of 6.4 with the words או התירוש and runs to the word הלחם in 6.5. This entire phrase then is repeated, ending with הלחם in 6.6 where the next word is again והתירוש. ⁸ להפץ = לחפץ. ⁹ Possibly to be read יכיל, which is better syntactically than וכול. ¹⁰ 4QS MS B: ידבר וכול המת[נדב]. ¹¹ The first י was corrected from ל. ¹² ירחק ... וכאשר is probably missing in 4QS MS B. ¹³ 4QS MS B: שנה תמימה יש[אלו]. ¹⁴ 4QS MS G: [אשר ישפטו על פי]הם.

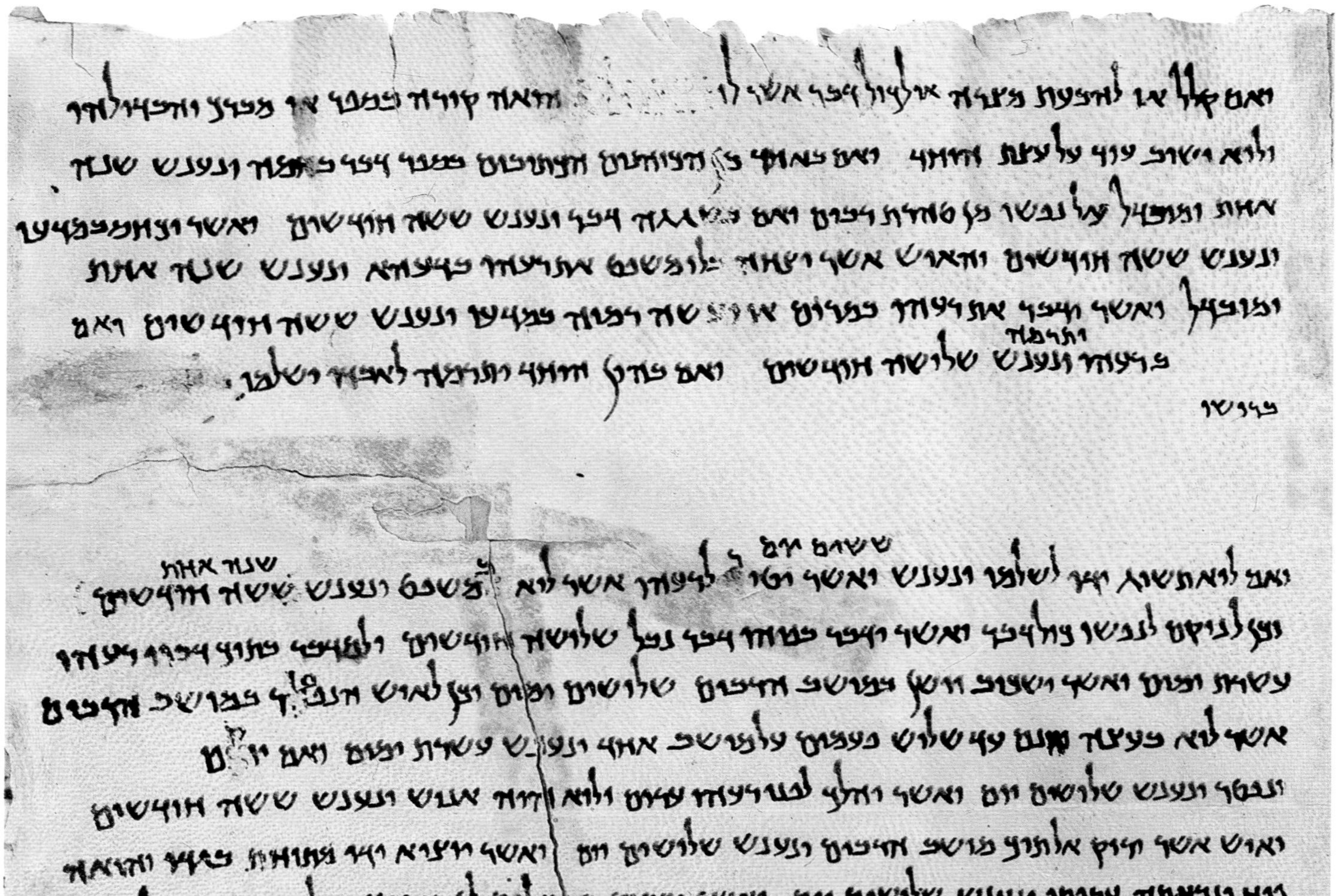

1 ואם קלל או להבעת מצרה ¹או לכול דבר אשר לו¹ (   ) הואה קורה בספר או מברך והבדילהו

2 ולוא ישוב עוד על עצת היחד   ואם באחד מן הכוהנים הכתובים בספר דבר בחמה ונענש שנה

3 אחת ומובדל על נפשו מן טהרת רבים ואם בשגגה דבר ונענש ששה חודשים   ואשר יכחס במדעו

4 ונענש ששה חודשים והאיש אשר יצחה בלו משפט את רעהו בדעהא ונענש שנה אחת

5 ²ומובדל² ואשר ידבר את רעהו במרום או יעשה רמיה במדעו ונענש ששה חודשים ²ואם²

6 ברעהו ונענש שלושה חודשים ואם בהון היחד יתרמה לאבדו ושלמו (ב   ) יתרמה

7 ²ברושו²

8 ואם לוא תשיג ידו לשלמו ונענש ונענש ואשר יטו( ) לרעהו אשר לוא ( )משפט ונענש (ששה חודשים) שנה אחת / ששים יום ³

9 וכן לנוקם לנפשו כול דבר ואשר ידבר בפיהו דבר נבל שלושה חודשים ולמדבר בתוך דברי רעהו

10 עשרת ימים ואשר ישכב וישן במושב הרבים שלושים ימים וכן לאיש הנפ( )ר ⁴במושב הרבים

11 אשר⁵ לוא בעצה וחנם עד שלוש פעמים על מושב אחד ונענש עשרת ימים ואם יז( )פו

12 ונפטר ונענש שלושים יום ואשר יהלך לפני רעהו ערום ולוא היה אנוש ונענש ששה חודשים

13 ואיש אשר ירוק אל תוך מושב הרבים ונענש שלושים יום   ואשר יוציא ידו מתוחת בגדו והואה

14 פוח ונראתה ערותו ונענש שלושים יום ואשר ישחק בסכלות להשמיע קולו ⁵ונענש שלושים⁵

15 יום והמוציא את יד שמאולו לשוח בה ונענש עשרת ימים והאיש אשר ילך רכיל ברעהו

16 והבדילהו שנה אחת מטהרת הרבים ונענש ואיש ברבים ילך רכיל ⁶לשלח הואה מאתם

17 ולוא⁶ ישוב עוד והאיש אשר ילון על ⁷יסוד היחד ישלחהו ולוא⁷ ישוב ואם על רעהו ילון

18 אשר לוא במשפט ונענש ששה חודשים והאיש אשר תזוע רוחו מיסוד היחד לבגוד באמת

19 וללכת בשרירות לבו אם ישוב ונענש שתי שנים ברשונה ( )לוא יגע בטהרת הרבים

20 (רבים) ובשנית לוא יגע (בטהרת) הרבים ואחר כול אנשי היחד ישב ובמלואת / משקה

21 לו שנתים ימים ישאלו הרבים   על דבריו ואם יקרבהו ונכתב בתכונו ואחר ישאל אל המשפט

22 (כ)ול איש אשר יהיה ⁸בעצת היחד (   ) על מלואת⁸ עשר שנים (   )

23 (   )   ושבה רוחו לבגוד ביחד ויצא מלפני (   )

24 הרבים ללכת בשרירות לבו לוא ישוב אל עצת היחד עוד ואיש מאנשי היח[ד אשר ית]ערב

25 עמו בטהרתו או בהונו אש[ר   הרבים] והיה משפטו כמוהו ל[שלחו

¹ או ... לו is written by a different hand than the rest of this column. ² The words ברושו, ואם, and ומובדל in lines 5-7 were perhaps added by a different hand. ³ 4QS MS E: [ששים [יום (?); but the text is very fragmentary. ⁴ 4QS MS E: הנפטר. ⁵ ממוש הרבים אש]ר 4QS MS E: [קולו ונענש שלשים. ⁶ 4QS MS G: י]שלחוהו מאתם ול[א. ⁷ 4QS MS G: יסו]ד היחד לשלח. ⁸ 4QS MS E: בעצ]ת היחד עד מלאות לו 4QS MS E: ול[א.

45

[*apparatus criticus* continued from page 47]

8.15b-9.11 is missing in 4QS MS E. [20] Differences between 4QS MS D and 1QS 8.24-27 require extended citation:
והבדילהו מן הטהרה ומן העצה ומן המשפט שנת[ים ימי]ם ושב במדרש ובעצה אם לא הלך עוד בשגגה עד מלאות לו שנתים
[21] במושב: read as בם ושב see M. Kister, *Tarbiz* 57 (1988): 324-25.

1   בעצת היחד שנים עשר ¹איש וכוהנים שלושה¹ תמימים בכול הנגלה מכול

2   התורה לעשות ²אמת וצדקה ומשפט² ואהבת חסד והצנע לכת איש אם רעהו

3   לשמור ³אמונה בארץ ביצר סמוך³ ורוח ⁴נשברה ולרצת עוון⁴ בעושי משפט

4   וצרת ⁵מצרף ולהתהלך עם כול⁵ ב( )מדת האמת ובתכון העת בהיות אלה ⁶בישראל

5   נכונה (ה)עצת היחד⁶ באמת⁷   ⁸למעّת עולם⁷ בית קודש לישראל וסוד קודש

6   קודשים לאהרון עדי אמת למשפט וב(י)חרי רצון⁸ לכפר בעד הארץ ולהשב

7   לרשעים ⁹גמולם   היאה חומת הבחן פנת יקר בל⁹

8   יזדעזעו¹⁰ יסודותיהו ובל יחישו ממקומם   מעון קודש קודשים

9   לאהרון¹⁰ בדעת כולם לברית משפט ¹¹ולקריב ניחוח ובית תמים ואמת בישראל¹¹

10   ¹²ולהקם ברית לחוّ()ת עולם¹² בהכון אלה ביסוד היחד שנתים ימים ¹³בתמים דרך   (והיו לרצון לכפר בעד הארץ ולחרוץ משפט רשעה ואין עולה) (בתמים דרך)

11   קודש בתוך עצת אנשי¹³ היחד וכול דבר נסתר ¹⁴מישראל ונמצאו לאיש¹⁴   יבדלו

12   הדורש אל יסתרהו מאלה מיראת רוח נסוגה   ובהיות אלה בישראל ליّחד

13   ¹⁶יבדלו מתוך מושב ¹⁷הנשי¹⁶ העול ללכת למדבר ¹⁸לפנות שם את דרך הואהא   בתכונים האלה¹⁵

14   כאשר כתוב במדבר פנו¹⁸ דרך °°°° ישרו בערבה מסלה לאלוהינו

15   היאה מדרש התורה א[ש]ר ¹⁹צוה ביד מושה¹⁹ לעשות ככול הנגלה עת בעת

16   וכאשר גלו הנביאים ברוח קודשו וכול איש מאנשי היחד ברית

17   היחד אשר יסור מכול המצוה דבר ביד רמה אל יגע בטהרת אנשי הקודש

18   ואל ידע בכול עצתם עד אשר יזכו   מעשיו מכול עול להלכ בתמים דרך וקרבהו

19   בעצה על פי הרבים ואחר יכת(ב) בתכונו וכמשפט הזה לכול הנוספ ליחד

20   ואלה המשפטים אשר ילכו בם אנשי התמים קודש איש את רעהו

21   כול הבא בעצת הקודש ההולכים בתמים דרך כאשר צוה צוה כול איש מהמה

22   אשר יעבר דבר מתורת מושה ביד רמה או ברמיה ישלחהו מעצת היחד

23   ולוא ישוב עוד ולוא יתערב איש מאנשי הקודש בהّנו ועם עצתו לכול

24   דבר ואם בשגגה יעשה ²⁰והובדל מן הטהרה ומן העצה ודרשו המשפט

25   אשר לוא ישפוט איש ולוא ישאל על כול עצה שנתים ימים אם תתם דרכו

26   ²¹במושבו במדרש ובעצה [על פי ה]רבים אם לוא שגג עוד עד מולאת לו שנתים

27   ²⁰ימים

---

¹ 4QS MS E: א[מונה בארץ ביצר סמוך ובענוה. ² 4QS MS E: אמת צדקה ומשפט [. ³ 4QS MS E:]אנשים [ו]כוהנים שלושה. ⁴ 4QS MS E: נ]שברה ולרצת עו[וו]ן. ⁵ 4QS MS E:] מצרף והתהלך עם כול. ⁶ 4QS MS E:]ישראל נכונה עצת היחד. ⁷ 4QS MS E:]ב[ישראל נכונה עצת היחד. ⁸ 4QS MS E:]ומטעת עולם בית] קודש קודשים לאהר[ון] עדי אמת למשפט] ובחיר[י] רצו[ן. ⁹ 4QS MS E:]ל יחושו ממקומם מעון קודש קו[ד]שים לאהר[ון. 4QS MS D: מ]מקומם; ¹⁰ 4QS MS E:]גמולם היא חומת] הבחן פנת יקר ב[ל. ¹¹ 4QS MS E:]ל [ולקריב] ניחוח ובית תמים ואמת ב[ישרא]ל. ¹² 4QS MS D: להקים ברית לחוקות עולם. ¹³ A מעון קודש קודשים scribe originally wrote בתמים דרך above the end of 1QS 8.10. Subsequently, בתמים דרך was erased and rewritten at the end of 8.10 following the words שנתים ימים where the word יבדלו was erased to make room for the phrase. Note that בתמים דרך is slightly lower than the rest of the line and that the ב in בתמים is the unerased ב of the original יבדלו which stood at the end of the line. The same corrector then rewrote יבדלו as a supralinear at the beginning of 1QS 8.11 to complete the phrase יבדלו בתוך עצת אנשי היחד ¹⁴ 4QS MS D:]מ[ישראל ונמצא לאיש. ¹⁵ Apparently the two supralinear words over יבדלו מתוך מושב are missing in 4QS MS D and MS E. ¹⁶ 4QS MS E:]יבדלו מ[ו]שב. ¹⁷ 4QS MS 1QS: מו יבדלו מן[ ]שב. ¹⁸ 4QS MS E: שמ]ה את דרך האמת כאשר] כתוב במד[בר פנ]ו. ¹⁹ 4QS MS E:]וקים אלה החן[וקים; 4QS MS D:]צוה ביד משה אלה הח[וקים D: אנשי].

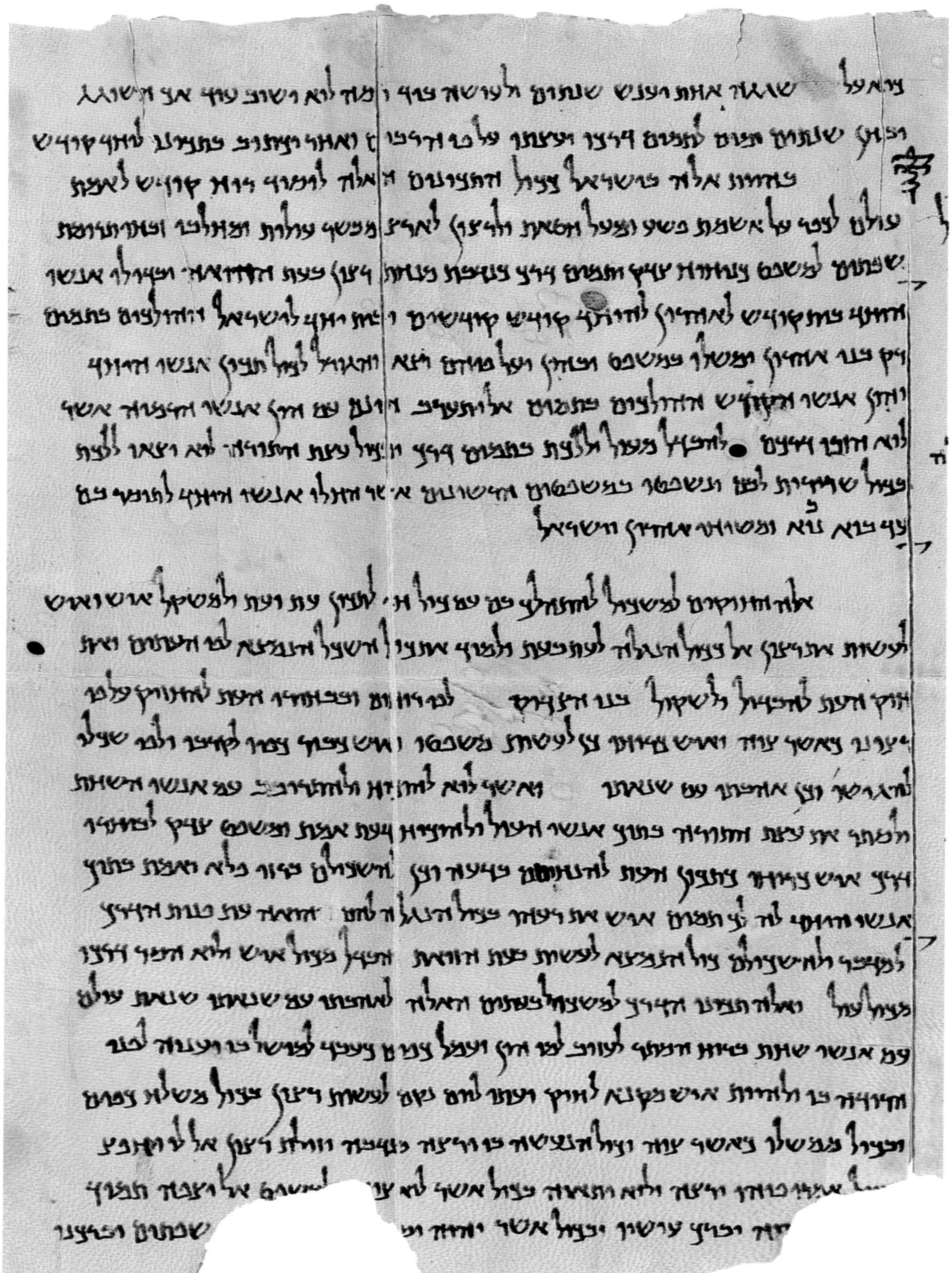

1 ¹כיא על ( ) שגגה אחת יענש שנתים ולעושה ביד רמה לוא ישוב עוד אך השוגג

2 יבחן שנתים ימים לתמים דרכו ועצתו על פי הרבים ואחר יכתוב בתכונו ליחד קודש

3 בהיות אלה בישראל ככול התכונים האלה ליסוד רוח קודש לאמת

4 עולם לכפר על אשמת פשע ומעל חטאת ולרצון לארצ¹ מבשר ²עולות ומחלבי ³זבח ותרומת³

5 שפתים למשפט ²כניחוח צדק ותמים דרך כנדבת מנחת ⁴רצון בעת ההיאה יבדילו אנשי

6 היחד בית קודש לאהרן להיחד קודש קודשים ובית יחד ⁵לישראל⁴ ההולכים בתמים⁵

7 רק בני אהרן ימשלו במשפט ובהון ועל פיהם יצא והגורל לכול תכון אנשי היחד

8 והון אנשי הקודש ההולכים בתמים אל יתערב עם הון אנשי הרמיה אשר

9 לוא הזכו דרכם להבדל מעול וללכת בתמים דרך ומכול עצת התורה לוא ⁶יצאו ללכת

10 בכול⁶ שרירות לבם ונשפטו במשפטים הרשונים אשר החלו אנשי היחד לתיסר בם

11 עד בוא נביא ומשיחי אהרון וישראל

12 ⁷אלה החוקים למשכיל ⁷להתהלך בם עם כול חי לתכון עת ועת ולמשקל איש ואיש

13 לעשות את רצונ⁸ אל ככול הנגלה לעת בעת ולמוד את כול השכל הנמצא לפי העתים ואת

14 חוק העת להבדיל ולשקול בני הצדוק   לפי רוחום ובבחירי העת להחזיק על פי

15 רצונו כאשר צוה ואיש כרוחו כן לעשות משפטו ואיש כבור כפיו לקרבו ולפי שכלו

16 להגישו וכן אהבתו עם שנאתו   ⁹ואשר לוא להוכיח ולהתרובב עם אנשי השחת⁹

17 ⁱ⁰ולסתר את עצת התורה¹⁰ בתוך אנשי העול ולהוכיח דעת אמת ומשפט צדק לביחרי

18 דרך איש כרוחו כתכון העת להנחותם בדעה וכן להשכילם ¹¹ברזי פלא ואמת¹¹ בתוך

19 אנשי היחד ¹²לה( )( )לכל¹² תמים איש את רעהו בכול הנגלה להם (ה)היאה עת פנות הדרך

20 למדבר ¹³ולהשכילם כול¹³ הנמצא לעשות בעת הזואת והבדל מכול איש ולוא הסר דרכו

21 מכול עול   ואלה תכוני הדרך למשכיל בעתים האלה לאהבתו עם שנאתו שנאת עולם

22 ¹⁴עם אנשי שחת ברוח הסתר לעזוב למו הונ¹⁴ ועמל כפים כעבד למושל בו וענוה לפני

23 הרודה בו ולהיות איש מקנא לחוק ועתי ליום נקם לעשות רצון בכול משלח כפים

24 ובכול ממשלו כאשר צוה וכול הנעשה בו ירצה בנדבה וזולת רצון אל לו יחפץ

25 [ובכו]ל אמרי פיהו ירצה ולוא יתאוה בכול אשר צו[ה] למשפ[ט] אל יצפה תמיד

26 [ ] ¹⁵ובצו]קה יברך עושיו ובכול אשר יהיה יספ]ר הסדיו [שפתים¹⁵ יברכנו

---

¹ For 1QS 9.1-4 cf. 4QS MS D: כי על שגגה אחת יענש שנתים וליד הרמה לא ישוב עוד אך שנתים [י]מים יבחן לתמים דרכו ולעצתו על פי הרבים ונכתב בתכונו ליחד קודש [בהיו]ת אלה בישראל ליחד כתכונים האלה ל[י]סד רוח קודש לאמת עולם לכפר על [.]. ³ This is written עלות וחלבי זבחים ותרומות ונדבת שפתים למ[שפ]ט ² 4QS MS D: אשמת פשע ומע]ל [חטא]ת ולרצון לארן]ץ as if one word in 1QS 9.4; 4QS MS D reads here וחלבי זבחים ותרומות ונדבת. This might lead one to speculate that 1QS may have a slightly corrupted text which should read: ר]צון בעת ההיא יבדלו בית אהרן לקודש ⁴ 4QS MS D: זבחי תרומות. ⁵ 4QS MS D: [יצאו] להתהלך ב]כול. ⁶ 4QS MS D: ליש]ראל ההלכים בתו]ם. ⁵ 4QS MS E: צוה ביד משה אשר [לכל]]אל[א]נשי 4QS MS E: לע]שות רצונ. ⁹ 4QS MS E: אלה החן]וקים] למש]כיל; note that 1QS 8.15b-9.11 is missing in 4QS MS E. ⁸ 4QS MS E: השחת. Note that השחת in 4QS MS D = 1QS השחת. In 4QS MS D: ואשר לא יוכיח איש ולא יתרובב עם אנשי ה]חעת. In 4QS MS D, the scribe originally wrote הרעת, then corrected it by placing a dot signifying erasure over the ע, writing a supralinear ש between the original הר of the word and finally by forming a ח from the original ר by adding a left vertical stroke to the letter. ¹⁰ 4QS MS D: ולסתר עצתו. is probably a corrup- tion of ¹¹ 4QS MS E: ב]רזי פלא ואם תומם דרך סור. ¹² 4QS MSS B and D: להלך; 4QS MS E: [ו]להשכילם בכל. ¹³ 4QS MS B: להשכילם בכול; 4QS MS D: בכל ¹⁴ 4QS MS D: עם אנשי השחת ברוח הסתר ולעזוב למו הון ובצע. ¹⁵ שפתים ... ובצו]קה is missing in 4QS MS D. ואמת ותם D. ¹⁴ 4QS MS D: ולהמשילם בכול

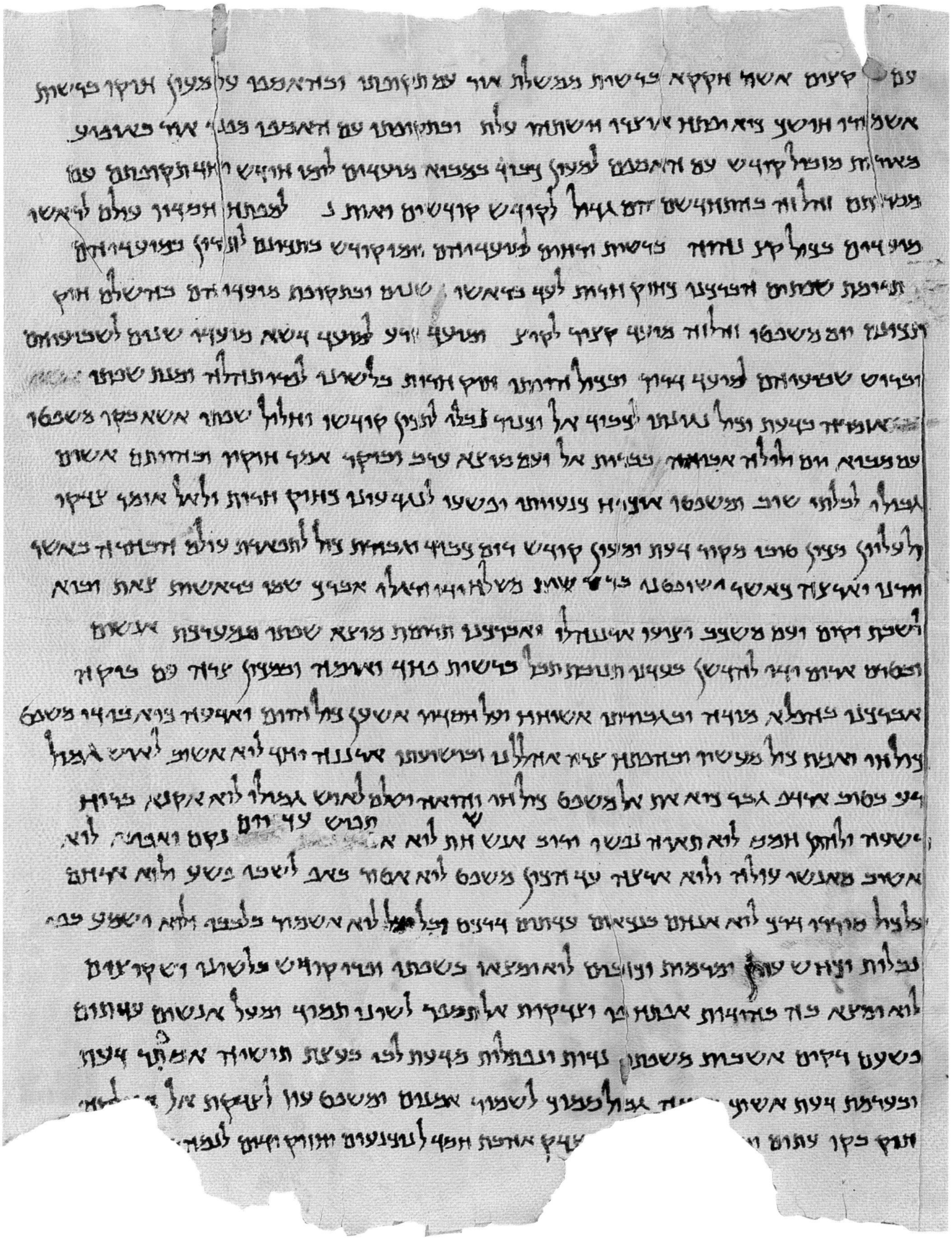

1 עם קצים אשר חקקא ברשית ממשלת אור [1]עם תקופתו ובהאספו על מעון חוקו [2]ברשית

2 אשמורי[2] חושך כיא יפתח אוצרו וישתהו עלת   ובתקופתו עם האספו מפני אור באופיע

3 [3]מאורות מזבול קודש עם האספם למעון כבוד במבוא מועדים לימי [4]חודש יחד תקופתם[4] עם

4 מסרותם זה לזה בהתחדשם [5]יום גדול לקודש קודשים ואות נ למפתח[5] חסדיו עולם לראשי

5 מועדים בכול קץ נהיה [6]ברשית[6] ירחים למועדיהם וימי קודש בתכונם לזכרון במועדיהם

6 ( ) תרומת שפתים [7]הברכנו[7] כחוק חרות לעד בראשי[7] שנים ובתקופת מועדיהם בהשלם חוק

7 תכונם יום משפטו זה לזה מועד קציר לקיץ ומועד זרע למועד דשא מועדי שנים לשבועיהם

8 וברוש שבועיהם למועד דרור ובכול היותי חוק חרות בלשוני לפרי תהלה ומנת שפתי (אשא)

9 ( ) אזמרה בדעת וכול נגינתי לכבוד [8]אל וכנור נבלי[8] לתכון קודשו וחליל שפתי אשא בקו משפטו

10 עם מבוא יום ולילה אבואה בברית אל ועם מוצא ערב ובוקר אמר חוקיו [9]ובהיותם אשים[9]

11 גבולי לבלתי שוב ומשפטו אוכיח כנעוותי ופשעי לנגד עיני כחוק חרות ולאל אומר צדקי

12 ולעליון מכין טובי מקור דעת ומעון קודש רום כבוד וגבורת כול לתפארת עולם הבחרה באשר

13 יורני וארצה כאשר ישופטני בר( )שית משלח ידי ורגלי אברכ שמו בראשית צאת ובוא

14 לשבת וקום ועם בשכב יצועי ארננה לו ואברכנו תרומת מוצא שפתי במערכת אנשים

15 ובטרם אריס ידי להדשן בעדני תנובת תבל ברשית פחד ואימה ובמכון [10]צרה עם בוקה[10]

16 אברכנו [11]בהפלא מודה[11] ובגבורתו אשוחח ועל חסדיו אשען כול היום ואדעה כיא בידו משפט

17 כול חי ואמת כול מעשיו ובהפתח צרה אהללנו ובישועתו ארננה יחד לוא אשיב לאיש גמול

18 רע בטובי[12] ארדפ גבר כיא את אל משפט כול חי [13]והואה[13] ישלם לאיש גמולו לוא אקנא ברוח

19 רשעה ולהון המס לוא תאוה נפשי [14]וריב אנש חת לוא[14] א(טור) באף לשבי[15] נקם[16] ואפיא לוא[16]   [15]תפוש עד יום[15]

20 אשיב מאנשי עולה ולוא ארצה עד הכון משפט לוא [17]אטור באף לשבי פשע[17] ולוא ארחם

21 על כול סוררי דרך לוא [18]אנחם בנכאים עד תום דרכם[18] ובליעל לוא אשמור בלבבי ולוא ישמע בפי

22 נבלות וכחש עוון ומרמות [19]וכזבים[19] לוא ימצאו בשפתי ופרי קודש בלשוני ושקוצים

23 לוא ימצא בה בהודות אפתח פי וצדקות אל תספר לשוני תמיד ומעל אנשים עד תום

24 פשעם רקים אשבית משפתי נדות ונפתלות מדעת לבי בעצת תושיה אסתֵר דעת

25 ובערמת דעת אשוך [בעדה] גבול סמוך לשמור אמנים ומשפט עוז לצדקת אל [אחל]קה

26 חוק בקו עתים [ ]   [ ]צדק אהבת חסד לנוכנעים וחזוק ידים לנמהר[ים להודיע]

---

[1] 4QS MS D: [ובה[אספו אל מעון חק[ו]. [2] 4QS MS F: ע[ם ת]קופתו ובה[ ]. [2] 4QS MS B: בראשית אשמורות. [3] 4QS MS B: מאורות מזבול קודשו.
[4] 4QS MS B: בר[אשית; 4QS. [5] 4QS MSS B and D: חדש יחד תקופתיהמה. [5] 4QS MS B: יום גדול לקודש קודשים ואות למפתח. [6] 4QS MS B: בר[אשית.
[7] 4QS MS B: אברכנו. [8] 4QS MS D: אל אכה נבל[י]. [9] 4QS MS D: ובהיותם אשיב. [10] 4QS MS F:] צרה עם
בוקה [. [11] 4QS MS F:] בהפלא מודה; 4QS MS B: והפלא מאדה. [12] 4QS MS F: רע לטוב. [13] 4QS MS F: הוא. [14] 4QS MS F:
אטור לש[בי]. [15] 4QS MS F:] נפשי ור[יב אנש]י שחת ל[ו]א. [16] 4QS MS F:]ר[ ]אפי לוא. [17] 4QS MS F: פשע ור[ ]. [18] 4QS
MS F: אנחם בנכוחים עד תום ד[רכ]ם. [19] 4QS MS F: וכזבין.

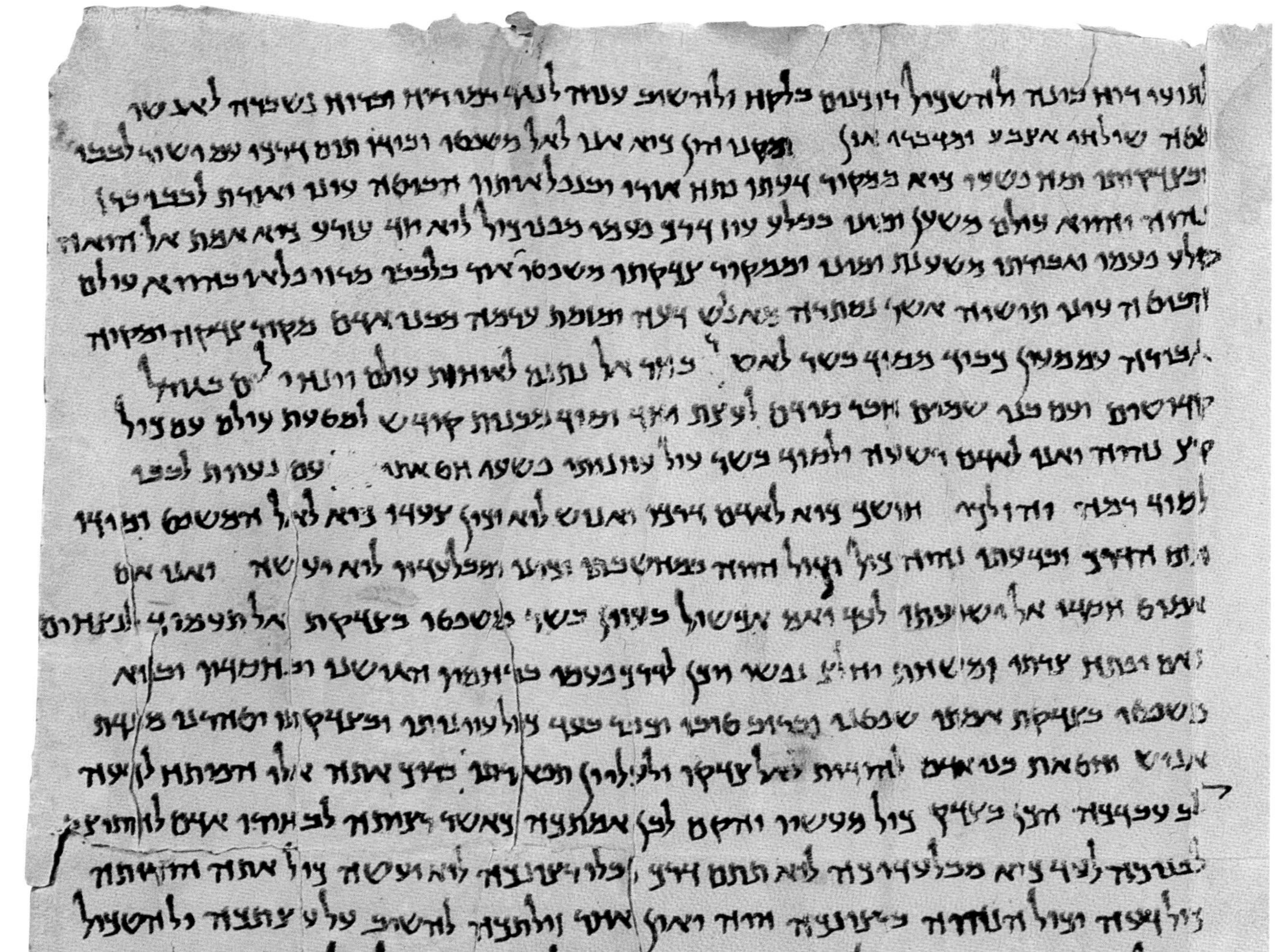

1   לתועי רוח בינה ולהשכיל רוכנים בלקח ולהשיב ענוה לנגד רמי רוח וברוח נשברה לאנשי

2   מטה שולחי אצבע ומדברי און   ומקני הון כיא אני לאל משפטי ובידו תום דרכי עם ישור לבבי

3   ובצדקותו ימח פשעי כיא ממקור דעתו פתח אורי ובנפלאותיו הביטה עיני ואורת לבבי ברז

4   נהיה והויא עולם משען ימיני בסלע עוז דרך פעמי מפני כול לוא יזד עזרע כיא אמת אל היאה

5   סלע פעמי וגבורתו משענת ימיני וממקור צדקתו משפטי אור בלבבי מרזי פלאו בהויא עולם

6   הביטה עיני תושיה אשר נסתרה מאנ֯ש דעה ומזמת ערמה מבני אדם מקור צדקה ומקוה

7   גבורה עם מעין כבוד מסוד בשר לאש֯י֯ ( ) בחר אל נתנם לאוחזת עולם וינחי֯()ם בגורל

8   קדושים ועם בני שמים חבר סודם לעצת יחד וסוד מבנית קודש למטעת עולם עם כול

9   קץ נהיה ואני לאדם רשעה ולסוד עול בשר עוונותי פשעי חטאתי ( ) עם נעוות לבבי

10   לסוד רמה והולכי   חושך כיא לאדם דרכו ואנוש לוא יכין צעדו כיא לאל המשפט ומידו

11   תום הדרך ובדעתו נהיה כול ודו֯ול הויה במחשבתו יכינו ומבלעדיו לוא יעשה   ואני אם

12   אמוט חסדי אל ישועתי לעד ואם אכשול בעוון בשר משפטי בצדקת אל תעמוד לנצחים

13   ואם יפתח צרתי ומשחת יחלץ נפשי ויכן לדרך פעמי ברחמיו הגישני ובחסדיו יביא

14   משפטי בצדקת אמתו שפטני וברוב טובו יכפר בעד כול עוונותי ובצדקתו יטהרני מנדת

15   אנוש וחטאת בני אדם להודות לאל צדקו ולעליון תפארתו ברוך אתה אלי הפותח לדעה

16   לב עבדכה הכן¹ בצדק כול מעשיו והקם לבן אמתכה כאשר רציתה לבחירי אדם להתיצב

17   לפניכה לעד כיא מבלעדיכה² לוא תתם דרך ובלו רצונכה לוא יעשה כול אתה הוריתה

18   כול דעה וכול הנהיה ברצונכה היה ואין אחר זולתכה להשיב על עצתכה³ ולהשכיל

19   בכול מחשבת קודשכה ולהביט בעומק רזיכה ולהתבונן בכול נפלאותיכה⁴ עם כוח

20   גבורתכה⁵ ומי יכול להכיל את כבודכה ומה אף הואה בן א֯דם במעשי פלאכה⁶

21   וילוד אשה מה ישב לפניכה והואה מעפר מגבלו ולחם רמה מדורו והואה מצירוק

22   חמר קורץ ולעפר תשוקתו מה ישיב חמר ויוצר יד ולעצת מה יבין

---

¹ 4QS MS J: הכן. לב עבדך ². 4QS MS J: מבלעדיך. ³ 4QS MS J: עצ]תך. ⁴ 4QS MS J: נפלאותיך. ⁵ 4QS MS J: גבורתך. ⁶ 4QS MS J: פלאך.

…they shall separate themselves from the session of the men of deceit in order to depart into the wilderness to prepare there the Way of the Lord as it is written: "In the wilderness prepare the way of the Lord, make level in the desert a highway for our God."

English Translation

RULE OF THE COMMUNITY

COLUMN I

Preamble

1 To the [...]*šym* for his life [the Book of the Rul]e of the Community: In order to seek

2 God with [all the heart and with all the soul] doing what is good and right before him, as

3 he commanded through Moses and all his servants the prophets; in order to love all

4 which he has chosen, and to hate all which he has rejected, keeping away from all evil

5 and adhering to all good works; in order to perform truth and righteousness and justice

6 upon the earth; in order to walk no longer with the stubbornness of a guilty heart, (nor with) lustful eyes

7 doing all evil; in order to receive all those who devote themselves to do God's statutes

8 into the covenant of mercy, to be joined to God's Council, and to walk perfectly before him (according to) all

9 revealed (laws) at their appointed times; in order to love all the Sons of Light each

10 according to his lot in God's Council, and to hate all the Sons of Darkness each according to his guilt

11 at God's vengeance; thus all those devoting themselves to his truth shall bring all their knowledge, strength,

12 and property into God's Community in order to purify their knowledge by the truth of God's statutes, and discipline their strength

13 according to the perfection of his ways, and all their property according to his righteous counsel; in order not to deviate from any one

14 of all God's commands in their times; in order that they not be early (in) their times, nor late

15 from all their seasons; in order not to turn aside from his true statutes (by) walking either (to) the right or (to) the left,

Entering the Covenant Community

16 and thus all those who are entering shall cross over by the Rule of the Community into the covenant before God in order to act

17 according to all which he has commanded. But they must not turn back from following after him because of any terror, dread, (or) fiery-testing

18 during the reign of Belial. And when they cross over into the covenant the priests

19 and the Levites shall praise the God of salvation and all his true works, and all

20 those who cross over into the covenant shall say after them: "Amen, amen."

21 Then the priests shall report God's righteousness along with its wondrous works,

22 and recount all (his) merciful acts of love towards Israel. And then the Levites shall enumerate

23 the iniquities of the sons of Israel and all their guilty transgressions and their sins during the dominion of

24 Belial. [Then al]l those who cross over into the covenant shall confess after them (by) saying: "We have perverted ourselves,

25 we have [reb]elled, we have [sin]ned, we have acted impiously, we [and] our [fath]ers before us, by our walking

26 [... .] True and righte[ous (is the) God of Israel and] his [ju]dgment against us and [our] fathers;

1 but he has bestowed his loving mercy upon us from eternity to eternity." And then the priests shall bless all

2 the men of God's lot who walk perfectly in all his ways, and say: "May he bless you with all

3 good and keep you from all evil, and may he enlighten your heart with insight for living. May he favor you with eternal knowledge,

4 and may he lift up his merciful countenance toward you for eternal peace." Then the Levites shall curse all the men of

5 Belial's lot, and they shall respond and say: "Cursed be you in all your guilty (and) wicked works. May God give you up

6 (to) terror through all the avengers, and may he visit upon you destruction through all those who take

7 revenge. Cursed be you without compassion according to the darkness of your works, and may you be damned

8 in everlasting murky fire. May God not be compassionate unto you when you cry out, and may he not forgive (you) by covering over your iniquity.

9 May he lift up his angry countenance to wreak his vengeance upon you, and may there not be peace for you according to all who hold fast to the fathers."

10 Then all those who cross over into the covenant shall say after those who bless and those who curse: "Amen, amen."

11 Then the priests and the Levites shall continue and say: "Because of his heart's idols which he worships cursed be

12 the one who enters into this covenant and puts the stumbling-block of his iniquity before him so that he backslides, (stumbling) over it, and

13 when he hears the words of this covenant, he blesses himself erroneously, saying: 'Peace be with me,

14 for I walk in the stubbornness of my heart.' May his spirit be destroyed, (suffering) thirst along with saturation, without

15 forgiveness. May God's wrath and his angry judgments flare up against him for everlasting destruction, and may all

16 the curses of this covenant stick to him. May God set him apart for evil that he may be cut off from all the Sons of Light because of his backsliding

17 from God through his idols and the stumbling-block of his iniquity. May he put his lot among those who are cursed forever."

18 Then all those who enter the covenant shall respond and say after them: "Amen, amen."

Renewal Ceremony, Denunciations, Atonement

19 Thus they shall do year after year, (during) all the days of Belial's reign. The priests shall cross over

20 first into the order, according to their spirits, one after the other. Then the Levites shall cross over after them,

21 then all the people shall cross over thirdly into the order, one after the other, by thousands, hundreds,

22 fifties, and tens, so that every single Israelite may know his standing place in God's Community

23 for an eternal council. No one shall either fall from his standing place or rise from the place of his lot,

24 for they shall all be in the Community of truth, of virtuous humility, of merciful love, and of righteous intention

25 [towa]rds one another, in a holy council, and members of an eternal assembly. And every one, who refuses to enter

26 [the covenant of God (so as)] to walk in the stubbornness of his heart, [shall] no[t...] his true [Commun]ity, for his soul detests

Column III

1 instructions about knowledge of righteous precepts. He is unable to repent, (so that) he might live, and with the upright ones he is not to be accounted.

2 His knowledge, his strength, and his property shall not come into the Community's Council, for in the filth of wickedness (is) his plowing, and (there is) contamination

3 in his repentance. And he is not righteous when he walks in the stubbornness of his heart. Darkness he considers the ways of light. In the fount of the perfect ones

4 he cannot be accounted. He cannot be purified by atonement, nor be cleansed by waters of purification, nor sanctify himself in streams

5 and rivers, nor cleanse himself in any waters of ablution. Unclean, unclean is he, as long as he rejects God's judgments,

6 so that he cannot be instructed within the Community of his (God's) counsel. For it is by the spirit of God's true counsel that the ways of the human — all his iniquities —

7 are atoned, so that he can behold the light of life. And it is by the Community's Holy Spirit in his (God's) truth that he can be cleansed from all

8 his iniquities. It is by an upright and humble spirit that his sin can be atoned, and it is by humbling his soul to all God's statutes, that

9 his flesh can be cleansed, by sprinkling with waters of purification, and by sanctifying himself with waters of purity. May he establish his steps for walking perfectly

10 in all God's ways, as he commanded at the appointed times of his fixed times, and not turn aside, to the right or to the left, and not

11 transgress a single one of all his commands. Then he will be accepted by an agreeable atonement before God, and it shall be unto him

12 a covenant of the everlasting Community.

Qumran's Fundamental Dualism

13 (It is) for the Master to instruct and teach all the Sons of Light concerning the nature of all the sons of man,

14 (with respect) to all the kinds of their spirits with their distinctions for their works in their generations, and (with respect) to the visitation of their afflictions together with

15 their times of peace. From the God of knowledge comes all that is occurring and shall occur. And before they came into being he established all their designs;

16 when they come into existence in their fixed times they carry through their task according to his glorious design. Nothing can be changed. In his hand (are)

17 the judgments of all things; and he is the one who sustains them in all their affairs. He created the human for the dominion of

18 the world, and designed for him two spirits in which to walk until the appointed time for his visitation, namely the spirits of

19 truth and deceit. In a spring of light emanates the nature of truth and from a well of darkness emerges the nature of deceit.

20 In the hand of the Prince of Lights (is) the dominion of all the Sons of Righteousness; in the ways of light they walk. But in the hand of the Angel of

21 Darkness (is) the dominion of the Sons of Deceit; and in the ways of darkness they walk. By the Angel of Darkness comes the aberration of

22 all the Sons of Righteousness; and all their sins, their iniquities, their guilt, and their iniquitous works (are caused) by his dominion,

23 according to God's mysteries, until (the Angel of Darkness') end. And all their afflictions and the appointed times of their suffering (are caused) by the dominion of his hostility.

24 All the spirits of his lot cause to stumble the Sons of Light; but the God of Israel and his Angel of Truth help all

25 the Sons of Light. He created the spirits of light and darkness, and he founded every work upon them,

26 l[…]bn every action, and upon their ways (are) [all…]wdh. The one God loves for all

Column IV

1 [app]ointed times of eternity, and takes pleasure in all its doings forever; (but concerning) the other he loathes its assembly; all its ways he hates forever.

2 These are their ways in the world: (The Spirit of Truth) shall illuminate the human heart and level before him all the ways of true righteousness; and make his heart fear God's judgments;

3 and (he shall inspire) a spirit of humility, patience, great compassion, constant goodness, prudence, insight, and (the) wonderful wisdom (which is) firmly established in all

4 God's works, (thereby helping the Son of Light) lean on his great mercy. And (the Son of Light shall possess) a spirit of knowledge in all work upon which he is intent, zeal for righteous precepts, a holy intention

5 with a steadfast purpose, great affection towards all the Sons of Truth, a glorious purity, loathing all unclean idols, walking with reservation

6 by discernment about everything, and concealing the truth of the mysteries of knowledge. The (preceding) are the principles of the spirit for the Sons of Truth (in) the world. And the visitation of all those who walk in it (will be) healing,

7 great peace in a long life, and multiplication of progeny together with all everlasting blessings, endless joy in everlasting life, and a crown of glory

8 together with a resplendent attire in eternal light.

9 Concerning the Spirit of Deceit, however, (these are the principles): greed and slackness in righteous activity, wickedness and falsehood, pride and haughtiness, atrocious disguise and falsehood,

10 great hypocrisy, fury, great vileness, shameless zeal for abominable works in a spirit of fornication, filthy ways in unclean worship,

11 a tongue of blasphemy, blindness of eyes and deafness of ear, stiffness of neck and hardness of heart, walking in all the ways of darkness, and (wallowing in) evil craftiness. The visitation of

12 all who walk in it (will be) many afflictions by all the angels of punishment, eternal perdition by the fury of God's vengeful wrath, everlasting terror

13 and endless shame, together with disgrace of annihilation in the fire of the dark region. All their times for their generations (will be expended) in dreadful suffering and bitter misery in dark abysses until

14 they are destroyed. (There will be) no remnant nor rescue for them.

15 In these (two spirits are) the natures of all the sons of man, and in their (two) divisions all their hosts of their generations have a share; in their ways they walk, and the entire task of

16 their works (falls) within their divisions according to a man's share, much or little, in all the times of eternity. For God has set them apart until the Endtime;

17 and he put eternal enmity between their (two) classes. An abomination to truth (are) the doings of deceit, and an abomination to deceit (are) all the ways of truth. (There is) a fierce

18 struggle between all their judgments, for they do not walk together. But God, in his mysterious understanding and his glorious wisdom, has set an end for the existence of deceit. At the appointed time

19 for visitation he will destroy it forever. Then truth will appear forever (in) the world, for it has polluted itself by the ways of ungodliness during the dominion of deceit until

20 the appointed time for judgment which has been decided. Then God will purify by his truth all human works and purge for himself some of the sons of man. He will utterly destroy the spirit of deceit from the veins of

21 his flesh. He will purify him from all ungodly acts by the Holy Spirit and sprinkle upon him the Spirit of Truth like waters of purification, (to purify him) from all the abominations of falsehood and from being polluted

22 by a spirit of impurity, so that upright ones may have insight into the knowledge of the Most High and the wisdom of the sons of heaven; and the perfect in the Way may receive understanding. For those God has chosen for an eternal covenant,

23 and all Adam's glory shall be theirs without deceit. All false works will be put to shame. Until now the spirits of truth and deceit struggle in the heart of humans,

24 and (so) they walk in wisdom or vileness. According to a man's share in truth shall he be righteous and thus hate deceit, and according to his inheritance in the lot of deceit he shall be evil through it, and thus

25 loathe truth. For God has set them apart until the time of that which has been decided, and the making of the new. He knows the reward of their works for all the end of

26 [appointed tim]es; he allots them to the sons of man for knowledge of good [… and thus de]ciding the lots for every living being, according to his spirit b[…the] visitation.

COLUMN V

Rules for Life in the Community

1 This (is) the rule for the men of the Community who devote themselves to turn away from all evil and hold fast to all which he has commanded as his will: they shall separate themselves from the congregation of

2 the men of deceit, in order to become a Community, with Torah and with property, and answerable to the Sons of Zadok, the priests who keep the covenant, according to the multitude of the men of

3 the Community who hold fast to the covenant. According to their order shall go forth the determination of the lot about everything concerning Torah, property, and judgment, to perform truth (in) unity, humility,

4 righteousness, justice, merciful love, (and thus) circumspectly walking in all their ways. No man shall wander in the stubbornness of his heart, to err following his heart,

5 his eyes, and the plan of his inclination. He shall rather circumcise in the Community the foreskin of the inclination (and) a stiff neck. They shall lay a foundation of truth for Israel, for the Community of an eternal

6 covenant. They shall atone for all those who devote themselves for a sanctuary in Aaron and for a house of truth in Israel, and for those who join them for a Community. In a lawsuit and judgment

7 they shall pronounce guilty all those who transgress the statute. These are the determinations of their ways, according to all these statutes, when they are gathered to the Community: every one who enters into the Community's Council

8 shall enter into God's covenant in the sight of all those who devote themselves. He shall take upon his soul by a binding oath to return to Moses' Torah, according to all which he has commanded with all

9 (his) heart and soul, according to everything which has been revealed from it to the Sons of Zadok, the priests who keep the covenant and seek his (God's) will, and according to the multitude of the men of their covenant

10 who devote themselves together to his truth and to walking in his will. He shall take upon his soul by covenant to separate from all the men of deceit who walk

11 in the way of wickedness. For they cannot be accounted in his (God's) covenant, since they have neither sought nor inquired after him through his statutes, in order to know the hidden (ways) in which they erred,

12 incurring guilt, nor the revealed (ways) in which they treated with an arrogant hand, (thus) arousing anger for judgment and taking vengeance by the curses of the covenant. In them he (God) will execute great

13 judgments resulting in eternal destruction without a remnant. He must not enter the water in order to touch the purity of the men of holiness, for they cannot be cleansed

14 unless they turn away from their wickedness, since (he remains) impure among all those who transgress his words. No one must be united with him in his duty or his property, lest he burden him

15 (with) guilty iniquity. But he shall keep far away from him in everything, for thus it is written: "Keep far away from everything false." No man of the men of

16 the Community shall respond to their utterance (with respect) to any law or judgment. No one must either eat or drink anything of their property, or accept from their hand anything whatever

17 without payment, as it is written: "Have nothing to do with the man whose breath is in his nostrils, for wherein can he be accounted?" For

18 all those who are not accounted within his (God's) covenant, they and everything they have must be excluded. The man of holiness must not lean on any worthless works,

19 for worthless are all who do not know his covenant. But all those who spurn his word he will destroy from the world, and all their works are impure

20 before him, and all their property is unclean. And therefore he shall enter into the covenant in order to act according to all these statutes for the Community (which is) a holy Congregation. And they shall examine

21 their spirits within the Community, between (each) man and his neighbor according to his insight and his works in the Torah, under the authority of the Sons of Aaron who dedicate themselves within the Community to establish

22 his covenant and to observe all his statutes which he commanded (them) to do, and upon the authority of the multitude of Israel who dedicate themselves to return to his (God's) covenant through the Community.

23 They shall register them in the rule, each before his companion, according to his insight and his works. Everyone shall obey his companion; the lower one (in rank obeying) the higher one (in rank). In order to examine

24 their spirit and their works year after year, so as to elevate each according to his insight and the perfection of his way, or to keep him back according to his perversity. Each shall admonish

25 his companion in t[ru]th, humility, and merciful love (one) to another. He must not speak to his fellow with anger or with a snarl,

26 or with a [stiff] neck [or in a jealous] spirit of wickedness. And he must not hate him [in the foreskin of] his heart, for he shall admonish him on (the very same) day lest

Column VI

1 he bear iniquity because of him. And also let no man accuse his companion before the Many without a confrontation before witnesses. According to these (precepts)

2 they shall behave themselves in all their dwelling-places. Wherever they are found, each one and his companion, the lesser one shall obey the greater with respect to work and money. And (in) unity they shall eat,

3 and (in) unity they shall say benedictions, and (in) unity they shall give counsel. And in every place where there are ten men (belonging to) the Community's Council, there must not be lacking among them a man (who is)

4 a priest. And each member shall sit according to his rank before him, and thus they shall be asked for their counsel concerning every matter. When the table has been prepared for eating, or the new wine

5 for drinking, the priest shall be the first to stretch out his hand, in order to bless the first (produce of) the bread

6 and the new wine. And where there are ten (members) there must not be lacking there a man who studies the Torah day and night

7 continually, each man relieving his companion. In unity the Many shall spend the third part of every night of the year, reading the Book, studying judgment,

8 and in unity saying benedictions. This is the rule for the session of the Many: each (member) in his order: The priests shall sit first, the elders second, and the rest of

9 all the people shall sit each (member) in his order. And thus they shall be asked concerning judgment, concerning any counsel, and (any)thing which is for the Many, each man presenting his knowledge

10 to the Community's Council. No man may speak during the speech of his fellow before his brother has finished speaking. He may not also speak before one whose rank is registered

11 before him. The man, who is asked, may speak only in his turn. At a session of the Many no man may say anything which is not according to the interest of the Many. And if the man

12 (who is) the Examiner over the Many should restrain a man who has something to say to the Many, which is not while the one who questions the Community's Council

13 is standing, then the man may stand on his feet and say: "I have something to say to the Many." If they say to him "Speak," then he may speak. And (regarding) each one who freely offers himself from Israel

14 to join the Community's Council, the Examiner at the head of the Many shall examine him with respect to his insight and his works. If he is suited to the discipline he (the Examiner) shall permit him to enter

15 into the covenant to turn to the truth and depart from all deceit; he shall instruct him in all the Community's precepts. And later, when he enters to stand before the Many, then they shall all be asked

16 concerning his affairs, and as the lot comes out according to the Many's counsel, he shall approach or withdraw. When he approaches the Community's Council he must not touch the Many's pure-food,

17 until he has been examined concerning his spirit and his work until one full year is completed, nor shall he have any share in the Many's property.

18 When he has completed one year within the Community, the Many shall be asked about his affairs with regards to his insight and his works in Torah. If the lot should go out to him

19 that he should approach the assembly of the Community according to the priests and the multitude of the men of their covenant, then both his property and his possessions shall be given to the hand of the man (who is)

20 the Examiner over the Many's possessions. And he shall register it into the account with his hand, and he must not bring it forth for the Many. He must not touch the Many's drink until

21 he has completed a second year among the men of the Community. When that second year has been completed he shall be examined according to the Many. If the lot goes out to him

22 to approach the Community, he shall be registered in the order of his rank among his brothers, for Torah, judgment, and purity, and his property shall be assimilated (into that of the Many). His counsel

23 and his judgment shall belong to the Community.

Rules for Punishment

24 These (are) the precepts by which they shall judge in an inquiry of the Community according to the cases: If a man among them is found who lies

25 about property, and he knows (his deception), he shall be excluded from the midst of the Many's pure-food (for) one year, and be fined one fourth of his food. And one who answers

26 his companion with stubbornness, addresses him impatiently, disregards the position of his associate by rebelling against the word of his companion who is registered before him,

27 [or takes the l]aw into his own hand shall be punished (for) on[e] year [and excluded. The o]ne who mentions anything in the name honored above all *h*[… .]

Column VII

1 If he blasphemed — either because of being terrified with affliction or because of any other reason, while he is reading the Book or saying benedictions — he shall be excluded

2 and never again return to the Community's Council. But if (it is) against one of the priests who are registered in the Book (and) he speaks in anger, he shall be punished (for) one year

3 and be excluded alone from the Many's pure-food. If he spoke unintentionally, however, he shall be punished (for) six months. Whoever lies knowingly

4 shall be punished (for) six months. The man who unjustly and knowingly insults his fellow shall be punished (for) one year,

5 and be excluded (from the Many's pure-food?). Whoever speaks with deceit or acts neglectfully with knowledge to his fellow shall be punished (for) six months; but if

6 he is neglectful against his fellow, he shall be punished (for) three months. If (it is) with the Community's property that he is neglectful and he wastes it, then he shall refund it

7 in its original value.

8 But if he cannot afford to refund it, he shall be punished (for) sixty days. Whoever bears a grudge against his fellow unjustly, shall be punished (for) one year,

9 and the same (applies) to one who takes any revenge for himself. Whoever utters with his mouth a foolish word (shall be punished for) three months. Whoever speaks during his companion's speech (the fine is)

10 ten days. Whoever lies down and sleeps at a session of the Many (shall be punished for) thirty
days; the same (applies) to the man who goes away at a session of the Many

11 without permission. And whoever falls asleep up to three times at a session shall be punished
(for) ten days, but if they should be standing

12 and he departs then he shall be punished (for) thirty days. Whoever walks naked before his
fellow without being forced (to do so) shall be punished (for) six months.

13 And a man who spits into the midst of the session of the Many, shall be punished (for) thirty
days. Whoever causes his penis to come out from under his garment, or it (the garment has)

14 holes so his nakedness is seen shall be punished (for) thirty days. Whoever guffaws improperly,
and makes his voice heard, shall be punished (for) thirty

15 days. Whoever stretches out his left hand in order to recline on it shall be punished (for) ten
days. The man who slanders about his companion

16 shall be excluded (for) one year from the Many's pure-food, and be punished. If it is against the
Many, however, that he slanders then he shall be banished from them,

17 and he is never to come back again. The man who grumbles against the Community's authority
shall be banished and never come back, but if it is against his companion that he grumbles

18 unjustly then he shall be punished (for) six months. The man whose spirit swerves from the
Community's authority, by dealing treacherously with the truth

19 and by walking in the stubbornness of his heart, if he returns he shall be punished (for) two
years: in the first (year) he must not touch the Many's pure-food

20 and in the second he must not touch the Many's pure-drink, and he shall sit behind all the men
of the Community. When he has completed

21 two years, the Many shall be asked concerning his affairs. If they allow him to draw near he shall
be enlisted in his place, and afterwards he may be asked concerning judgment.

22 Every man who has been in the Community's Council for as long as a period of ten years,

23 and whose spirit then backslides by being treacherous towards the Community, and he leaves
the teachers of

24 the Many to walk in the stubbornness of his heart shall never again return to the Community's
Council. And a man from the men of the Communi[ty who sh]ares

25 with him his pure-food or his property wh[ich...] the Many, his judgment shall be the same: he
shall be b[anished... .]

COLUMN VIII

Rules for the Holy Congregation

1 In the Community's Council there (are to be) twelve (lay)men and three priests, perfect in
everything which has been revealed from the whole

2 Torah, to perform truth, righteousness, justice, merciful love, and circumspect walking, each one
with his companion

3 to keep faithfulness in the land with a steadfast purpose and a broken spirit, and to pay for
iniquity by works of judgment

4 and suffering affliction, and to walk with all by the measure of truth and the norm of the Endtime.
When these become in Israel

5 — the Community's Council being established in truth — an eternal plant, the House of Holiness
consisting of Israel, a most holy assembly

6 for Aaron, (with) eternal truth for judgment, chosen by (divine) pleasure to atone for the land and
to repay

7 the wicked their reward, it shall be the tested wall, the costly cornerstone.

8 Its foundations shall neither be shaken nor be dislodged from their place. (It shall be) a most holy
dwelling

9 for Aaron, with all-encompassing knowledge of the covenant of judgment, and offering up a
sweet odor. (It shall be) a house of perfection and truth in Israel

10 to uphold the covenant of eternal statutes. They will be accepted to atone for the land and to decide judgment over wickedness; and there will be no more iniquity. When these are established in the Community's principles for two years among the perfect of the Way

11 they shall be set apart (as) holy in the midst of the Council of the men of the Community. Everything which has been concealed from Israel and is found by someone

12 who studies — he shall not conceal it from these out of fear of a backsliding spirit. When these become the Community in Israel

13 they shall separate themselves from the session of the men of deceit in order to depart into the wilderness to prepare there the Way of the Lord

14 as it is written: "In the wilderness prepare the way of the Lord, make level in the desert a highway for our God."

15 This (concerns) the study of the Torah wh[ic]h he commanded through Moses to do, according to everything which has been revealed (from) time to time,

16 and according to that which the prophets have revealed by his Holy Spirit. No man of the men of the Community — of the covenant of

17 the Community — who strays from any one of the ordinances deliberately may touch the pure-food of the men of holiness

18 nor know any of their counsel, until his works have become purified from all deceit by walking with those perfect of the Way. Then he may approach

19 the council according to the Many, and afterwards he may be enlisted in his rank. This precept (shall be) for every one who joins the Community.

20 These (are) the precepts according to which the men of perfect holiness shall behave each with his companion:

21 all who enter into the Council of Holiness of those who walk with the perfect of the Way as he commanded, (indeed) every man of them

22 who transgresses one word of Moses' Torah deliberately or through negligence, shall be banished from the Community's Council

23 and never come back again. No one from the men of holiness shall associate with his property or with his counsel concerning any

24 matter. But if it is through inadvertence that he does it, then he shall be excluded from the pure-food and from the Council, and they shall study the judgment:

25 "He must neither judge a man, nor be asked for any counsel for two years." If his way is perfect

26 (he may return to participate) in the session, in study, and in the Council [according to the] Many provided that he commit no further inadvertence until he has completed two

27 years.

COLUMN IX

1 For (it is because) of one inadvertence that he can be punished two years, but for the one who acts deliberately he shall never return. Only the one who (errs) inadvertently

2 shall be tested for two years as to the perfection of his way and his counsel according to the Many, and afterwards be enlisted in his rank for the Community of Holiness.

3 When, according to all these norms, these (men) become in Israel a foundation of the Holy Spirit in eternal truth,

4 they shall atone for iniquitous guilt and for sinful unfaithfulness, so that (God's) favor for the land (is obtained) without the flesh of burnt-offerings and without the fat of sacrifices. The proper offerings of

5 the lips for judgment (is as) a righteous sweetness, and the perfect ones of the Way (are as) a pleasing freewill offering. At that time the men of the Community shall separate themselves

6 (as) a House of Holiness for Aaron, for the Community of the most Holy Ones, and a house of the Community for Israel; (these are) the ones who walk perfectly.

7 The Sons of Aaron alone shall rule over judgment and property. According to them the lot shall be cast concerning every norm of the men of the Community.

8 And (concerning) the property of the men of holiness who walk perfectly, it must not be merged with the property of the men of deceit who

9 have not cleansed their way by separating themselves from deceit and walking with the perfect ones of the Way. They shall not depart from any counsel of the Torah in order to walk

10 in all the stubbornness of their heart. They shall be judged by the first judgments in which the men of the Community began to be instructed,

11 until the coming of the prophet and the Messiahs of Aaron and Israel.

12 These are the statutes, by which the Master shall walk with every living being, according to the norm of every time and the weight of every man.

13 He shall do God's will, according to everything which has been revealed from age to age. He shall learn all the understanding which has been found according to the times

14 and the statute of the Endtime. He shall separate and weigh the Sons of Righteousness according to their spirits. He shall keep hold of the chosen ones of the Endtime according to

15 his will as he has commanded. According to a man's spirit (is) justice to be done (to him), and according to the cleanness of a man's hands he may approach, and upon the authority of his insight

16 he may draw near, and thus (establish) his love along with his hatred. But one must not argue nor quarrel with the men of the pit,

17 so that the counsel of the Torah might be concealed in the midst of the men of deceit. One must argue with true knowledge and righteous judgment (only with) the chosen of

18 the Way, each according to his spirit and according to the norm of the Endtime. He shall guide them with knowledge, and instruct them in the mysteries of wonder and truth in the midst of

19 the men of the Community, so that they may walk perfectly each one with his companion in everything which has been revealed to them. That is the time to prepare the way

20 to the wilderness. He shall instruct them (in) all that is found to be performed in this time. He shall separate himself from each man who has not turned his way

21 from all deceit. These are the norms of the way for the Master in these times with respect to his love and his hate. Eternal hatred

22 against the men of the pit in the spirit of concealment. He shall leave to them property and labor of hands, as a slave does to the one who rules over him, and one oppressed before

23 the one who dominates over him. He shall be a man zealous for the statute and prepared for the day of vengeance. He shall perform (God's) will in every enterprise

24 and in all his dominion, as he (God) has commanded. And (in) all that befalls him he shall delight willingly and desire only God's will,

25 [and in al]l the words of his (God's) mouth he shall delight. He desires nothing which he (God) has not command[ed, for] God's [judgme]nt always keeps watch.

26 [...And in afflic]tion he praises his creator. And in every circumstance he shall rec[ount his (God's) mercies... (with the offering of)] the lips. He shall praise him

Column X

1 (in accord) with the times which he has decreed: at the beginning of the dominion of light, at its turning-point when it withdraws itself to its assigned dwelling, at the beginning of

2 the watches of darkness when he (God) opens its treasure and spreads it over (the earth), and at its turning-point when it withdraws itself before the light, when

3 luminaries shine forth from the realm of holiness, when they withdraw themselves to the dwelling of glory, at the commencement of the seasons on the days of the new moon, together with their turning-point and

4 their transmitting to one another — when they are renewed (it is) a great day for the most holy and a sign of the release of his eternal mercies, at the heads of

5 seasons in every time to come, at the beginning of months at their appointed times, and on holy days in their fixed order, as memorials at their appointed times.

6 (With) the offering of the lips I will praise him according to a statute engraved forever: at the beginnings of years and at the turning-point of their seasons by the completion of the statute of

7 their norm — (each) day (having) its precept — one after another, (from) the season for harvest until summer; (from) the season of sowing until the season of grass; (from) the seasons for years until their seven-year periods;

8 at the beginning of their seven-year period until the Jubilee. As long as I live (there shall be) an engraved statute on my tongue as a fruit of praise, the portion of my lips.

Hymn of Praise

9 I will sing with skill, and all my song (will be) to the glory of God. The strings of my harp (will be tuned) to the norm of his holiness, and the flute of my lips I will play in tune with his judgment.

10 As the day and night enter I will enter into God's covenant, and as evening and morning depart I will recite his statutes. Where they are I will establish

11 my boundary without backsliding. (By) his judgment I am chastened according to my iniquities, and my transgressions are before my eyes as an engraved statute. To God I call, "My Righteousness!"

12 and to the Most High, "Foundation of my Goodness," "Fountain of Knowledge," "Spring of Holiness," "Pinnacle of Glory," "The Power of All with Eternal Glory." I will choose what

13 he teaches me, and I will delight (in) however he judges me. When I stretch out (my) hands and feet I will praise his name. When I go out and come in,

14 (when I) sit and rise, and when laid on my couch, I will cry for joy to him. I will praise him with the offering of the utterance of my lips in the row of men,

15 and before I lift my hand to enjoy the delights of the world's produce. In the beginning of terror and dread, and in the abode of affliction and distress

16 I will bless him exceedingly. I will meditate upon his power, and upon his mercies I will lean all day. For I know that in his hand is the judgment of

17 every living being, and (that) all his works (are) truth. When affliction starts I will laud him, and for his salvation I will cry out for joy thoroughly. I will pay no one the reward

18 of evil; with good I will pursue humankind. For the judgment of every living being (resides only) with God, and he (alone) shall pay man his reward. I will not envy through a spirit of

19 wickedness, and my soul will not desire the wealth of violence. And until the Day of Vengeance I will not be engaged (in) the strife against a man of the pit. But my anger I will not

20 turn away from the men of deceit, and I will not feel satisfied until he (God) has accomplished judgment. I will not hold anger towards those who turn away from transgression; but I will not have compassion

21 for all those who deviate from the Way. I will not console those who are being obstinate until their way is perfect. I will not keep Belial in my heart. Neither shall be heard from my mouth

22 lewdness and iniquitous deceit, nor craftiness and lies be found on my lips. But the fruit of holiness (shall be) on my tongue, and abominations

23 shall not be found on it. I will open my mouth with thanksgiving hymns, and my tongue shall enumerate always God's righteousness and men's unfaithfulness to the point of their complete

24 sinfulness. I will remove vanities from my lips, impure and tortuous thoughts from the thought of my heart. With wise counsel I will conceal knowledge,

25 and with prudent knowledge I will hedge [(it) with a] firm boundary, keeping the faithfulness and the strong judgment of God's righteousness. [I will measu]re

26 a statute by the measuring-line of times […] righteous, merciful love towards the lowly, and to strengthen the hands of the anxio[us, to cause to know]

Column XI

1 discernment to those erring of spirit, to teach understanding to those that grumble, to respond humbly before the haughty of spirit and with a contrite spirit towards the men of

2 oppression who stretch forth a finger, speak iniquity, and acquire wealth. But as for me, the judgment concerning me (belongs) to God. The perfection of my way and the uprightness of my heart is in his hand.

3 He shall blot out my transgression by his righteousness. For he has released his light from the fountain of his knowledge, so (that) my eye beheld his wonders, and the light of my heart beheld the mystery of

4 what shall occur and is occurring, forever. A support is at my right hand, on a firm rock (is) the way of my footstep. It shall not be shaken on account of anything, for the truth of God is

5 the rock of my footstep, and his strength is the staff (in) my right hand. My justice (is) from the fountain of his righteousness. A light from his wondrous mysteries (comes) into my heart. With the eternal Being

6 my eye beheld a salvation which is hidden from humankind, knowledge and prudent discretion (which is hidden) from Adam's sons, a fountain of righteousness and a well of

7 strength as well as a spring of glory (hidden) from the assembly of flesh. Those whom God has chosen he has set as an eternal possession. He has allowed them to inherit the lot of

8 the holy ones. With the sons of heaven he has joined together their assembly for the Council of the Community. Their assembly (is) a House of Holiness for the eternal plant during every

9 time to come. And I (belong) to wicked Adam, to the assembly of deceitful flesh. My iniquities, my transgressions, my sins, as well as the perverseness of my heart

10 (belong) to the assembly of maggots and of those who walk in darkness. For my way (belongs) to Adam. A human cannot establish his step; for to God (alone) belongs the judgment and from him is

11 the perfection of the Way. All shall occur by his knowledge. All which is occurring he establishes by his design, and without him (nothing) shall work. And I, when

12 I totter, God's mercies (are) my salvation forever. When I stumble over fleshly iniquity, my judgment (is) by God's righteousness which endures forever.

13 When my affliction starts, he rescues my soul from the pit. He establishes my footsteps for the Way. By his compassions he draws me near, and by his mercies he brings

14 my judgment. By the righteousness of his truth he judges me. By his great goodness he atones for all my iniquities. By his righteousness he cleanses me of the impurity of

15 the human and (of) the sins of Adam's sons, in order (that I might) praise God (for) his righteousness, and the Most High (for) his glory. Blessed are you, my God, who opens for knowledge

16 the heart of your servant. Establish in righteousness all his works. Raise up the son of your handmaid, as you are pleased (to establish) those chosen from Adam to stand firmly

17 before you forever. For no way can be perfect without you. And no(thing) shall work without your will. You have taught

18 all knowledge. All which shall occur is by your will. There is no one besides you to dispute your counsel, or to give instruction

19 in anything of your holy design, to behold the depth of your mysteries, to discern all your wonders along with the power of

20 your strength. Who can grasp your glory? What, indeed, is Adam's son among your wondrous works?

21 Born of a woman, how can he dwell before you, he whose kneading (is) from dust and whose corpse (is) food for maggots? He is (but) a discharge, (mere)

22 pinched-off clay whose urge is for the dust. What can clay and that which is shaped (by) hand dispute; what counsel does it comprehend?

The facing foldout of the *Rule of the Community* shows the full Scroll from column one to eleven, from right to left. The right column is the first column, as Hebrew is written from right to left — that is why the right margins are even and the left ones ragged.

The stitching to the right of column one indicates that something preceded it. Most likely what came first was the title of the Scroll. This title has been recovered; it begins with the words the "Rule of the Community." This foldout of the Scroll is reproduced at 50% of its actual size. The top of the Scroll is worn away, especially in columns one to three.

Major sections of the document are often indicated; for example, the fundamental teaching regarding the "two ways" is preceded on column three by a space (3.12), a mark in the margin (3.13), and an indentation (3.13).

Also, note that the scribes who copied the Dead Sea Scrolls made mistakes; note in particular column eight in which there are erasures and corrections above the line (possibly indicating mistakes from copying and a word or passage incorrectly overlooked). The space at the end of column eleven shows that the *Rule of the Community* ended here.

RULE

OF THE

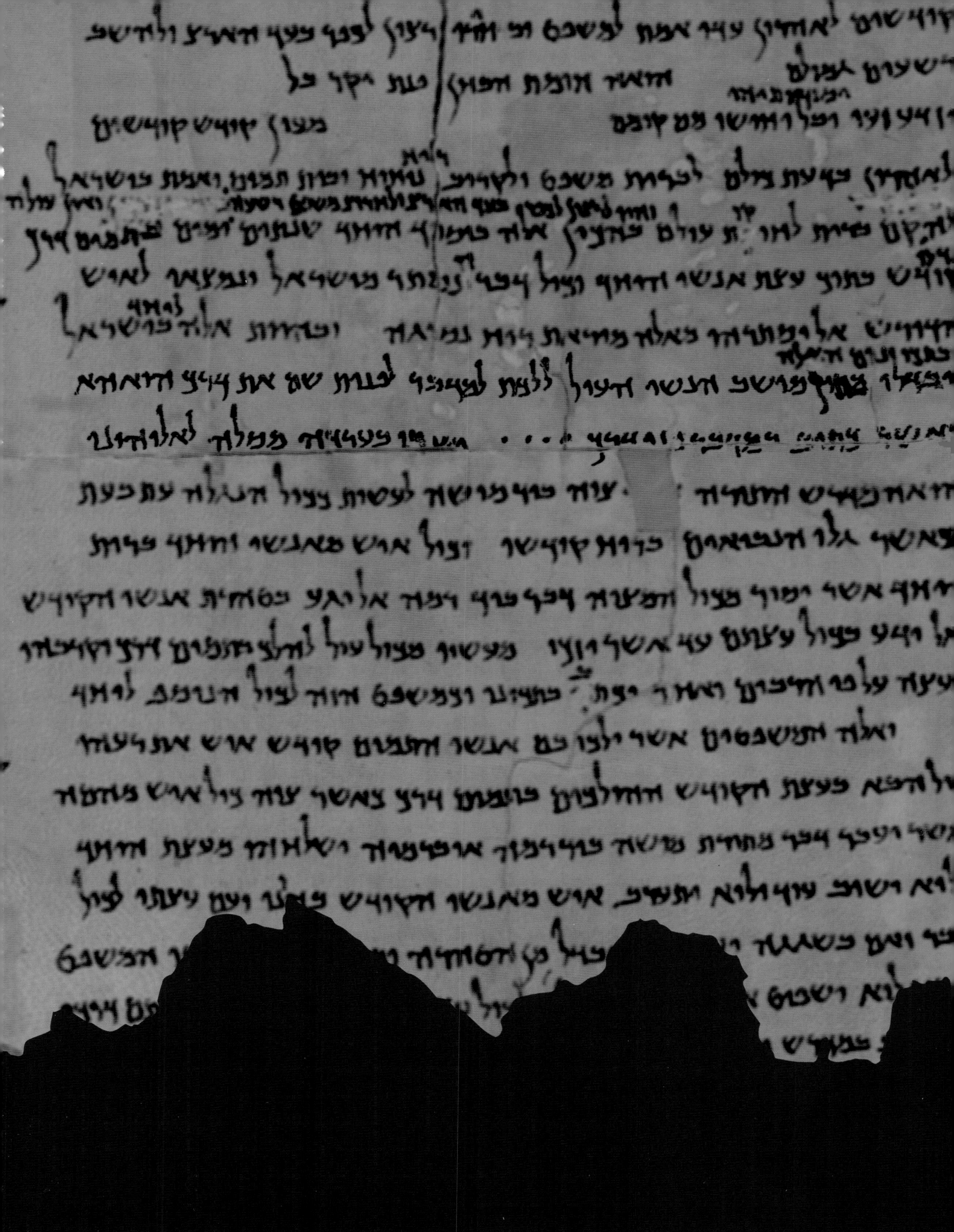

...ייבדלו (אנשי החבורה) ממקום אנשי העוול וילכו למדבר לפנות שם את דרך ה'

COMMI

UNITY

Modern Hebrew
Translation

(חובותיהם של באי הברית)

1 ל[...]שים לחייו. [ספר סר]ך היחד: ידרוש

2 את ה' ב[כל לב ובכל נפש.] ויעשה מה שטוב ומה שישר בעיני ה' כמו

3 שציוה (ה') ביד משה וביד כל עבדיו הנביאים. ויאהב את כל

4 מה ש(ה') בחר בו וישנא את כל מה ש(ה') מאס בו. וירחק מכל רע

5 וידבק במעשים טובים. ויקיים אמת וצדקה ומשפט

6 בארץ. ולא יתנהג לפי תאוותיו

7 לעשות רע. כל מי שמתנדב לקיים את חוקי ה'

8 יובא בברית חסד להתקבל לחבורת ה'. ויתנהג לפני ה' בתום (על פי) המצוות הידועות

9 כהתגלותן בזמנן המיועד. ויאהב את כל בני אור לפי

10 חלקם בחבורת ה'. וישנא את כל בני החושך לפי עונשם

11 מיד ה'. וכל המתנדבים לברית ה' יצרפו את כל דעתם וכוחם

12 ורכושם לחבורת ה', לחזק את דעתם בחוקי האמת של ה' ולכונן

13 את כוחם במצוותיו המושלמות ואת כל רכושם כעצת צדקו. ולא יעברו על איזו

14 מצוה ממצוות ה' בזמניהן ולא יקדימו את מועדיהם ולא יאחרו

15 את חגיהם, ולא יסורו מחוקי ה' במאומה.

(הברכות והקללות)

16 וכל המתקבלים לחבורה יעברו בברית לפני ה' (ויתחייבו) לעשות

17 את כל מצוות ה' ולא לסור מאחריו מחמת פחד ואימה

18 וייסורים בעת שלטון כוחות הרשע. וכאשר יעברו (המתקבלים) בברית יברכו הכוהנים

19 והלויים את ה' ואת כל מעשיו. וכל

20 העוברים בברית יענו: אמן אמן.

21 והכוהנים ימנו את צדקות ה' ומעשי גבורתו

22 ואת חסדיו עם ישראל. והלויים ימנו

23 את עוונות בני ישראל ואת כל פשעיהם וחטאיהם בזמן שלטון

24 כוחות הרשע. [וכ]ל העוברים בברית יתוודו ויאמרו: עווינו

25 [פ]שענו [חט]אנו והרשענו אנו [וא]בותינו כאשר מרדנו בחוקים,

26 וצוד[ק ה' שהע]ניש אותנו ואת אבותי[נו]

78

1 (אבל את) חסדיו גמל עלינו לעולמים. והכוהנים יברכו את כל

2 אנשי חבורת ה' הדבקים במצוות ה', ויאמרו: יברכך (ה') בכל

3 טוב וישמורך מכל רע ויחכימך בשכל לאורך ימים ויתן לך תבונה נצחית,

4 וישים לך שלום עולמים. והלויים יקללו את כל חבורת אנשי

5 הרשע ויאמרו: ארור תהיה בשל מעשי רשעתך. יביא

6 ה' עליך חלחלה ביד נקמים (=מלאכי נקמה) ויכלה אותך ביד פורעים (=מלאכי פורענות).

7 ארור תהיה לאין רחמים בחשכת מעשיך, ומקולל תהיה

8 באפלת אש (השאול) הנצחית. לא ירחם עליך ה' כאשר תתפלל (אליו) ולא יסלח ולא יכפר על עוונותיך.

9 ייפרע ממך בכעסו, ולא יהיה לך שלום בפי כל מלמדי זכות אבות (=ממליצים).

10 וכל העוברים בברית יענו אחר המברכים והמקללים: אמן אמן.

11 ויוסיפו הכהנים והלויים ויאמרו: ארור יהיה מי מבאי הברית שיפר בכוונה רעה

12 את הברית הזאת בפנייתו אחר עוונותיו.

13 וכאשר ישמע את קללות הברית הזאת יאמר בלבו: שלום יהיה לי

14 גם אם אנהג כרצון לבי; ותיספה רוחו הצמאה עם הרווה ולא

15 ייסלח לו. כעס ה' ושפטיו יבערו בו לכליון נצח, וידבקו בו כל

16 קללות הברית הזאת. ויבדילהו ה' לרעה, והוא ייבדל מחבורת בני האור בגלל שנסוג

17 מאחרי ה' בכוונתו הרעה ובפנייתו אחר עוונותיו. יתן (ה') את חלקו בחבורת ארורי נצח.

18 וכל באי הברית יאמרו: אמן אמן.

19 ככה יעשו כל שנה בכל ימי שלטון הרשעה. הכוהנים יעברו

20 ראשונים בשורה זה אחרי זה לפי מעלתם הרוחנית, והלויים יעברו אחריהם (שניים),

21 וכל העם יעברו שלישיים בשורה, זה אחר זה, (בקבוצות ש)ל אלפים ומאות

22 וחמישים ועשרות. וידע כל איש ישראל את מקומו בחבורת ה'

23 שתתקיים לעד. ולא ירד איש בדרגה ולא יעלה בדרגה,

24 אלא הכל יהיו בחבורת ה', (וינהגו) בענוה, באהבה שאינה תלויה בדבר ובכוונות טובות

25 כלפי הזולת, בתוך חבורת ה' שתתקיים לעד. וכל מי שמסרב לבוא

26 [בברית ה'] וינהג על פי תאוותיו ל[א יימנה על חבו]רת ה' כי מאס

1 במצוות ובמשפטי צדק לא החזיק כדי לחיות. (לכן) לא יימנה בעדת צדיקים

2 ודעתו וכוחו והונו לא יתקבלו לחבורה. כי מחשבת רשע מחשבתו וטומאה

3 במנהגיו. לא ייחשב לצדיק בהתנהגותו על פי תאוותיו, ובחשכה יביט לדרכי אור. במקום תמימים

79

4 לא ייחשב. לא יוכל להיזכות על ידי קרבנות כיפורים ולא יוכל להיטהר במי חטאת (מאפר הפרה האדומה), ולא יטהר בימים

5 ובנהרות ובכל מי רחיצה (מקוואות). טמא יהיה כל עוד הוא מואס במצוות

6 ה' ואינו מתייסר במשפטי החבורה. כי ברוח חבורת האמת האלוהית יכופרו כל

7 עוונות האדם ויראה באור החיים, וברוח קודש המיוחדת לחבורת ה' יטהר מכל

8 עוונותיו וברוח יושר וענווה יתכופר חטאתו, ובהיכנעותו למצוות ה' יטהר

9 בשרו ויכשר להיטהר במי חטאת ולהתקדש במי טהרה, ויתחזק לקיים

10 את חוקי ה' כאשר צוה, (חוקים הנקבעים) בתקופות (שקבע) ה'. ולא יסטה מן החוקים במאומה ולא

11 יעבור על שום מצוה ממצוות ה'. אז יתרצה ה' לו בקרבנות כיפורים. והוא יזכה להיכלל בברית

12 החבורה הקיימת לעד.

(תכונות האנוש)

13 למשכיל, ללמד את כל בני האור על תכונות כל בני האדם

14 על פי מיני יצריהם לסימניהם, למעשיהם בדורותיהם בתקופות הרע

15 ובתקופות השלום שלהם. מה' כל מה שהיה וכל מה שיהיה, ולפני שנוצרו הוא תכנן אותם.

16 ובהתהוותם בזמנם כפי שתכנן אותם ה' יתקיימו הדברים ולא יוכל איש לשנותם.

17 ה' מנהיג את כל היצורים והוא דואג להם לכל צורכיהם. ה' ברא את האדם למשול

18 בתבל ונתן לו שני יצרים להתנהג על פיהם עד המועד שהוא יפקוד את הארץ (באחרית הימים). הם יצר

19 האמת (=הטוב) ויצר הרע. במקור האור תכונת הטוב ובמקור החושך תכונת הרוע.

20 מלאך האור מושל בבני הצדק והם נוהגים בדרך הטוב, ומלאך

21 החושך מושל בני הרשע והם נוהגים בדרך הרוע. ב(זמן שלטון) מלאך החושך שוגגים

22 כל בני צדק, וכל חטאיהם ועוונותיהם ואשמותיהם ופשעיהם מתקיימים בעת שלטונו

23 לפי התוכנית הנסתרת של ה' עד קצו (של שלטון מלאך החושך). וכל נגעיהם ומועדי צרותם בעת שלטונו.

24 וכל מלאכי חבורתו נועדו להכשיל את בני האור. אבל ה' ומלאכו מסייעים לכל

25-26 בני אור. ה' ברא יצר טוב ויצר רע ועל פיהם ייסד כל דבר. את האחד אוהב ה'

עמוד ד

1 לעולמים וכל מנהגיו תמיד רצויים לו. ואת האחד הוא מתעב, ושונא לנצח את כל מנהגיו.

(רוח האמת)

2 ואלה מנהיגהם בעולם: (היצר הטוב) יאיר את עיני האדם ויכוונהו בדרכי האמת ויביאהו לפחוד ממשפטי

3 ה' (ויתן לו) ענוותנות וסבלנות ורחמים וטוב נצחי ושכל ובינה וחכמה וגבורה נסמכת על כל

4 מעשי ה' ונשענת על כל חסדיו ודעת להבין את תכניות ה', ונאמנות למשפטי הצדק ותוכניות

80

5 ה' כלפי נאמניו והתנהגות במידת החסד עם כל בני החבורה ושמירת הטהרה, שנאת כל
העוונות, והתנהגות

6 בזהירות ובתבונה, והסתרת רזי ה'. אלה היסודות של רוח בני האמת וכל ההולכים בדרך
האמת יזכו לבריאות

7 ורוב שלום ואריכות ימים וריבוי צאצאים וכל ברכות עד ושמחת עולמים בחיי נצח ועטרת
כבוד

8 ולבוש הדר באור נצחי.

(רוח העוולה)

9 (ואלה התכונות) של רוח העוולה: תאוותנות והתרשלות במנהגי האמת, רשע ושקר, גאוה
והתנשאות, כחש ורמיה, אכזריות

10 ורוב חנופה, חוסר סבלנות והרבה אוולת וקנאות לזדון, מעשי תועבה ורוח זנות ומנהגי
טומאה

11 ושפת גידופים, אי ראיית האמת ואי שמיעת (תוכחת), עקשנות וטמטום, הליכה בכל דרכי
חושך וחכמה להרע.

12 כל ההולכים בדרך רוח העוולה נידונים לרוב נגעים ביד כל מלאכי החבלה, לפגעים
תמידיים מכעס אל נקמות, ולחלחלה נצחית ולחרפת

13 עולם ולכלמת כליון באש מחשכים (שבשאול). וכל תקופותיהם יהיו באבל ויגון ורעה גדולה
בזמן קיומו של החושך,

14 עד שיכלו ללא שארית ופליטה.

(נחלת האדם באמת ובעוולה)

15 על פי (שני היצרים) הללו (נקבעות) תכונות כל בני האדם, והם נוחלים מהם תמיד ונוהגים
על פיהם וכל

16 מעשיהם לפי נחלתם בהם, לפי חלקו של כל איש (בכל אחד מהם) אם מעט אם הרבה. כי ה'
נתנם זה בצד זה עד המועד

17 האחרון (עת הגאולה), ונתן שנאה נצחית ביניהן. (רוח) הטוב מתעבת את מנהגי (רוח) הרוע,
ו(רוח) הרוע מתעבת את כל מנהגי (רוח) הטוב, וקנאת

18 ריב בכל משפטיהן כי דרכיהם שונות זו מזו. וה' בתוכניתו הנסתרת ובחוכמתו קצב זמן
לקיומה של (רוח) הרוע ובמועד

19 שנקבע ישמיד אותה לתמיד. אז תכונן רוח האמת כי נטמאה בדרכי רשע בזמן שלטון הרוע
עד

20 מועד המשפט. ואז יטהר ה' בחסדו את בני האדם ויזקק את האנשים לכלות את יצר הרע
מתוך

21 גופם ולטהר אותם ברוח ה' מכל מנהגי הרשעה. ויזה עליהם רוח אמת כמי חטאת (לטהר
אותם) מכל תועבות שקר והיטמאות

22 ברוח נידה. ויתבוננו הישרים בדעת ה', ותמימי הדרך בחוכמת המלאכים, כי בהם בחר ה'
ל(בני) ברית עולמים.

23 ולהם (יתן ה') את כל התהילה שניתנה לאדם (הראשון). ותכלה הרשעה ויהיו לבושת.כל
מעשי הרמיה. עד הנה רבים יצר הטוב ויצר הרע בלב האנשים.

24 (לכן) מתנהגים האנשים בחכמה ובאוולת. ככל שאדם נוחל יותר מן היצר הטוב כן הוא
שונא את הרע. וככל שהוא נוחל יותר מחלק הרע כן הוא נוהג ברשעות

25 ומתעב את האמת. כי זה בצד זה שם אותם ה' עד המועד שקבע לשינוי הדברים. והוא יודע
את כל אשר יעשו היצרים בכל הזמנים

26 והנחיל אותם לבני האדם לדעת טוב [ורע ול]תת לכל איש את חלקו לפי מעלתו הרוחנית
ב[... עד המועד] שנקבע.

81

(תקנון המתנדבים)

1. וזה התקנון של אנשי החבורה המתנדבים: ישובו מכל רע ויחזיקו במצוות ה' וייבדלו מעדת

2. הרשעים וייעשו חבורה אחת בלימוד התורה ובשיתוף הרכוש. ויסורו למרות בני צדוק הכוהנים שומרי הברית וראשי

3. החבורה המחזיקים בברית. על פיהם ייקבע כל דבר בתורה וברכוש ובמשפט. וינהגו בדרך אמת שיתוף וענוה

4. צדקה ומשפט ואהבה שאינה תלויה בדבר וצנעה בכל מנהיגהם. לא ינהג איש על פי תאוותיו

5. ויצריו. אלא ימולו כולם את עורלת הלב ואת העקשות. ייסדו יסוד נאמן של ישראלים לחבורת ברית

6. נצח. ויכופר לכל המתנדבים (להיות) כמקדש של כוהנים וכבית נאמן של ישראלים והמצטרפים אליהם לחבורה ולריב ולמשפט

7. ולהעניש את כל העברייניים.

(מנהגי המתנדבים)

ואלה מנהגיהם על פי כל החוקים האלה בהתכנסם לחבורה: כל המתקבל לחבורה

8. יבוא בברית ה' בנוכחות כל המתנדבים ויישבע בשבועת אסר לשוב אל תורת משה, ככל אשר ציוה (ה'), בכל

9. לב ובכל נפש, (כפירוש התורה) הנגלה לכוהנים בני צדוק שומרי הברית ומפרשי מצוות ה' ולאנשי החבורה

10. המתנדבים כולם לברית ה' ולהתנהג על פי מצוותיו. המתקבל יישבע להיבדל מכל הרשעים הנוהגים

11. ברשעות שאינם משתייכים לבני ברית ה', כי לא חקרו היטב את חוקי ה' להכיר את המצוות הנעלמות מהם (שנתגלו לבני החבורה) ועברו עליהן בשגגה

12. המחייבת קרבן אשם. ועל המצוות הנגלות והברורות לכל עברו בזדון והביאו לכך שייעשו בהם שפטים כקללות הברית שיביאו עליהם

13. כיליון מוחלט לעולמים. הרשעים מנועים מלהיטהר במים כדי לאכול ממזונם הטהור של אנשי החבורה. כי לא יוכלו להיטהר

14. אלא אם ישובו מרעתם כי הטומאה שורה בקרב העברייניים. הם מנועים מלהשתתף עם אנשי היחד ברכוש ובהון כדי שלא ישיאו אותם

15. עוון. יש לרחוק מהם כמו שכתוב "מכל דבר שקר תרחק". איש מאנשי

16. החבורה לא ינהג על פי מנהיגהם וחוקיהם, ולא יאכל מרכושם ולא ישתה ולא יקבל מהם דבר

17. ללא תשלום כמו שכתוב "חדלו לכם מן האדם אשר נשמה באפו כי במה נחשב הוא".

18. יש להבדיל את כל מי שאינם משתייכים לברית ה' ואת כל אשר להם. ולא יסתייע איש מאנשי החבורה באנשי

19. ההבל כי הבל כל מי שאינם יודעים את מצוות ה'. וה' ישמיד את כל מנאצי דברו, וכל מעשיהם (נחשבים) טמאים בעיניו

20. וטומאה בכל רכושם. וכאשר המועמד לחבורה יבוא בברית (ויתחייב) לעשות ככל החוקים האלה כדי להתקבל לחבורה יחקרו

21. את מעלתו הרוחנית בקרב בני החבורה, לפי שכלו ודבקותו במצוות התורה על פי הכוהנים המתנדבים לחבורה כדי לקיים

22 את חוקי ה' ועל פי ראשי הישראלים המתנדבים לקיים את ברית ה' במסגרת החבורה.

23 ויקבעו את סדר מעלתם בחבורה איש לפי שכלו ודבקותו במצוות. הקטן במעלה יציית לגדול ממנו. וראשי החבורה

24 יבחנו את הסדר כל שנה ויעלו בדרגה את מי שראוי להעלות ויורידו בדרגה את מי שראוי להוריד. בריבם יוכיחו

25 החברים זה את זה בא[מ]ת ובענוה ובאהבה שאינה תלויה בדבר. ולא ידברו זה אל זה בכעס או בהתרסה

26 או בע[קשות או בקנאות] מרושעת ולא ישנא איש את אחיו [... ב]לבבו אלא ביום המקרה (לפני שקיעת השמש) יבוא בדין עם רעהו כדי שלא

עמוד ו

1 ייענש בגללו. כמו כן לא יתבע איש את רעהו לדין לפני החבורה ללא ראיות שעל פי עדים.

(מנהגי החבורה)

2 על פי התקנות הללו יתנהגו זה עם זה בכל מקומות מגוריהם. ויצייתו הקטן במעלה לגדול ממנו בענייני רכוש והון. ויחד יאכלו

3 ויחד יברכו ויחד יקיימו כינוסים (למשפט וללימוד התורה) ובכל מקום שיש בו עשרה מאנשי החבורה יהיה עמהם

4 כוהן. ואיש לפי מעלתו (בחבורה) ישבו לפניו, ובסדר הזה יישאלו לדעתם בכל דבר משפט. וכאשר יערכו את השולחן כדי לאכול (מביכורי הדגן) או לשתות (מביכורי) התירוש,

5 הכוהן יברך ראשון על ביכורי הלחם או על ביכורי התירוש.

6 ובמקום שיש בו העשרה (מאנשי החבורה) יעסקו (האנשים) בלימוד התורה יומם ולילה,

7 איש בתורו. ובני החבורה יהיו ערים במושב החבורה במשך שליש מכל לילה מלילות השנה כדי לקרוא בתורה וללמוד את החוקים

8 ולומר ברכות.

(סדר הישיבה והדיון)

וזה סדר ישיבת החבורה איש לפי מעלתו. הכוהנים ישבו ראשונים והזקנים שניים ושאר

9 כל העם ישבו [אחריהם] איש לפי מעלתו, וכן יישאלו למשפט ולכל התייעצות ודבר הנידון בין

10 אנשי החבורה. אל ייכנס איש לתוך דברי חברו, וכמו כן לא ידבר לפני מי שגדול ממנו במעלה.

11 כל איש יישאל בתורו ואז ידבר. ולא ידבר איש במושב החבורה כל דבר שאינו נוגע לחבורה ואפילו

12 המפקח של החבורה. וכל מי שמעוניין להביא איזה דבר לדיון בפני החבורה שלא במעמד האיש השואל את החבורה.

13 האיש הזה יקום ויאמר. אני מעוניין להביא איזה דבר לדיון בפני החבורה. (רק) אם יתירו לו ידבר.

(קבלת חברים חדשים)

וכל מי שמתנדב מישראל

14 להיווסף לחבורה ייחקר על ידי האיש המופקד על הרבים על הבנתו ועל דבקותו במצוות. אם ישגה (?) בחוק

83

15 ישביענו (הפקיד) לשוב לאמת ולסור מכל רע וילמד אותו את כל חוקי החבורה. ואחר כך כאשר יתייצב המועמד לפני הרבים יישאלו

16 הכל בעניינו ולפי החלטתם יתקבל (כמועמד) או יידחה. וכאשר יתקבל (המועמד) לחבורה לא יגע במזון הטהור

17 של החבורה עד אשר ייחקר על הבנתו ועל דבקותו במצוות במשך שנה תמימה. ובתקופה זו לא ישתתף בהון החבורה.

18 וכעבור שנה יישאלו בני החבורה בעניינו באשר להבנתו ודבקותו במצוות. ואם יוחלט

19 לקבלו לחבורה יובא גם את כספו ורכושו אל המפקח על רכוש החבורה,

20 והלה יערוך רשימה (של הרכוש והממון), והכסף לא ישמש לצורכי הרבים. (המתקבל) לא יגע במשקה (הטהור) של אנשי החבורה עד

21 שתמלא לו שנה שנייה בקרב החבורה. ובתום השנה השנייה ייבדק עניינו על פי הרבים ואם יוחלט לצרפו

22 לחבורה הוא ייכלל לפי דרגתו ברשימת בני החבורה לצורך (התכנסויות ללימוד) התורה ולקיום המשפט ולסעודות המשותפות ולשיתוף הממון. והוא יהיה דן

23 בחבורה ונידון על ידיה.

(העונשים)

24 ואלה העונשים אשר ייענשו בהם לפי חקירת החבורה בכל מקרה. מי מאנשי החבורה שימעל ביודעין

25 בכספי החבורה לא ישתתף בסעודות החבורה במשך שנה, ויקנסו אותו ברבע ממכסת המזון. ומי שיתנהג עם

26 רעהו בסרבנות או בחוסר סבלנות ויפגע בזכות חברו; משום שהמרה את פי רעהו הכתוב לפניו (ברשימת הדרגות)

27 [וע]שה דין לעצמו, יוטל עליו קנס בשיעור רבע ממזונו במשך שנה, [והוא לא ישתתף בסעודת בני החבורה. ומי ש]יזכיר את השם המפורש על כל ה]

עמוד ז

1 אם (הזכירו כאשר) קלל או כאשר נחרד מצרה או מכל סיבה אחרת, או כשהוא קורא בתורה או מברך – ייבדל

2 לתמיד מחבורת היחד. מי שיספר לשון הרע בכוונה על אחד מן הכוהנים הרשומים ברשימת החברים – ייענש שנה

3 אחת (בשיעור רבע ממזונו ולא ישתתף בסעודות החבורה (במשך השנה הזאת); ואם בהיסח הדעת סיפר לשון הרע – ייענש ששה חודשים (בשיעור רבע ממזונו ולא ישתתף בסעודת החבורה בזמן הזה). ומי שישקר לרעהו

4 ייענש ששה חודשים (כנ"ל). מי שיקלל בלא סיבה ובכוונה את רעהו ייענש שנה אחת (בשיעור רבע ממזונו)

5 ולא ישתתף בסעודת החבורה (בשנה הזאת). מי שידבר עם רעהו בהתנשאות או יזלזל בחברו, ייענש ששה חודשים (כנ"ל).

6 ומי שיתרשל ב(כבוד) רעהו ייענש שלושה חודשים (כנ"ל). ואם יתרשל בהון החבורה ויגרום לאובדנו, ישלם

7 את מלוא סכום הקרן.

8 אם לא יהיו לו אמצעים לשלם ייענש ששים יום (כנ"ל). מי שישמור טינה לרעהו שלא כמצות (התורה) ייענש שנה אחת (כנ"ל).

84

9 אותו העונש יוטל על מי שיעשה דין לעצמו. מי שינבל את פיו ייענש שלושה חודשים (כנ"ל). ומי שייכנס לתוך דברי חברו

10 ייענש במשך עשרה ימים (כנ"ל). מי שיישכב ויי3שן באסיפה של החבורה ייענש שלושים יום (כנ"ל). אותו קנס יוטל על מי שישב ברישול (ויירדם) בעת האסיפה

11 בלי כוונה ומי שיתנמנם באסיפה אחת עד שלוש פעמים ייענש עשרה ימים (כנ"ל). ואם לאחר שזקפוהו (כלומר: התרו בו)

12 ישב ברישול – ייענש שלושים יום (כנ"ל). מי שיתהלך ערום לפני הבריות, מבלי שהיה אנוס, ייענש ששה חודשים (כנ"ל).

13 מי שיירק אל תוך מושב החבורה ייענש שלושים יום (כנ"ל). מי שיוציא את ידו מתחת כסותו כשאין הוא

14 לבוש כראוי כך שתיגלה ערוותו ייענש שלושים יום (כנ"ל). מי שיצחק צחוק פרוע ייענש שלושים

15 יום (כנ"ל). ומי שיוציא את יד שמאלו לשוח בה ייענש עשרה ימים (כנ"ל). ומי שילשין על רעהו

16 יובדל שנה אחת מן הסעודה המשותפת וייענש (בתקופה הזאת בשיעור רבע ממזונו). ומי שילשין על כלל החבורה יגורש מן החבורה

17 לתמיד. ומי שינהג במרי נגד מוסדות היחד יגורש לתמיד. ואם נגד רעהו ינהג

18 במרי ללא הצדקה ייענש ששה חודשים (כנ"ל). ומי שיסור ממוסדות החבורה ויפר את הברית

19 וינהג על פי תאוותיו, כאשר ישוב (לחבורה) ייענש שנתיים. בשנה הראשונה הוא לא ישתתף בסעודת החבורה,

20 ובשנה השניה לא יגע במשקה (הטהור) של החבורה, וישב אחרי כל אנשי החבורה. ובמלאת

21 לו שנתיים יישאלו החברים על מעשיו ואם יקבלוהו ייכתב בדרגה שנקבעה לו, ואחרי כן יישאל בענייני משפט.

22 וכל איש מאנשי החבורה שמלאו עשר שנים

23 לקבלתו וחזר לבגוד בחבורה, ויתנהג על

24 פי תאוותיו, לא ישוב עוד אל מועצת החבורה. וכל מי מאנשי החבו[רה שיש]תתף

25 אתו במזונו הטהור או ברכושו ש[לא ברשות]החברים יהיה דינו כדין המשתלח וי[שולח אף] הוא מן החבורה.]

עמוד ח

(הרכב החבורה)

1 במועצת החבורה יהיו שנים עשר ישראלים ושלושה כוהנים, מקיימים בשלמות את כל

2 המצוות שנגלו לחבורה, ומקיימים אמת וצדקה ומשפט ואהבה שאינה תלויה בדבר, ונוהגים במידת הצניעות זה עם זה.

3 מקיימים את ברית ה' בעולם בנאמנות ובהכנעה ומכפרים עוון בחבורת מקיימי המצוות

4 בעת היסורים שלפני הגאולה, ומתנהגים עם הכל לפי החוקים הנצחיים והתקנות הזמניות. בהיות אלה בישראל

5 תתקיים מועצת החבורה לנצח, חבורת קודש של ישראלים ויסוד קודש

6 קודשים של כוהנים, עדי אמת למשפט ובחירי רצון (ה') לכפר בעד הארץ ולהשיב

85

7 לרשעים גמולם. (מועצת החבורה) היא חומת המגדל, אבן הפנה שלא

8 יזועו יסודותיהם ולא ימושו ממקומם. מעון קודש קודשים

9 של כהנים, בדעת כולם לברית משפט ולהקריב ריח ניחוח ובית ישר ונאמן בישראל,

10 להקים ברית נצחית ויהיו לרצון לכפר בעד הארץ ולחרוץ משפט רשעה. כאשר יתקיימו הכללים האלה ביסוד החבורה שנתים בתום דרך וללא עולה,

11 ייבדלו קודש בתוך אנשי החבורה. וכל דבר הנסתר מישראל שיתגלה למי

12 שדורש (בתורה) אל יסתיר אותו משאר ישראל בשל חשש מפני תגובה שלילית

(ההליכה במדבר)

כאשר יתקיימו התקנות הזמניות הללו בישראל

13 ייבדלו (אנשי החבורה) ממקום אנשי העוול וילכו למדבר לפנות שם את דרך ה'

14 כמו שכתוב "במדבר פנו דרך ה' ישרו בערבה מסילה לאלהינו".

15 (הדרך) היא לימוד החוקים א[ש]ר צוה ה' ביד משה, לקיים את החוקים כפי שיתגלו (ללומדים) מעת לעת,

16 וכפי שגילו הנביאים ברוח הקודש. וכל איש מאנשי החבורה

17 אשר יעבור על איזו מצוה בזדון לא ישתתף בסעודת החבורה

18 ובאסיפתם עד שירחק מכל מעשה רע וילך בדרך האמת. אז יתקבל

19 לחבורה על פי החלטת החברים, ואחר תיקבע דרגתו. וככה ייעשה לכל מי שמצטרף לחבורה.

(עונשים)

20 ואלה העונשים אשר ינהגו על פיהם אנשי החבורה זה עם זה.

21 כל המתקבלים לחבורה הנוהגים בחוקי האמת כאשר צוה ה'. כל

22 מי שיעבור על מצוה ממצוות התורה בזדון או מתוך זלזול יגורש מן החבורה

23 ולא ישוב עוד. ולא ישתתף איש מאנשי החבורה בהונו ולא ידון אתו

24 בדבר משפט. ואם בשגגה עבר על המצוות יובדל מסעודת החבורה ומן הכינוסים ולימוד החוק.

25 ולא ישפוט ולא יישאל על כל עצה שנתים. אם ישוב להיות תמים בקיום המצוות

26-27 ישוב להשתתף במושב החבורה ובמדרש התורה ובהתכנסויות [על פי החלטת ה]חברים, בתנאי שלא עבר (אפילו) בשגגה על המצוות במשך השנתיים הללו.

עמוד ט

1 כי מי שעובר בשגגה על אחת ממצוות התורה ייענש שנתים. ומי שעובר על המצוות בזדון (יגורש מן העדה ו)לא ישוב. מי שעבר בשגגה על המצוה

2 ייבחן שנתים לתום דרכו והבנתו, על פי הרבים, ואחר תיקבע דרגתו בחבורה.

(הרכב החבורה)

3 כאשר יתקיימו התקנות הזמניות הללו בישראל ייקבע רצון ה' כאמת

4 נצחית, ויכופר על אשמת פשע ומעל חטאת, והארץ תירצה יותר מבשר עולות ומחלבי זבח ותפילה

5 תיחשב בעיני ה' כקורבנות, ותום דרך יהיה כנדבת מנחת רצון. בעת ההיא ייבדלו אנשי

6 החבורה, כמוסד של כוהנים הנבדלים כקודש קודשים וכמוסד של ישראלים הנוהגים בתום.

7 הכוהנים ישלטו במשפט ובהון ועל פיהם ייקבע חלק כל אנשי החבורה.

8 והון אנשי החבורה ההולכים בדרך האמת לא ישותף עם הון (האנשים) המקילים ראש

9 שלא הקפידו בקיום המצוות ולא נבדלו מעוול על מנת ללכת בדרך האמת, אך עם זה הם לא נפרדו מכלל החבורה משום שלא נהגו על

10 פי תאוותיהם – הם, מקילי הראש, ייענשו בעונשים הראשונים שאנשי החבורה נענשים בהם

11 עד אשר יבוא נביא ומשיחי אהרון וישראל.

(מנהגי המשכיל)

12 אלה החוקים למשכיל להתנהג על פיהם עם כל האדם לפי החוק התקף באותה העת ולפי חשיבותו של כל איש.

13 יקיים את מצוות ה' כפי שהן מתגלות (ללומדים) בכל עת, ויחקור את כל ידע התורה המתגלה בעתים השונות ואת

14 החוקים של הקופת שלטון הרשע. יבדיל וימדוד את בני החבורה לפי מעלתם הרוחנית, ויתמוך בבחירים שבתקופת הרשע

15 כרצון ה', כאשר ציווה. וידון כל איש לפי מעלתו הרוחנית ויקרב כל איש לפי צדיקותו, ולפי מדע תורתו,

16 וכן ינהג באשר לאהבתו או שנאתו (את כל איש). לא יריב או יתווכח איש עם הרשעים (שמחוץ לכת).

17 ויסתיר את החוקים המיוחדים לכת מאותם הרשעים. וילמד חוקי אמת ומשפטי צדק לבחירים (אנשי הכת),

18 איש כמעלתו הרוחנית כחוק העת (של שלטון הרשע). ינחה אותם בדעה וילמדם סתרי חוקי ה' בקרב

19 אנשי החבורה. וינהגו זה עם זה ביושר בכל המצוות הנגלות להם בעת הזאת שהחבורה פרשה

20 למדבר. וילמדם את כל מה שראוי לעשות בעת הזאת, ולהיבדל מכל מי שלא סר

21 מרע. ואלה התקנות למשכיל בעתים הללו לאהבתו (את בני החבורה) ולשנאתו הנצחית

22 את הרשעים (שמחוץ לחבורה), שנאה מסותרת. יוותר להם על הון ורכוש כ(מנהג) עבד כלפי מי שמושל בו, וישפיל רוחו בפני

23 מי שרודה בו. ויהיה דבק בקנאות בחוקי (התורה) ומוכן ליום נקם. יעשה רצון ה' בכל מלאכתו

24 ובכל יכולתו כמו שציווה (ה'). וכל מה שייעשה בו יקבל ברצון וחוץ מן המצוות לא יחפץ בדבר.

25 [ובכ]ל דברי ה' ירצה ולא יתאוה במה שלא ציו[ה] (ה'). למשפ[ט ה' יצפה תמיד

26 [גם בעת צ]רה יברך את ה' ותמיד יספ]ר חסדיו...] יברך את ה'

87

1   בזמנים אשר קבע ה': בתחילת הופעת האור ובצהרי היום ובהיאסף האור למעוני הקבוע. בתחילת

2   אשמורות החושך ובזמן הלילה בעת שה' פותח את אוצרו של החושך ומפזרו (על פני הארץ), ובחצות הלילה, ובהיאסף החושך מפני האור, בעת הופעת

3   המאורות בשמי ה' ובהיאספם למעון ה'; בהתחדשות של (ארבע) עונות השנה, ובמחציתן וכאשר הן נפגשות

4   זו עם זו. מועד התחדשות הוא יום גדול לה' וסימן להופעת חסדיו, בראשי

5   ארבע עונות השנה בכל הזמנים.

(ברכות בגוף ראשון)

בראשי החודשים לתקופותיהם ובחגים בזמנם לזכרון במועדיהם,

6   כתרומת שפתים אני מברך את ה', כמנהג קבוע לנצח. בראשי שנים ובארבע עונות השנה ובסופן כאשר הן

7   נפגשות זו עם זו: עונת האביב עם עונת הקיץ ועונת הסתיו עם עונת החורף. מועדי השנים לתקופות שמיטותיהן

8   ובראש השמיטות מועד היובל. וכל עוד אני חי מנהג קבוע בידי להלל את ה'.

9   אני מזמר בדעת ומנגן לכבוד ה'; מכה נבלי לומר חוקיו וחלילי לספר משפטיו.

10   בתחילת היום והלילה אני בא בברית ה' ובצאת הערב והבוקר אני אומר חוקיו. אני נוהג על פיהם ואיני סר מהם.

11   אל משפט ה' אני מביט כאשר אני חוטא ופשעי לנגד עיני בקביעות. לה' אני קורא צדקי

12   ולעליון מכון טובי, מקור דעת ומעין קודש רום כבוד וגבורת כל לתפארת עולם. אני בוחר

13   לקיים את מצוות ה' ומקבל ברצון את ייסוריו. בכל צעדיי אני מברך את ה',

14   בשבתי ובקומי ובשכבי לישון. אני מברך אותו בביטוי שפתיי בקהילת אנשים.

15   ולפני שאני מתחיל לאכול מטוב הארץ (אני מברך על המזון?). כאשר נופלים עליי פחד ואימה ורעות

16   אני מברך אותו במאוד, ועל גבורתו אני מספר ועל חסדיו אני נסמך תמיד. ידוע לי כי כי הוא משגיח

17   על כל היצורים וכל פעולתו אמת. וכאשר באה עליי צרה אני מהלל את ה' וכשהוא מושיע אותי אני מרנן לו בקהל. איני מעניש איש על

18   רעתו אלא נוהג בטוב עם הכל. כי ה' שופט את כל הבריות ומשלם לכל איש כגמולו. איני מקנא

19   ברשעות (או: ברשעים), ואיני מתאוה להון שלא נעשה במשפט (או: להון הרשעים), לא אבוא בריב עם הרשעים עד יום הדין (של ה'), אבל איני חדל

20   לשנוא אותם (בסתר) ולא אהיה שבע רצון עד יום המשפט (של ה'). איני שומר שנאה לאנשי החבורה ואיני מרחם

21   על כל מי שאינם נוהגים במנהגיהם. איני מרחם על הרשעים כל עוד אינם נוהגים בדרך האמת. אין רשעות בלבי ואין דבר

22   נבלות ושקר בפי, ועוון ושקר אינם נמצאים בשפתיי. דברי קודש בלשוני ותועבות

23   אינן נמצאות בה. פי מדבר תשבחות וצדקות ה' מספרת לשוני תמיד כנגד עוונות האדם עד תום

פעם. אני מסיר דברי ריק משפתי ודברי ניבול מלבי. בחכמה אני מסתיר (תוקן: מספר) את דעת ה'

ובערמה אני מסוכך [עליה,] חוק נאמן לשמור אמונים ומשפט עוז לצדקת ה'. [אני מל]מד

את החוק הנקבע בכל עת ועת [... אני נוהג] באהבה שאינה תלויה בדבר עם אנשי החבורה ומחזק את ידיהם [כדי להודיע]

עמוד יא

לתועי רוח בינה. ללמד את הנרגנים לקח, ולהשיב בענוה לגאותנים, וברוח נשברה לאנשי

מוטה שולחי אצבע ומדברי און ורוכשי הון. ואני ביד ה' משפטי ותום דרכי עם יושר לבי

ובצדקות ה' נמחק פשעי כי ה' מאיר את עיני בדעת ומראה לי את נפלאותיו וממלא את לבבי אור בגלותו לי את רזיו,

וסומך אותי בידיעת סודות הבריאה הנצחיים. רגליי עומדות איתן ולא יתמוטטו. כי אני נשען על חוקי האמת של ה'

ועל גבורתו. בצדקתו אני נושע ורזיו מאירים את עיני ואני מביט בסודות הבריאה הנצחיים.

חכמה ודעת הנסתרות מבני האדם, מקור צדקה

גבורה וכבוד הנסתרים מבני אנוש – את אלה נתן ה' לבחיריו לנחלת עולם והנחילם בחלק

המלאכים לחבורה קדושה וליסוד מבנה קודש הנטוע לעד.

אני שייך לזרע האדם הנמשך אל הרשע וליסוד האנוש הנפשע, ועוונותיי ופשעיי וחטאתיי ונעוותיי הם מתכונות האדם

שנידון להיות משכן רימה וסופו לחשכת הקבר. כי האדם אינו קובע את מעשיו אלא ה'.

ההנהגה וההתנהגות ביושר ממנו היא, והוא תכנן ויצר את הכל ודבר לא ייעשה מבלעדיו. ואשר לי,

כאשר אני נופל חסדי האל מושיעים אותי לעד, וכאשר אני נכשל בעוונות האדם, ה' בצדקתו אשר קיימת לעולמים

הוא אשר דן אותי. וכאשר הוא מביא עליי צרה אין הוא ממיתני אלא מדריכני בחוקיו. הוא מקרב אותי ברחמיו ושופט אותי בחסדיו

ובצדקתו ומכפר ברוב טובו על כל עוונותיי. בצדקתו הוא מטהר אותי מטומאת

האדם ומחטאותיי כדי שאודה לו על צדקתו (ואהלל) את תפארתו.

(תהלת ה')

ברוך אתה ה' הפותח לדעה את

לבי. עשה נא שכל מעשיי יהיו טובים, וקיים לי מה שניאות לעשות לבחיריך, שאתייצב

לפניך לנצח. כי מבלעדיך אין מנהגי יושר ובלא רצונך אין נעשה דבר. אתה הורית

כל דעה וכל מה שקיים ברצונך נהיה, ואין אחר זולתך לטעון כנגדך ולהבין את

כל תוכניותיך ואת רזיך וכל נפלאותיך וכוחך.

ומי יכול להבין אותך ומה אפוא הוא בן האדם בפלאי יצירתך

ילוד אשה אינו דר במחיצתך. והוא מעפר יסודו ומאכל רימה גופו.

והוא מחומר קורץ ולעפר ישוב. מה ישיב חומר ומעשה יד ומה יוכל להבין?

French Translation

RÈGLE DE LA COMMUNAUTÉ

COLONNE I

Introduction

1 Pour […]*šym* pour sa vie [le Livre de la Règ]le de la Communauté. Pour chercher

2 Dieu de [tout (son) coeur et de tout (son) être], faisant ce qui est bon et droit devant lui, selon

3 ce qu'il a ordonné par Moïse et par tous ses serviteurs les prophètes; pour aimer

4 tout de qu'il a choisi et haïr tout ce qu'il a rejeté, s'éloignant de tout mal

5 et s'attachant à toute bonne oeuvre; pour accomplir la vérité, la justice et la droiture

6 dans le pays et ne plus marcher dans l'obstination d'un coeur coupable et d'yeux luxurieux

7 s'adonnant à tout mal; pour faire entrer tous ceux qui veulent accomplir les décrets de Dieu

8 dans l'alliance de grâce, s'unir au Conseil de Dieu, et marcher parfaitement devant lui (conformément aux)

9 révélations, en leurs temps déterminés; pour aimer tous les Fils de Lumière, chacun

10 selon son lot dans le Conseil de Dieu, et haïr tous les Fils de Ténèbres, chacun selon sa (part de) culpabilité

11 à la vengeance de Dieu; tous ceux qui sont volontaires pour sa vérité apporteront leur connaissance, leur puissance

12 et leurs biens dans la Communauté de Dieu, pour purifier leur connaissance par la vérité des décrets de Dieu, régir leur puissance

13 selon la perfection de ses voies, et tous leurs biens selon le conseil de sa justice; pour ne s'écarter d'aucun

14 de tous les commandements de Dieu au sujet de leurs temps, pour n'être ni en avance sur leurs moments, ni en retard

15 par rapport à toutes leurs saisons; pour ne pas dévier de ses décrets de vérité en allant à droite ou à gauche.

L'entrée dans l'alliance

16 Ainsi, tous ceux qui entrent, (c'est) par la Règle de la Communauté (qu'ils) passeront dans l'alliance, devant Dieu, pour agir

17 selon tout ce qu'il a ordonné, sans cesser de le suivre à cause d'une quelconque terreur, d'un effroi ou d'un creuset

18 d'épreuves durant la domination de Bélial. Quand ils passeront dans l'alliance, les prêtres

19 et les lévites béniront le Dieu des délivrances et toutes ses oeuvres de vérité; et tous

20 ceux qui passeront dans l'alliance diront après eux: "Amen, amen".

21 Les prêtres raconteront comment la justice de Dieu (s'est manifestée) par des oeuvres puissantes

22 et proclameront toutes les grâces de sa miséricorde en faveur d'Israël. Et les lévites raconteront

23 tous les péchés des fils d'Israël et toutes leurs transgressions coupables et leurs fautes (commises) durant la domination de

24 Bélial. [Et tou]s ceux qui passeront dans l'alliance confesseront après eux en disant: "Nous avons péché,

25 nous avons commis des [tr]ansgressions et des [fau]tes, nous avons été méchants, nous [et] nos [pè]res avant nous, par notre comportement

26 [… .] (Il est) vrai et just[e, (le) Dieu d'Israël et] son [ju]gement contre nous et contre [nos] pères,

COLONNE II

1 mais il exerce sur nous la miséricorde de sa grâce, depuis toujours et pour toujours". Alors les prêtres béniront tous

2 les hommes du lot de Dieu, qui marchent parfaitement en toutes voies, et ils diront: "Qu'il te bénisse de tout

3 bien et te garde de tout mal. Qu'il illumine ton coeur par l'intelligence de vie et te favorise de la connaissance éternelle.

4 Qu'il lève vers toi le visage de sa grâce pour (que tu aies) la paix éternelle". Alors les lévites maudiront tous les hommes

5 du lot de Bélial, ils prendront la parole et diront: "Malheur à toi en toutes tes oeuvres méchantes, coupables. Que Dieu te livre

6 (à) la terreur par les agents de vengeance. Qu'il te punisse de destruction par tous ceux qui dispensent

7 les rétributions. Malheur à toi, sans miséricorde, selon les ténèbres de tes oeuvres. Damné sois-tu

8 dans l'obscurité du feu éternel. Que Dieu ne te favorise pas quand tu crieras vers lui. Qu'il ne te pardonne pas en effaçant tes péchés.

9 Qu'il lève le visage de sa colère pour se venger de toi et qu'il n'y ait aucune (parole) de paix pour toi dans la bouche de tous les intercesseurs".

10 Et tous ceux qui passent dans l'alliance diront après ceux qui bénissent et ceux qui maudissent: "Amen, amen".

11 Et les prêtres et les lévites poursuivront et diront: "Malheur, à cause des idoles qu'il sert en son coeur,

12 à celui qui entre dans cette alliance en mettant devant lui l'obstacle de son péché pour s'y égarer. Voici

13 qu'en entendant les paroles de cette alliance, il se bénira en lui-même en disant: 'Que je sois en paix

14 même si je marche dans l'obstination de mon coeur". Que soit arraché son esprit, (qui est) soif en même temps que saturation, sans

15 pardon. Que la colère de Dieu et ses ardents jugements s'enflamment contre lui pour une destruction éternelle. Que s'attachent à lui toutes

16 les imprécations de cette alliance. Que Dieu le mette à part, pour le mal, et qu'il soit retranché du milieu de tous les fils de lumières, parce qu'il s'est égaré

17 loin de Dieu avec ses idoles et l'obstacle de son péché. Qu'il lui donne son lot au milieu des malheureux pour toujours".

18 Et tous ceux qui entrent dans l'alliance prendront la parole et diront après eux: "Amen, amen".

Cérémonie de renouvellement, dénonciations, expiation

19 Ainsi feront-ils année après année, tout le temps de la domination de Bélial. Les prêtres passeront

20 en premier dans l'ordre, selon leurs esprits, l'un après l'autre. Et les lévites passeront après eux,

21 et tout le peuple passera en troisième dans l'ordre, l'un après l'autre, par milliers, centaines,

22 cinquantaines et dizaines, pour que chaque Israélite connaisse le rang qu'il tient dans la Communauté de Dieu

23 pour un Conseil éternel. Et nul ne descendra du rang qu'il tient ou ne s'élèvera du lieu (où se trouve) son lot.

24 Car ils seront tous dans la communauté de vérité, d'humilité vertueuse, d'amour loyal et d'intention juste,

25 chacun à l'égard de son prochain, dans un Conseil de sainteté, et les membres d'une assemblée éternelle. Et quiconque refuse d'entrer

26 [dans l'alliance de Dieu,] marchant dans l'obstination de son coeur, [qu'il] n[e … pas] sa [Communa]uté véritable, car

COLONNE III

1 son âme déteste les admonitions (au sujet) de la connaissance des préceptes justes. Il n'a pas la force de convertir sa vie, et ne sera pas compté avec les (hommes) droits.

2 Sa connaissance, sa puissance et ses biens ne viendront pas dans le Conseil de la Communauté, car il laboure dans la fange de la méchanceté, et (il y a de) la contamination

3 dans sa conversion. Il ne sera pas justifié quand il est entraîné dans l'obstination de son coeur et qu'il perçoit les ténèbres comme des voies de lumière. A la source des parfaits,

4 il n'est pas compté. Il ne sera pas nettoyé par l'expiation, ni purifié par les eaux lustrales, ni sanctifié dans les mers

5 ou les fleuves, ni purifié par toutes les eaux d'ablution. Impur, il reste impur, tant qu'il rejette les jugements

6 de Dieu, en sorte qu'il ne peut être corrigé dans la Communauté de son conseil. Car c'est par l'esprit du vrai conseil de Dieu que les voies de l'homme — tous ses péchés —

7 sont effacés, pour qu'il perçoive la lumière de vie. C'est par l'Esprit Saint de la Communauté en Sa vérité qu'il peut être purifié de tous ses

8 péchés. C'est par un esprit droit et humble que sa faute peut être effacée. C'est par l'humilité de sa personne à l'égard de tous les décrets divins que

9 sa chair peut être purifiée, par l'aspersion d'eaux lustrales, et en se sanctifiant par des eaux de purification. Qu'il affermisse ses pas pour marcher parfaitement

10 dans toutes les voies de Dieu, ainsi qu'il l'a ordonné en ses temps déterminés, ne déviant ni à droite ni à gauche, et ne

11 s'écartant d'aucun de tous ses commandements. Alors, il plaira à Dieu par des expiations apaisantes, et cela deviendra pour lui une alliance

12 de Communauté éternelle.

Le dualisme fondamental de la Communauté de Qumrân

13 C'est au Maître d'instruire et d'enseigner à tous les Fils de Lumière la nature de tous les fils d'homme,

14 selon toutes leurs sortes d'esprits et les caractéristiques de leurs oeuvres en leurs générations, et selon la visite où ils seront affligés ainsi que

15 les temps de leur bonheur. Du Dieu de connaissance provient tout ce qui est et sera. Avant qu'ils ne viennent à l'existence, il a établi tous leurs plans;

16 et quand ils viennent à l'existence, en leurs temps déterminés, ils accomplissent leurs activités selon son plan glorieux, sans pouvoir rien y changer. En sa main

17 sont les jugements de toutes choses: c'est lui qui pourvoit à tous leurs besoins. Il a créé l'humanité pour qu'elle domine

18 le monde; il lui a mis deux esprits en qui elle marche jusqu'au moment de sa visite, qui sont les esprits de

19 vérité et de perversion. D'une source de lumière (émane) la nature de la vérité, et d'une fontaine de ténèbres (émerge) la nature de la perversion.

20 En la main du Prince de Lumières (est) la domination de tous les fils de justice: ils marchent dans les voies de lumière. Mais en la main de l'Ange de

21 Ténèbres (est) la domination des fils de perversion: ils marchent dans les voies de ténèbres. Par l'Ange de Ténèbres (est provoqué) l'égarement de

22 tous les fils de justice: toutes leurs fautes, leurs péchés, leur culpabilité et les transgressions de leurs oeuvres (s'effectuent) sous sa domination,

23 conformément aux mystères de Dieu, jusqu'à son terme. Et toutes leurs afflictions, et les moments de leur détresse (se passent) sous sa domination hostile.

24 Et tous les esprits de son lot font trébucher les Fils de lumière; mais le Dieu d'Israël et son Ange de Vérité viennent en aide à tous

25 les Fils de Lumière. Il a créé les esprits de lumière et de ténèbres, et sur eux il a fondé toute oeuvre,

26 *l[…]hn* toute action, et sur leurs voies [toute…]*wdh*. L'un, Dieu l'aime pour toute

1 [...]'dy d'éternité, se plaisant en toutes ses activités à jamais; quant à l'autre, il déteste son assemblée, et toutes ses voies, il les hait à perpétuité.

2 Et voici leurs voies dans le monde: pour illuminer le coeur de l'homme et pour aplanir devant lui toutes les voies de vraie justice; et pour faire redouter à son coeur les jugements de

3 Dieu; et un esprit d'humilité et de longanimité, de grande miséricorde et de bonté constante, et d'intelligence, d'instruction et de puissante sagesse solidement fondée sur la foi en toutes

4 les oeuvres de Dieu, prenant appui sur sa grâce abondante; et un esprit de connaissance en tout plan d'oeuvre, un zèle pour les justes préceptes, une intention sainte

5 dans un penchant ferme; et une grande affection pour tous les Fils de Vérité; et une pureté glorieuse, détestant toutes les idoles souillées, et se conduisant modestement

6 avec discernement à tout propos, dissimulant la vérité des mystères de connaissance. Tels sont les principes de l'esprit pour les Fils de Vérité (dans) le monde. Et la visite de tous ceux qui marchent en lui (sera): la guérison,

7 une grande paix dans une longue vie, une postérité florissante ainsi que toutes les bénédictions durables, et une joie éternelle dans la vie perpétuelle, et une couronne de gloire

8 ainsi qu'un vêtement d'honneur dans la lumière éternelle.

Sur l'esprit de perversité

9 Mais (voici les caractéristiques) de l'esprit de perversité: ambition personnelle et laisser-aller dans le service de la justice, méchanceté et mensonge, orgueil et arrogance, perfidie et tromperie cruelles,

10 grande hypocrisie, prompte colère, grande folie, un zèle insolent pour des oeuvres abominables dans un esprit de débauche, des voies souillées dans un service impur

11 une langue blasphématoire, l'aveuglement des yeux et la dureté d'oreille, la raideur de nuque et la dureté de coeur, marchant dans toutes les voies de ténèbres, et la ruse maligne. La visite

12 de tous ceux qui marchent en lui (sera): de nombreux coups de tous les anges de destruction, la perdition éternelle par l'ardeur de la colère vengeresse de Dieu, une terreur perpétuelle et une honte

13 durable, avec l'opprobre de l'extermination dans le feu des régions ténébreuses. Et tous leurs temps, pour leurs générations, (s'écoulera) dans l'affliction douloureuse et le malheur amer, dans les sombres abysses, jusqu'à

14 ce qu'ils soient détruits. (Il n'y aura) ni reste ni rescapé pour eux.

Les deux natures de toute l'humanité

15 En ces (deux esprits sont) donc les natures de tous les fils d'homme, et en leur (deux) catégories toutes leurs armées ont une part, en leurs générations; elles marchent en leurs voies, et tout l'effet

16 de leurs oeuvres (se situe) en leurs catégories, suivant le partage de l'homme, selon qu'il a beaucoup ou peu, en tous les temps éternels. Car Dieu les a mis en parts égales, jusqu'au temps

17 final, et il a posé une haine éternelle entre leurs catégories. Les activités de perversité sont une abomination pour la vérité, et les voies de vérité sont une abomination pour la perversité. (Il y a) une féroce

18 lutte entre tous leurs jugements, car ils ne marchent pas ensemble. Mais Dieu, dans son intelligence mystérieuse et sa sagesse glorieuse, a prévu un terme à l'existence de la perversité. Au moment

19 de la visite, il l'anéantira à jamais. Alors la vérité paraîtra à perpétuité (dans) le monde, qui s'est pollué dans les voies de la méchanceté durant la domination de la perversité jusqu'au

20 moment du jugement fixé. Alors Dieu purifiera par sa vérité toutes les oeuvres de l'humain, et s'affinera des fils d'homme, détruisant totalement tout esprit de perversité de leurs membres

21 charnels, les purifiant par l'Esprit Saint de toute activité méchante. Il fera jaillir sur lui l'Esprit de Vérité comme les eaux lustrales (qui nettoient) toutes les abominations mensongères et la pollution

22 par un esprit de souillure, et pour instruire les (hommes) droits de la connaissance du Très-Haut, et faire comprendre la sagesse des fils du ciel à ceux dont la voie est parfaite. Car Dieu les a choisis pour une alliance éternelle

23 et toute la gloire d'Adam leur appartiendra, sans perversité. Toutes les oeuvres trompeuses seront (couvertes) de honte. Jusqu'à présent, les esprits de vérité et de perversion combattent dans le coeur humain,

24 et (ainsi) ils marchent dans la sagesse ou la folie. Selon son partage dans la vérité, un homme est donc juste et hait la perversité; et selon son héritage dans le lot de la perversion, il en est méchant et donc

25 déteste la vérité. Car Dieu les a mis en parts égales jusqu'au temps fixé et au renouvellement. Il connaît les effets de leurs oeuvres jusqu'à la fin complète des

26 [moments prév]us, et il les a partagés aux fils d'homme pour la connaissance du bien [… et pour dé]cider les lots pour tout vivant, selon son esprit, *b*[… la] visite.

COLONNE V

Règles pour la vie en Communauté

1 Ceci (est) la règle pour les hommes de la Communauté, qui sont volontaires pour se convertir de tout mal et pour s'attacher à tout ce qu'il a commandé selon sa volonté: ils se sépareront de la Congrégation

2 des hommes de perversion, pour devenir une communauté, en Loi et biens, s'en remettant aux Fils de Sadoq, les prêtres qui gardent l'alliance, et à l'ensemble des hommes

3 de la communauté attachés à l'alliance. Sur leur ordre se décidera la détermination des lots en toute chose concernant la loi, les biens, et le droit, pour accomplir ensemble la vérité, l'humilité

4 la justice et la droiture, l'amour loyal, et la modestie de conduite en toutes leurs voies. Que personne ne marche dans l'obstination de son coeur, pour errer en suivant son coeur,

5 ses yeux, et l'intention de son penchant. Il circoncira plutôt dans la Communauté le prépuce du penchant et de la nuque raide. Ils poseront une fondation de vérité pour Israël, pour la communauté d'alliance

6 éternelle. Ils expieront pour tous les volontaires pour un sanctuaire en Aaron et une maison de vérité en Israël, et pour ceux qui se joignent à eux en une Communauté. Dans un procès et jugement,

7 ils déclareront coupable tous ceux qui transgressent le décret. Voici la détermination de leurs voies, selon tous ces décrets, lorsqu'ils s'assemblent en Communauté. Quiconque entre au Conseil de la Communauté,

8 (il) entrera dans l'alliance de Dieu à la vue de tous les volontaires. Il s'engagera, par un serment d'obligation sur sa personne, à se convertir à la Loi de Moïse, selon tout ce qu'il a commandé, du fond de

9 son coeur et de son être, d'après tout ce qui en a été révélé aux Fils de Sadoq, les prêtres qui gardent l'alliance et cherchent ce qui lui plaît, et d'après l'ensemble des hommes de leur alliance

10 qui sont ensemble volontaires pour (accomplir) sa vérité et marcher selon ce qui lui plaît. Il s'engagera par alliance, sur sa personne, à se séparer de tous les hommes de perversion qui marchent

11 dans les voies de la méchanceté. Ils ne peuvent compter dans son alliance, puisqu'ils l'ont pas recherché et ne l'ont pas consulté, à travers ses décrets, pour connaître les choses cachées en quoi ils se sont égarés,

12 se rendant coupables, et les choses révélées en quoi ils ont agi avec arrogance, excitant (ainsi) la colère du jugement et l'exercice de la vengeance par les imprécations de l'alliance. Contre eux (Dieu) exécutera de grands

13 jugements (aboutissant) à une destruction éternelle, sans reste. Il n'entre pas dans les eaux pour toucher la pureté des hommes de sainteté. Car ils ne peuvent être purifiés

14 à moins de se détourner de leur mal, car (il demeure) impur avec tous ceux qui transgressent sa parole. Que nul ne s'unisse à lui dans son service ou ses biens, de peur qu'il ne le charge

15 d'un péché de culpabilité. Mais il se tiendra loin de lui en toute chose, ainsi qu'il est écrit: "Tiens-toi loin de toute chose mensongère". Nul des hommes de

16 la communauté ne s'en remettra à eux pour toute (affaire de) loi ou de droit. Personne ne doit manger ni boire rien (provenant) de leurs biens, ni accepter quoi que ce soit de leur main

17 sans l'avoir payé, ainsi qu'il est écrit: "Rompez avec l'homme qui n'a qu'un souffle dans les narines, car pour combien peut-il compter?" Car

18 tous ceux qui ne sont pas comptés dans son alliance doivent être exclus, eux et tout ce qu'ils ont. L'homme de sainteté ne doit prendre appui sur aucune oeuvre de

19 vanité, car ils sont vanité tous ceux qui ne connaissent pas son alliance. Mais tous ceux qui méprisent sa parole, il les éliminera du monde, et toutes leurs oeuvres sont de la souillure

20 devant lui, et tous leurs biens sont impurs. Ainsi entrera-t-il dans l'alliance pour agir conformément à tous ces décrets pour la Communauté (qui est) une sainte Congrégation. Ils examineront

21 leurs esprits en commun, (distinguant) chacun de son prochain, selon sa compréhension et ses oeuvres dans la Loi, sous l'autorité des Fils d'Aaron qui sont volontaires dans la Communauté pour établir

22 son alliance et pour observer tous ses décrets, qu'il a commandé d'accomplir, et sous l'autorité de la multitude d'Israël qui est volontaire pour revenir à son alliance grâce à la Communauté.

23 Ils les inscriront en ordre, chacun devant son prochain, selon sa compréhension et ses oeuvres. Chacun obéira à son prochain, l'inférieur au supérieur. Ils passeront

24 en revue leur esprit et leurs oeuvres année après année, pour élever chacun selon sa compréhension et la perfection de sa voie, ou le rétrograder selon ses défaillances. Chacun

25 réprimandera son prochain en vé[ri]té, humilité, amour loyal pour chacun. Qu'on ne lui parle pas avec colère, ou en grondant,

26 ou avec une nuque [raide, ou la jalousie] d'un esprit méchant. Il ne doit pas le haïr [dans le prépuce de] son coeur, mais il le réprimandera le jour (même), sous peine

COLONNE VI

1 d'être chargé de péché à cause de lui. De même, que personne n'amène une affaire qui concerne son prochain devant les Nombreux sans (l'avoir) confronté devant témoins. Selon ces (règles)

2 ils marcheront, partout où ils habitent, partout où chacun se trouve avec son prochain. L'inférieur obéira au supérieur en matière de travail et d'argent. Et ils mangeront ensemble,

3 prononceront les bénédictions ensemble, et tiendront conseil ensemble. Et en tout lieu où il y a dix hommes (faisant partie) du Conseil de la Communauté, qu'il ne manque pas, parmi eux,

4 un prêtre. Et chacun s'assoeira devant lui, selon son rang, et ainsi ils se demanderont conseil en toute chose. Et quand on aura préparé la table pour manger ou le vin nouveau

5 pour boire, le prêtre étendra sa main en premier pour bénir les prémices du pain

6 et le vin nouveau. Et qu'il ne manque pas, là où il y a dix (membres), un homme qui étudie la Loi jour et nuit

7 continuellement, chacun relayant son prochain. Les Nombreux veilleront ensemble, pendant la troisième partie de chaque nuit de l'année, lisant le Livre, étudiant le droit,

8 et prononçant les bénédictions ensemble. Et voici la règle pour la session des Nombreux: chacun à sa place. Les prêtres s'assoieront d'abord, les anciens en deuxième, ensuite le reste

9 de tout le peuple, chacun à son rang. Ils se demanderont jugement et tout conseil, et tout ce qui concerne les Nombreux, chacun faisant part de ce qu'il sait

10 au Conseil de la Communauté. Que personne ne parle au milieu des paroles de son prochain, avant que son frère n'ait fini de parler. De même, qu'il ne parle pas avant celui dont le rang est inscrit

11 avant le sien. L'homme interrogé, qu'il ne parle qu'à son tour. A une session des Nombreux, personne ne doit dire quelque chose sans l'accord des Nombreux. Et si

12 l'Intendant des Nombreux doit sévir (contre) un homme qui a quelque chose à dire aux Nombreux, sans que soit en poste celui qui interroge le Conseil

13 de la Communauté, cet homme se tiendra debout et dira: "J'ai quelque chose à dire aux Nombreux". Et s'ils le lui disent, il parlera. Et tout Israélite qui veut

14 se joindre au Conseil de la Communauté, l'Inspecteur qui est à la tête des Nombreux l'examinera sur sa compréhension et sur ses oeuvres. S'il est apte à la discipline, il lui permettra d'entrer

15 dans l'alliance pour qu'il se convertisse à la vérité et se détourne de toute perversion. Il l'instruira de tous les préceptes de la Communauté. Ensuite, quand il entrera pour se tenir devant les Nombreux, on les interrogera

16 tous sur son cas, et, selon le lot qui lui sera dévolu d'après le conseil des Nombreux, il s'approchera ou se retirera. Quand il s'approche du Conseil de la Communauté, il ne doit pas toucher à la pureté

17 des Nombreux, jusqu'à ce qu'il ait été examiné sur son esprit et son oeuvre, jusqu'à ce qu'une année entière ne soit écoulée; il ne doit pas non plus partager les biens des Nombreux.

18 Quand une année s'est écoulée pour lui au milieu de la Communauté, les Nombreux seront interrogés sur sa compréhension et sur ses oeuvres dans la Loi. Et si le lot lui est dévolu

19 de s'approcher de l'assemblée de la Communauté, d'après les prêtres et l'ensemble des hommes de leur alliance, alors ses biens et ses revenus seront remis aux mains de l'homme

20 qui est intendant des biens des Nombreux; (celui-ci) inscrira le (tout) de sa main dans le registre, mais ne le dépensera pas pour les Nombreux. Il ne doit pas toucher au breuvage des Nombreux jusqu'à ce

21 qu'une deuxième année ne soit écoulée pour lui au milieu des hommes de la Communauté. Quand cette deuxième année est écoulée, on l'examinera d'après (l'avis) des Nombreux. S'il lui est dévolu

22 comme sort de s'approcher de la Communauté, il sera inscrit selon l'ordre de son rang parmi ses frères, pour la Loi, le droit et la pureté, et le partage de ses biens. Son conseil sera (valide)

23 pour la Communauté, ainsi que son jugement.

Règles disciplinaires

24 Voici les préceptes d'après lesquels ils jugeront lors d'une enquête de la Communauté, suivant les cas. S'il se trouve parmi eux quelqu'un qui ment

25 à propos de ses biens, délibérément, il sera exclu de la pureté des Nombreux (pendant) une année, et sera privé du quart de sa nourriture. Et celui qui répond à

26 son prochain avec la nuque raide, lui parle avec une impatience colérique, néglige le rang de son associé en se rebellant contre la parole de son prochain qui est inscrit avant lui,

27 [ou qui se fait jus]tice par sa propre main, sera puni (pendant) un[e] année [et exclu. Ce]lui qui évoque quelque chose par le nom honoré au-dessus de tout *h*[... .]

COLONNE VII

1 Et s'il maudit (Dieu) — soit parce qu'il est assailli par la détresse ou pour toute autre raison — alors qu'il lit le Livre ou prononce les bénédictions, il sera exclu

2 et ne reviendra jamais au Conseil de la Communauté. Mais si (c'est) contre un des prêtres inscrits dans le livre (qu')il a parlé avec fureur, il sera puni (pendant) une année

3 et isolé individuellement de la pureté des Nombreux. Et s'il a parlé par inadvertance, il sera puni (pendant) six mois. Quiconque ment sciemment

4 sera puni (pendant) six mois. L'homme qui insulte son prochain, injustement (et) sciemment, sera puni (pendant) un an,

5 et exclu. Et quiconque parle à son prochain de façon trompeuse, ou commet une négligence (envers lui), sciemment, sera puni (pendant) six mois; mais s'il

6 est négligent envers son prochain, il sera puni (pendant) trois mois. Et si (c'est) avec les biens de la Communauté qu'il est négligent et qu'il les gaspille, il les remboursera

7 en entier.

8 Et s'il n'a pas les moyens de les rembourser, il sera puni (pendant) soixante jours. Quiconque garde rancune contre son prochain unjustement sera puni (pendant) un an;

9 de même pour celui qui se venge personnellement (en) quoi que ce soit. Quiconque prononce de sa bouche une parole stupide (sera puni pendant) trois mois. Celui qui parle au milieu des paroles de son prochain

10 (sera puni pendant) dix jours. Quiconque s'allonge et dort pendant une session des Nombreux (sera puni) pendant trente jours; de même pour l'homme qui s'absente pendant une session des Nombreux

11 sans permission. Et celui qui s'endort jusqu'à trois fois à la même session sera puni (pendant) dix jours, mais s'ils doivent se lever

12 et qu'il s'absente, alors il sera puni (pendant) trente jours. Quiconque marche nu devant son prochain sans obligation sera puni (pendant) six mois.

13 Et un homme qui crache au milieu d'une session des Nombreux sera puni (pendant) trente jours. Quiconque fait sortir son pénis de sous son vêtement, ou si (ce dernier a)

14 des trous et laisse voir sa nudité, sera puni (pendant) trente jours. Quiconque rit sottement et à voix haute sera puni (pendant) trente

15 jours. Quiconque tend la main gauche pour s'y appuyer sera puni (pendant) dix jours. L'homme qui calomnie son prochain

16 sera exclu (pendant) un an de la pureté des Nombreux et puni; mais s'il calomnie les Nombreux, il sera renvoyé d'entre eux

17 et ne reviendra pas à nouveau. L'homme qui gronde contre l'autorité de la Communauté sera renvoyé et ne reviendra pas; mais si c'est contre son prochain qu'il gronde

18 injustement, il sera puni (pendant) six mois. L'homme dont l'esprit déroge à l'autorité de la Communauté, en trahissant la vérité

19 et en marchant dans l'obstination de son coeur, s'il revient, il sera puni (pendant) deux années: durant la première, il ne doit pas toucher à la pureté des Nombreux

20 et durant la seconde, il ne doit pas toucher au breuvage des Nombreux, et il s'assoiera derrière tous les hommes de la Communauté. Quand sont accomplies

21 ses deux années, jour pour jour, les Nombreux seront interrogés sur ses actes. S'ils lui permettent de s'approcher, il sera inscrit à son rang, et on pourra ensuite l'interroger sur le droit.

22 Et tout homme qui a été dans le Conseil de la Communauté pendant au moins dix années complètes

23 et dont l'esprit se détourne pour trahir la Communauté, et qui s'éloigne de la présence

24 des Nombreux pour marcher dans l'obstination de son coeur, ne reviendra jamais au Conseil de la Communauté. Et s'il y a un des hommes de la Communau[té qui pa]rtage

25 avec lui sa pureté ou ses biens qu[e …]les Nombreux, son jugement sera le même: il sera r[envoyé… .]

COLONNE VIII

Règles pour la Congrégation sainte

1 Dans le Conseil de la Communauté, (il y aura) douze hommes et trois prêtres, parfaits en tout ce qui a été révélé de toute

2 la Loi, pour pratiquer la vérité, la justice, le droit, l'amour loyal et la modestie de conduite, chacun avec son prochain,

3 pour garder la fidélité dans le pays, avec un penchant ferme et un esprit contrit, pour acquitter le péché par des oeuvres de droiture

4 et (en supportant) la détresse du creuset, et pour marcher conformément à toute la mesure de vérité et la norme du temps (de la fin). Quand ces choses se produiront en Israël,

5 le Conseil de la Communauté sera établi en vérité, en plante éternelle, maison de sainteté pour Israël, et assemblée très sainte

6 pour Aaron, témoins de vérité pour le jugement, choisis selon la volonté (de Dieu) pour expier pour le pays et rendre

7 aux méchants leur rétribution. Ce sera le rempart éprouvé, la pierre d'angle de grande valeur.

8 Ses fondations ne seront pas ébranlée et ne changeront pas de place. (Ce sera) une demeure très sainte

9 pour Aaron, avec une connaissance totale pour l'alliance de droiture, présentant un parfum apaisant. (Ce sera) une maison de perfection et de vérité en Israël

10 pour maintenir l'alliance selon les décrets éternels. Ils seront agréés pour expier pour le pays et pour décider le jugement de la méchanceté; et il n'y aura plus de perversité. Quand ceux-ci seront établis dans les principes de la Communauté, depuis deux années, jour pour jour, parmi ceux dont la voie est parfaite,

11 ils seront mis à part (comme quelque chose de) saint au milieu du Conseil des hommes de la Communauté. Tout ce qui a été caché à Israël et qui est trouvé par l'homme

12 qui cherche, il ne devra pas le leur cacher par crainte d'un esprit d'égarement. Quand ceux-ci deviendront la Communauté en Israël,

13 ils se sépareront de la session des hommes de perversion pour aller au désert et y préparer la Voie du Seigneur,

14 ainsi qu'il est écrit: "Dans le désert, préparez la voie du Seigneur, nivelez dans la steppe une route pour notre Dieu".

15 Ceci (fait référence à) l'étude de la Loi q[u]'il a ordonné par Moïse d'accomplir, selon tout ce qui a été révélé, de période en période,

16 et selon ce que les prophètes ont révélés par son Esprit Saint. Aucun des hommes de la Communauté, de l'alliance

17 de la Communauté, qui dévie d'un commandement quelconque, avec arrogance, ne doit toucher à la pureté des hommes de sainteté,

18 ni connaître aucun de leur conseils, jusqu'à ce qu'il ait nettoyé ses oeuvres de toute perversion, pour marcher avec les parfaits de la Voie. Alors il pourra approcher

19 du conseil, d'après (l'avis) des Nombreux, et ensuite être inscrit à son rang. Et (il en sera) ainsi pour quiconque se joint à la Communauté.

20 Et voici les préceptes selon lesquels marcheront les hommes de parfaite sainteté, chacun avec son prochain.

21 Tout (individu) qui entre dans le Conseil de Sainteté de ceux qui marchent dans la perfection de voie, tel qu'il l'a commandé, tout homme parmi eux

22 qui transgresse un mot de la Loi de Moïse, avec arrogance ou négligence, sera renvoyé du Conseil de la Communauté

23 et ne reviendra pas à nouveau. Aucun des hommes de sainteté ne partagera ses biens ou son conseil en quoi

24 ce soit. Mais si c'est par inadvertance qu'il le fait, il sera exclu de la pureté et du Conseil, et ils scruteront le jugement:

25 "Qu'il ne juge personne et ne soit interrogé pour aucun conseil pendant deux années, jour pour jour". Si sa voie est parfaite,

26 (il pourra réintégrer) la session, l'étude, et le Conseil, [d'après (l'avis) des] Nombreux, pourvu qu'il n'ait pas commis d'autre inadvertance jusqu'à ce que soient accomplies ses deux années,

27 jour pour jour.

COLONNE IX

1 Car (c'est à cause) d'une inadvertance qu'il peut être puni (pendant) deux ans, alors que celui qui agit avec arrogance ne reviendra pas à nouveau. C'est seulement celui qui a agi par inadvertance

2 qui sera sondé pendant deux ans, jour pour jour, quant à la perfection de sa voie et de son conseil, d'après (l'avis) des Nombreux; ensuite il sera inscrit à son rang à la Communauté de Sainteté.

3 Quand ces (hommes) deviendront en Israël, selon toutes ces normes, une fondation de l'Esprit Saint dans la vérité

4 éternelle, ils expieront la culpabilité (due à) la transgression et l'infidélité (due à) la faute, et (obtiendront) la faveur (divine) pour la terre, sans la chair des holocaustes ni la graisse des sacrifices. L'offrande

5 des lèvres, selon le droit, (est) un apaisement juste, et les parfaits de la Voie (sont) une offrande volontaire agréable. En ce temps-là, les hommes de la Communauté

6 seront mis à part (comme) une Maison de Sainteté pour Aaron, pour (être) la Communauté des Saints par excellence, et (comme) une maison de Communauté pour ceux d'Israël qui marchent dans la perfection.

7 Seuls les fils d'Aaron auront autorité en (matière de) jugement et de biens. Sur leur ordre se décidera le lot pour toute norme des hommes de la Communauté.

8 Et (à propos) des biens des hommes de sainteté qui marchent dans la perfection: leurs biens ne doivent pas être partagés avec les biens des hommes de tromperie qui

9 n'ont pas nettoyé leur voie en se séparant de la perversion pour marcher avec les parfaits de la Voie. Ils n'abandonneront aucun conseil de la Loi pour marcher

10 dans l'obstination de leur coeur. Ils seront jugés selon les premiers jugements dans lesquels les hommes de la Communauté ont commencé à être corrigés

11 jusqu'à la venue du prophète et des Messies d'Aaron et d'Israël.

12 Voici les décrets pour le Maître, qui marchera d'après eux avec tout vivant, selon la norme de chaque période et le poids de chaque homme.

13 Il accomplira la volonté de Dieu, selon tout ce qui a été révélé, de période en période. Il apprendra toute la compréhension qui a été trouvée selon les périodes et

14 le décret du temps (de la fin). Il mettra à part et pèsera les Fils de Justice selon leurs esprits. Il s'attachera aux élus du temps (de la fin), conformément à

15 sa volonté, ainsi qu'il l'a commandé: selon l'esprit de chacun, il lui fera droit; selon la pureté de ses mains, il le fera approcher; et à proportion de sa compréhension,

16 il le fera avancer. Tels seront son amour et sa haine. Qu'il ne discute ni ne se querelle avec les hommes de la fosse,

17 pour que le conseil de la Loi reste caché au milieu des hommes de perversion. Qu'il discute la connaissance vraie et le juste jugement (seulement) avec les élus

18 de la Voie, chacun selon son esprit et selon la norme du temps (de la fin). Il les guidera avec connaissance et ainsi leur fera comprendre les mystères merveilleux et véridiques au milieu

19 des hommes de la Communauté, pour qu'ils marchent dans la perfection, chacun avec son prochain, en tout ce qui leur a été révélé. C'est le temps de préparer la voie

20 au désert. Il leur fera comprendre tout ce qu'on a trouvé pour (qu'ils le) fassent en ce temps. Il se séparera de tout homme qui n'a pas détourné sa voie

21 de toute perversion. Voici les normes de la voie pour le Maître, en ces temps, concernant son amour et sa haine. Haine éternelle

22 contre les hommes de la fosse, dans un esprit de secret. Il leur abandonnera ses biens et le labeur de ses mains, comme un esclave à qui le domine, et un opprimé devant

23 celui qui l'a soumis. Ce sera un homme zélé pour le décret et préparé pour le jour de la vengeance. Il accomplira la volonté (divine) en toute entreprise de ses mains

24 et en tout son domaine, ainsi qu'il l'a commandé. Et (en) tout ce qui lui arrive, il se plaira volontiers, et il ne désirera que ce qui plaît à Dieu,

25 [et en toute]s les paroles de la bouche (de Dieu) il se plaira. Et il ne convoitera rien que (Dieu) n'ait comman[dé,] étant toujours attentif [au jugeme]nt de Dieu.

26 [… Et dans l'angois]se, il bénira son créateur. Et en toute circonstance, il racon[tera ses grâces… (par l'offrande)] des lèvres. Il le bénira

COLONNE X

1 (en conformité) avec les temps qu'il a décrétés: au commencement de la domination de la lumière, à son point tournant, quand elle se retire vers la demeure qui lui a été assignée; au commencement

2 des veilles des ténèbres, quand il ouvre son trésor et qu'il les répand sur (la terre?), à leur point tournant, avec leur retrait devant la lumière; quand

3 les luminaires resplendissent depuis le domaine de sainteté, quand ils se retirent à la demeure de gloire; au début des saisons, aux jours de la nouvelle lune, tout comme à leur point tournant, lorsqu'ils

4 se succèdent l'un à l'autre; à leur renouvellement, (qui est) un grand jour pour le saint des saints et un signe pour l'ouverture de ses grâces éternelles; au commencement des

5 saisons en toute période à venir, au commencement des mois (tous) en leurs temps, et aux jours saints à leurs rangs, comme mémorials (tous) en leurs temps.

6 (Par) l'offrande des lèvres, je le bénirai, selon un décret gravé à jamais: au commencement des années et au point tournant de leurs saisons quand se complète le décret

7 de leur norme — chaque jour ayant son précepte — l'un après l'autre, (de) la saison de la récolte à l'été; de la saison des semailles à la saison des herbages; aux fêtes d'années jusqu'à leurs septénaires;

8 au début de leurs septénaires jusqu'au Jubilé. Tant que je vivrai, un décret gravé (sera) sur ma langue, comme un fruit de louange et la part de mes lèvres.

Hymne de louange

9 Je chanterai avec habileté, et mon chant (est) à la gloire de Dieu. Les cordes de ma harpe (sont ajustées) selon sa sainte norme, et (sur) la flûte de mes lèvres je jouerai en harmonie avec son jugement.

10 Quand le jour et la nuit arrivent, j'entrerai dans l'alliance de Dieu, et quand le soir et le matin sortent, je dirai ses décrets. Là où ils sont, je placerai

11 ma borne, sans retour. (Par) son jugement, je suis châtié selon mes défaillances, et mes transgressions sont sous mes yeux, comme un décret gravé. Et je dis à Dieu: "Ma Justice!"

12 et au Très-Haut "Fondement de mon bien", "Fontaine de connaissance", "Source de Sainteté", "Pinacle de Gloire", et "Toute-Puissance pour une Splendeur éternelle", Je choisirai ce

13 qu'il m'enseignera, je me plairai en (la manière) dont il me jugera. En commençant (toute) entreprise de mes mains ou mes pieds, je bénirai son nom; au commencement d'un aller ou d'un retour,

14 en (m')asseyant ou en me levant, et en m'allongeant sur ma couche, je lui crierai ma joie. Je le bénirai par l'offrande sortie de mes lèvres, dans l'alignement des hommes,

15 et avant que je ne lève les mains pour jouir des délicieux produits de la terre. Au commencement d'une terreur ou d'un effroi, et au fonds de la détresse et de la désolation,

16 je le bénirai extrêmement. Je méditerai sur sa puissance, et je prendrai appui sur ses grâces tout le jour. Car je sais qu'en sa main (est) le jugement

17 de tout vivant, et (que) toutes ses oeuvres (sont) vérité. Quand s'amorcera la détresse, je le louerai, et à son salut je crierai également de joie. Je ne rendrai à personne la rétribution

18 du mal, (mais) je poursuivrai l'humanité par le bien. Car c'est en Dieu que (se trouve) le jugement de tout vivant, et c'est lui qui dispensera à chacun sa rétribution. Je n'envierai pas par esprit

19 de méchanceté, et mon être ne convoitera pas les biens (acquis par) violence. Je ne participerai pas à la lutte des hommes de la fosse, jusqu'au Jour de Vengeance. Mais ma colère, je ne

20 la détournerai pas des hommes de perversité, et je ne serai pas satisfait tant qu'il n'aura pas établi leur jugement. Je ne garderai pas de rancune colérique envers ceux qui se détournent de la transgression; mais je n'aurai pas de compassion

21 pour tous ceux qui dévient de la Voie. Je ne consolerai pas ceux qui sont frappés, jusqu'à ce que leur voie soit parfaite. Je ne garderai pas Bélial en mon coeur. On n'entendra pas en ma bouche

22 d'obscénités ou de perfidie pécheresse, et ni ruses ni mensonges ne se trouveront sur mes lèvres. Mais le fruit de sainteté (sera) sur ma langue, et (rien de) détestable

23 ne s'y trouvera. J'ouvrirai la bouche en actions de grâce, et ma langue racontera continuellement les (oeuvres de) justice de Dieu, et l'infidélité des hommes, jusqu'à leur complète

24 transgression. J'enlèverai les (choses) vaines de mes lèvres, les (idées) impures et tortueuses de la pensée de mon coeur. Avec une sage intention, je cacherai la connaissance,

25 et avec une prudente connaissance, je dresserai [pour elle une] frontière solide, gardant fidélité et ferme droiture envers la justice de Dieu. [Je mesurer]ai

26 un décret avec le cordeau des temps […] justice et amour loyal pour les humiliés, et affermissant les mains de ceux qui s'affole[nt, pour faire connaître]

Colonne **XI**

1 le discernement aux égarés d'esprit. Pour faire comprendre l'enseignement à ceux qui murmurent; pour répondre humblement à l'esprit arrogant, et avec un esprit contrit aux hommes

2 d'oppression, qui pointent le doigt, parlent de méfaits et acquièrent des biens. Car pour moi, mon jugement (appartient) à Dieu. En sa main (est) la perfection de ma voie et la droiture de mon coeur.

3 Par sa justice, il effacera ma transgression. Car, de sa fontaine de connaissance, il a fait jaillir sa lumière. Mon oeil a perçu ses merveilles, et la lumière de mon coeur le mystère

4 de ce qui sera et qui est, éternellement. (Il y a) un soutien à ma droite, sur le roc ferme (est) le chemin de mes pas. Il ne sera pas ébranlé par quoi que ce soit, car la vérité de Dieu est

5 le roc de mes pas et sa puissance est le bâton (en) ma droite. De la fontaine de sa justice (vient) mon droit. (Il y a) en mon coeur la lumière de ses secrets merveilleux. Ce qui sera éternellement,

6 mon oeil (le) perçoit: la sagesse qui est cachée à l'humanité, la connaissance et le projet ingénieux (caché) aux fils d'Adam, une fontaine de justice et un réservoir

7 de puissance, ainsi qu'une source de gloire (cachée) à l'assemblée de la chair. Ceux que Dieu a choisis, il en a fait une possession éternelle. Il les a fait hériter du lot

8 des saints. Avec les fils du ciel, il a uni leur assemblée, pour le Conseil de la Communauté. (Leur) assemblée (est) un Édifice de Sainteté, pour la plante éternelle, durant toute

9 la période à venir. Moi, j'(appartiens) au méchant Adam, à l'assemblée de la chair perverse. Mes péchés, mes transgressions, mes fautes, ainsi que les défaillances de mon coeur

10 (appartiennent) à l'assemblée de la vermine et de ceux qui marchent dans les ténèbres. Car ma voie (est celle) d'Adam. L'être humain ne peut affermir sa marche; car à Dieu (seul est) le jugement, et de sa main

11 (vient) la perfection de voie. C'est par sa connaissance que tout existe. Et tout ce qui existe, il l'a établi dans son plan, et sans lui (rien) ne se fait. Et moi, si

12 je chancelle, les grâces de Dieu (sont) mon salut à jamais. Et si je trébuche sur le péché charnel, je suis jugé par la justice de Dieu, stable à perpétuité.

13 Si ma détresse s'amorce, il délivre mon être de la fosse. Il affermit mon pas pour la Voie. Par sa miséricorde, il me fait avancer, et par ses grâces, il fait venir

14 mon jugement. Dans la justice de sa vérité, il me juge. Dans sa grande bonté, il pardonne tous mes péchés. Dans sa justice, il me purifie de l'impureté

15 humaine et de la faute des fils d'Adam, pour (que je puisse) rendre grâce à Dieu (pour) sa justice, et au Très-Haut (pour) sa splendeur. Béni sois-tu, mon Dieu, qui ouvre pour la connaissance

16 le coeur de ton serviteur. Établis dans sa justice toutes ses oeuvres. Dresse le fils de ta servante, comme tu l'a voulu pour les élus d'Adam, afin qu'il se tienne

17 devant toi à jamais. Car sans toi, aucune voie n'est parfaite. Et en dehors de ta volonté, rien ne se fait. Toi, tu as enseigné

18 toute connaissance. Tout ce qui existera sera par ta volonté. Il n'y a personne en dehors de toi, pour répliquer à ton conseil, ou pour faire comprendre

19 tout ton dessein glorieux; pour percevoir la profondeur de tes mystères; pour discerner toutes tes merveilles, ainsi que la force

20 de ta puissance. Qui peut contenir ta gloire? Qu'est donc le fils d'Adam parmi tes oeuvres merveilleuses?

21 Né d'une femme, comment peut-il demeurer devant toi, lui, pétri de poussière, et dont le corps (est) de la nourriture à vers? Il n'est qu'une semence,

22 de la glaise pressée; et son instinct (le porte) vers la poussière. Que peut répliquer la glaise, et ce qui a été façonné à la main? Et de quoi peut-il discerner le conseil?

...devono separarsi dall'Assemblea degli uomini del Male, per andare nel deserto a spianarvi la via della Verità, come sta scritto: <<Nel deserto spianate la via del Signore, rendete diritto nella steppa il sentiero al

Italian Translation

Regola della Comunità

Colonna I

Preambolo

1 A[…] šym per la sua vita (?) [il Libro della Rego]la della Comunità. Bisogna cercare

2 Dio con [tutto il cuore e con tutta l'anima], facendo ciò che è buono e giusto davanti a Lui, secondo quanto

3 ha comandato per mezzo di Mosè e per mezzo di tutti i suoi servi i profeti; bisogna amare tutto ciò

4 che Egli ha scelto e odiare tutto ciò che Egli ha respinto, stando lontani da ogni male

5 e attaccati a tutte le opere buone; bisogna agire sulla terra secondo verità, giustizia e diritto;

6 bisogna smettere di comportarsi con la durezza del cuore peccaminoso e degli occhi lussuriosi,

7 commettendo ogni sorta di male; bisogna accogliere nel Patto di Grazia tutti coloro che si offrono spontaneamente per agire secondo i comandamenti di Dio,

8 per unirsi nell'Assemblea di Dio e per comportarsi perfettamente davanti a Lui <secondo> tutte

9 le cose rivelate nei tempi fissati; bisogna amare tutti i figli della Luce, ciascuno

10 secondo la sua sorte, nel progetto di Dio, e odiare tutti i figli della Tenebra, ciascuno secondo il suo peccato

11 nella vendetta di Dio. Tutti coloro che si offrono spontanei alla Sua Verità devono apportare tutta la loro conoscenza, (tutta) la loro energia

12 e (tutto) il loro patrimonio nella Comunità di Dio, per purificare la loro conoscenza per mezzo della verità dei comandamenti di Dio, per disciplinare la loro energia

13 secondo la perfezione delle Sue vie e (per impiegare) tutto il loro patrimonio secondo il consiglio della Sua giustizia. Essi non devono discostarsi

14 da nessuno dei comandamenti di Dio riguardanti i tempi (liturgici). Non bisogna anticiparli, né restare indietro

15 rispetto a tutti i loro momenti, né deviare dai comandamenti della Sua Verità, andando a destra o a sinistra.

L'entrata nella Comunità del Patto

16 Tutti coloro che sono accolti nella Regola della Comunità devono impegnarsi davanti a Dio a comportarsi

17 secondo tutto quello che Egli ha ordinato e a non allontanarsi da Lui per nessun timore o paura, afflizione

18 o prova (quali accadono) sotto il regno di Belial. Nel momento in cui essi entrano nel Patto, i sacerdoti

19 e i leviti benediranno il Dio della salvezza e tutte le opere della Sua Verità. Tutti

20 coloro che entrano nel Patto diranno, dopo di loro, «Amen, amen».

21 I sacerdoti, (poi), narreranno i benefici di Dio (operati) per mezzo delle opere della Sua potenza;

22 racconteranno tutti i Suoi privilegi d'amore verso Israele. I leviti, (invece), narreranno

23 le colpe dei figli d'Israele, tutte le loro ribellioni colpevoli e i loro peccati (commessi) sotto il regno

24 di Belial. Dopo di loro, [tut]ti coloro che entrano nel Patto confesseranno, dicendo: «Siamo stati malvagi,

25 ci siamo [ri]bellati, abbiamo [pec]cato, siamo stati empi, noi [e] i nostri [pa]dri prima di noi, perché siamo andati

26 […] verità. Gius[to è il Dio di Israele e (giusto) è il] Suo [gi]udizio contro di noi e contro i [nostri] padri.

1 Egli ci ha elargito il Suo amore misericordioso da sempre e per sempre. Allora i sacerdoti benediranno tutti

2 gli uomini del partito di Dio, che procedono perfettamente in tutte le Sue vie; diranno: «Ti benedica (Dio) con ogni

3 bene e ti preservi da ogni male; illumini il tuo cuore (concedendoti) l'intelletto della vita e ti faccia la grazia della conoscenza di (ciò che è) eterno.

4 Egli rivolga il Suo volto misericordioso verso di te (per concederti) la pace dell'eternità». Allora i leviti malediranno tutti gli uomini

5 del partito di Belial e a loro volta diranno: «Maledetto tu per tutte le tue opere malvagie ed empie. Che Egli ti consegni

6 al terrore per mezzo di coloro che esercitano la vendetta (di Dio). Che Egli ti perseguiti e ti mandi in rovina per mezzo di tutti coloro che danno

7 la retribuzione (di Dio). Che tu sia maledetto senza misericordia, secondo la tenebra delle tue opere. Che tu sia dannato

8 nell'oscurità del fuoco eterno. Che Dio non abbia pietà di te, quando tu lo invochi. Che Egli non ti perdoni purificando le tue colpe.

9 Volga contro di te il Suo volto adirato, esercitando la Sua vendetta contro di te, né ci sia pace per te sulla bocca degli intercessori».

10 Dopo (che hanno parlato) coloro che benedicono e coloro che maledicono, tutti coloro che entrano nel Patto diranno: «Amen, amen».

11-12 I sacerdoti e i leviti proseguiranno, allora, dicendo: «Sia maledetto colui che entra in questo Patto per gli idoli del suo cuore, se egli continua a servirli. (Così) egli pone davanti a sé l'inciampo della sua colpa, venendo meno a causa di essa.

13 Quando ascolterà le parole di questo Patto, egli penserà di essere benedetto e dirà: "Che io abbia la pace,

14 per quanto io proceda nella durezza del mio cuore". Ma che la sua anima assetata perisca nonostante l'abbondanza di acqua, in modo che non ci sia

15 perdono. Che l'ira di Dio e la collera dei Suoi giudizi divampino contro di lui (portandolo) alla rovina eterna. Gli restino attaccate tutte

16 le maledizioni di questo Patto. Che Dio lo separi per il male e sia sradicato di mezzo a tutti i figli della Luce, perché si è ritirato

17 dalla sequela di Dio a causa dei suoi idoli e dell'inciampo della sua colpa. Che Dio ponga la sua sorte in mezzo a quella di coloro che sono maledetti per l'eternità».

18 Dopo di loro tutti coloro che entrano nel Patto risponderanno e diranno: «Amen, amen».

Rinnovo annuale della cerimonia. Denunce varie. Espiazione.

19 Si farà così ogni anno per tutto il tempo del regno di Belial. I sacerdoti passeranno nella regola

20 per primi, uno dopo l'altro, secondo i loro spiriti. Dopo di loro passeranno i leviti

21 e (poi) tutto il popolo passerà nella regola per terzo, uno dopo l'altro, secondo le migliaia, le centinaia,

22 le cinquantine e le diecine, affinché ogni uomo di Israele conosca il suo posto nella Comunità di Dio,

23 per (formare) l'Assemblea eterna. Nessuno deve scendere dalla sua posizione, né prendere un posto superiore a quello della sua sorte;

24 perché tutti staranno in comunione di verità, di umiltà buona, di amore benigno, di pensieri giusti,

25 [cias]cuno verso il suo prossimo, nell'Assemblea santa, figli del progetto eterno. Chiunque rifiuti di entrare

26 [nel Patto di Dio,] procedendo nella durezza del suo cuore, no[n… Comun]ità della Sua Verità, perché egli ha disprezzato

1 le istruzioni riguardanti la conoscenza dei giusti precetti; non ha avuto la forza di convertire la sua vita. (Per questo) non può essere annoverato tra i giusti:

2 né la sua conoscenza, né la sua attività, né il suo patrimonio entreranno nell'Assemblea della Comunità, perché il suo pensiero è nel fango della malvagità

3 e nella sua conversione c'è impurità; egli non sarà giustificato per l'eccesso (?) di durezza del suo cuore, in quanto guarda la tenebra come vie della luce.

4 Non sarà annoverato nella fonte dei perfetti; non sarà purificato dai riti espiatori; non sarà reso puro dall'acqua lustrale; non sarà reso santo da(ll'acqua de)i mari, né da quella

5 dei fiumi; non diventerà puro nemmeno con tutte le acque di abluzione. Resterà completamente impuro per tutto il tempo che rifiuterà gli statuti

6 di Dio senza lasciarsi istruire nella Comunità della Sua Assemblea. Infatti è per mezzo dello spirito dell'Assemblea della Verità di Dio che sono espiate tutte le azioni dell'uomo,

7 tutte le sue colpe, cosicché egli possa contemplare la Luce della Vita. Per mezzo dello spirito santo della Comunità (fondata) sulla Sua Verità egli è purificato da tutte

8 le sue colpe. Il suo peccato sarà espiato in spirito di rettitudine e di umiltà; con l'umiltà del suo animo di fronte a tutti i comandamenti di Dio sarà purificato

9 il suo corpo, quando è asperso di acqua lustrale ed è santificato con l'acqua della contrizione. Egli stabilirà i suoi passi, per procedere perfettamente

10 in tutte le vie di Dio, come Egli ha ordinato riguardo ai momenti dei tempi da lui fissati, senza deviare né a destra, né a sinistra e senza

11 trasgredire nessuno dei Suoi comandamenti. Allora sarà accetto con espiazioni gradite a Dio. (Questo) sarà per lui il Patto

12 della Comunità eterna.

Il predeterminismo e il dualismo di Qumran

13 E' compito del *maśkil* istruire tutti i figli della Luce e dare loro insegnamenti riguardo alla natura di tutti gli uomini

14 (distinti) secondo il genere dei loro spiriti, (riconoscibili) dai loro segni di distinzione, (che dipendono) dalle loro opere (compiute) nelle loro generazioni, e secondo sia le loro punizioni

15 sia i loro tempi di pace mandati da Dio. Dal Dio della conoscenza (viene) tutto ciò che è e che sarà. Prima che gli uomini vengano all'esistenza, Egli ha stabilito ogni loro pensiero

16 cosicché, quando vengono all'esistenza secondo i tempi fissati per loro, essi compiono le loro azioni secondo il disegno della Sua gloria. Nulla può essere cambiato. Nella Sua mano

17 è il destino di tutto. E' Lui che ha cura degli uomini in tutte le loro cose. E' Lui che ha creato l'uomo per dominare

18 la terra, stabilendo per lui due spiriti, perché proceda in essi fino al momento del Suo intervento. Sono gli spiriti

19 del Bene e del Male. In una fonte di Luce è la stirpe del Bene e da una fonte di Tenebra (proviene) la stirpe del Male.

20 In mano al principe della Luce è il governo di tutti i figli della Giustizia, i quali camminano nelle vie della Luce. In mano all'Angelo

21 della Tenebra è tutto il governo dei figli del Male, i quali camminano nelle vie della Tenebra. Dall'Angelo della Tenebra (dipende) lo smarrimento di tutti i figli della Giustizia. Tutti i loro peccati, le loro colpe, le loro empietà, le loro azioni ribelli (sono causati) dal suo dominio

23 secondo la misteriosa volontà di Dio, finché (giunge) la sua fine. Tutte le sventure degli uomini e i tempi delle loro angosce (dipendono) dal dominio della sua ostilità.

24 Tutti gli spiriti del suo partito cercano di far cadere i figli della Luce, ma il Dio di Israele e l'Angelo della Sua Verità aiutano tutti

25 i figli della Luce. E' Lui che ha creato gli spiriti della Luce e della Tenebra e su di essi ha fondato ogni opera

26 *l[…]hn… […]wdh*. L'uno, Dio lo ama per tutti

Colonna IV

1 [i te]mpi dell'eternità, compiacendosi di tutte le sue azioni per sempre. In quanto all'altro, Dio ne detesta il pensiero e odia tutte le sue vie per sempre.

Le vie del principe della Luce

2 Queste sono le loro vie sulla terra: (il primo) ha il compito di illuminare il cuore dell'uomo, di appianare davanti a lui tutte le vie della vera giustizia e di incutere nel suo cuore il timore dei giudizi

3 di Dio. (Frutto di questa illuminazione) sono spirito di umiltà, pazienza, grande amore, bene eterno, intelletto, saggezza, sapienza somma che ha fiducia in tutte le

4 opere di Dio e si appoggia sulla grandezza della Sua misericordia; spirito di conoscenza in ogni progetto di azione, zelo per (mettere in pratica) i giusti precetti, intenzione

5 santa con fermo proposito; grande misericordia verso tutti i figli della Verità; purità gloriosa che aborre tutti gli idoli dell'impurità, umiltà di comportamento

6 accompagnata da prudenza in ogni occasione; capacità di nascondere la verità dei misteri di conoscenza. Questi sono i progetti dello spirito (del Bene) nei riguardi dei figli della Verità sulla terra. L'intervento divino in favore di tutti coloro che procedono secondo questo spirito (porta) salute

7 e grande pace con lunga vita e fecondità, accompagnate da tutte le benedizioni eterne; (porta) gioia eterna nella vita senza fine, la corona di gloria

8 con grande splendore nella Luce eterna.

Le vie del principe della Tenebra

9 Per quanto riguarda lo spirito cattivo, (da esso viene) avidità e pigrizia nelle opere giuste; malvagità e fraudolenza; orgoglio e superbia; falsità e rilassatezza; crudeltà

10 e grande empietà; grande irascibilità, grande stoltezza e zelo arrogante per (compiere) azioni abominevoli in spirito di impudicizia; vie impure al servizio dell'impurità

11 e lingua blasfema; cecità degli occhi e sordità delle orecchie; durezza di cervice e pesantezza di cuore; si procede in tutte le vie della Tenebra e dell'intelligenza rivolta al male. L'intervento di Dio

12 contro tutti coloro che procedono in questo spirito (si manifesta) in una grande quantità di colpi (inferti da Dio) per mezzo di tutti gli angeli della distruzione, a rovina eterna per mezzo del furore dell'ira vendicatrice di Dio, in terrore e obbrobrio

13 senza fine insieme con la vergogna della distruzione nel fuoco della regione delle Tenebre. Tutti i tempi delle loro generazioni saranno in dolorosa tristezza, in sofferenza amara e in sventure di Tenebra fino

14 al loro annientamento; per loro non ci sarà né resto, né scampato.

Le due nature degli uomini

15 Da questi (due spiriti dipende) la natura di tutti gli uomini e, in (questi due) campi separati, essi hanno in sorte di appartenere all'una o all'altra schiera per tutte le generazioni. (Gli uomini) procedono nelle vie di questi e tutta la retribuzione,

16 piccola o grande, per ciò che fanno è in questi (due) campi secondo il destino di ciascuno per tutti i tempi, perché Dio ha posto questi due spiriti l'uno di fronte all'altro fino al tempo

17 finale e ha posto un odio eterno fra i loro gruppi: le opere del Male sono abominio del Bene e abominio del Male tutte le opere del Bene. Ardore

18 di contesa reciproca è in tutte le loro decisioni, perché essi non procedono insieme. Nei misteri della Sua mente e nella sapienza della Sua gloria Dio ha posto un termine all'esistenza del Male e al momento

19 del (Suo) intervento lo distruggerà per sempre. Allora il Bene si affermerà per sempre sulla terra, per quanto essa si sia contaminata nelle vie della malvagità sotto il dominio del Male fino

20 al tempo del Giudizio che è già fissato. Allora Dio purificherà tutte le opere dell'uomo per mezzo della Sua Verità e purificherà per sé la struttura umana, distruggendo ogni spirito malvagio dall'intimo

21 della sua carne e purificando l'uomo per mezzo dello spirito santo da tutte le opere malvagie. Egli aspergerà sopra di lui lo spirito di Verità come acqua lustrale, (per purificarlo) da tutti gli abomini della Menzogna, (nei quali) si è contaminato

22 per lo spirito di impurità. Egli insegnerà ai giusti la conoscenza dell'Altissimo e ai perfetti nella condotta insegnerà la sapienza degli angeli, perché sono loro quelli che Dio ha eletto per costituire il Patto eterno.

23 A loro (appartiene) tutta la gloria di Adamo. Il male scomparirà e ogni opera di rilassatezza sarà una vergogna. Fino a quel momento lo spirito del Bene e quello del Male combatteranno nel cuore dell'uomo.

24 Gli uomini procederanno (gli uni) nella sapienza e (gli altri) nella stoltezza: se un uomo appartiene alla Verità e alla Giustizia, questo odia il Male; se è nel partito del Male e la malvagità è in lui,

25 questo ha in abominio il Bene, perché Dio ho posto questi due campi uno di fronte all'altro fino al tempo fissato e alla nuova creazione. Dio conosce la retribuzione delle opere di questi due spiriti per tutti i tempi

26 [...]n e li ha dati in sorte agli uomini, perché conoscano il bene [... e facendo cad]ere la sorte di ogni essere vivente secondo il suo spirito b[... fino a]l Suo intervento (finale).

COLONNA V

Regole per la vita comunitaria

1 Questa è la regola per gli uomini della Comunità, che si mostrano volenterosi a pentirsi di ogni male e ad aderire a tutto ciò che Egli ha ordinato secondo la Sua volontà. Essi si separeranno dall'Assemblea

2 degli uomini del Male per formare una comunità (fondata) sulla Torah e sul(la comunione de)l patrimonio. Si sottometteranno all'autorità dei Figli di Sadoq, i sacerdoti che osservano il Patto, e a quella della moltitudine dei membri

3 della Comunità, che aderiscono al Patto. Secondo il loro volere saranno prese le decisioni per ogni affare riguardante la Torah, il patrimonio e il comportamento. Essi devono praticare insieme la verità, l'umiltà,

4 la giustizia e il diritto, amore misericordioso, modestia in tutto ciò che essi fanno, cosicché nessuno proceda nella durezza del suo cuore, smarrendosi dietro ad esso,

5 ai suoi occhi e ai pensieri della sua inclinazione. Ma anzi, ciascuno deve circoncidere nella Comunità il prepuzio della natura e della dura cervice, per porre il fondamento della Verità per Israele, per la Comunità del Patto

6 eterno; per fare l'espiazione in favore di tutti coloro che si mostrano volenterosi (di raggiungere) la santità che è in Aronne e (di costruire) la casa della Verità in Israele e per coloro che si uniscono a loro per vivere insieme, per processare, per giudicare

7 e per perseguitare tutti coloro che trasgrediscono i comandamenti (di Dio). Questa è la regola della loro condotta riguardo a tutti questi comandamenti, quando sono accolti nella Comunità. Tutti quelli che entrano nell'Assemblea della Comunità,

8 entreranno nel Patto di Dio alla presenza di tutti coloro che si mostrano volonterosi. Egli si impegnerà su se stesso, con un giuramento vincolante, a convertirsi alla Torah di Mosè, secondo tutto quello che Egli ha ordinato, con tutto

9 il cuore e con tutta l'anima, secondo tutto ciò che di essa è stato rivelato ai Figli di Sadoq, i sacerdoti che osservano il Patto e che indagano la Sua volontà, e secondo (la volontà de)gli uomini del Patto,

10 che hanno scelto volentieri (di vivere) insieme secondo la Sua verità e di comportarsi secondo la Sua volontà. (Chi entra nella Comunità) si impegnerà sul Patto, (giurando) sulla sua vita, a separarsi da tutti gli uomini del Male, che procedono

11 sulla via malvagia; infatti essi non sono stati annoverati nel Suo Patto, perché non hanno cercato (Dio) e non hanno indagato su di Lui per mezzo dei Suoi comandamenti, per arrivare alla conoscenza di quelle cose occulte, a causa delle quali si sono smarriti

12 peccando. In quanto poi alle cose rivelate, le hanno trasgredite deliberatamente, cosicché l'ira (di Dio) crescerà (fino) a (provocare) il giudizio, che eseguirà la vendetta sulla base delle maledizioni del Patto. (Dio) farà contro di essi

13 grandi giudizi fino a distruggerli per sempre senza che vi sia resto. (Coloro che non entrano nella Comunità) non possono entrare nell'acqua, toccando (poi) la purità degli uomini santi, perché essi non sono puri,

14 a meno che non si convertano dalla loro malvagità, perché l'impurità rimane in tutti coloro che trasgrediscono la Sua parola. Che nessuno si unisca a uno di loro né nella sua attività, né nel suo patrimonio, per non addossarsi

15 la colpa di un peccato. Che si stia lontani da lui in ogni cosa, perché così sta scritto: «Starai lontano da ogni cosa menzognera» (Ex 23:7). Che nessuno degli uomini

16 della Comunità risponda (a lui) per dare il suo parere riguardo a (problemi de)lla Torah o del comportamento. Che nessuno mangi o beva nulla del loro patrimonio, né accetti assolutamente nulla dalle loro mani,

17 che non sia a prezzo, come sta scritto: «Non abbiate nulla a che fare con l'uomo, il cui soffio di vita sta nelle sue narici, perché "Quanto è stimato costui?"» (Is 2:22). Infatti

18 bisogna separare (da noi) tutti coloro che non sono annoverati nel Suo Patto, nonché tutto ciò che possiedono. Che nessun uomo santo si appoggi su nessuna creatura

19 vana, perché tutti coloro che non aderiscono al Suo Patto sono vanità. Egli sterminerà dalla terra tutti coloro che disprezzano la Sua parola; tutte le loro opere sono per Lui impurità

20 e impurità è in tutte le cose che appartengono a loro. Quando uno entra nel Patto, (impegnandosi) a comportarsi secondo tutti questi comandamenti e unendosi alla Comunità santa, (i membri della Comunità) esamineranno, tutti insieme,

21 il suo spirito (distinguendo) tra uno e un altro secondo la sua intelligenza e secondo le sue opere riguardo alla Torah, sotto l'autorità dei Figli di Aronne, che si sono mostrati volenterosi (di entrare) nella Comunità per realizzare

22 il Patto e per osservare tutti i comandamenti che Egli ha ordinato di mettere in pratica, e sotto l'autorità della moltitudine di Israele, cioè di coloro che si sono mostrati volenterosi nel pentirsi, (entrando) nella Comunità del Suo Patto.

23 Ciascuno sarà iscritto nel (libro del)la Regola in ordine secondo la sua intelligenza e secondo le sue opere, in modo che ciascuno obbedisca al suo compagno, il più piccolo al più grande. Bisogna

24 esaminare anno per anno il loro spirito e le loro opere, in modo da far salire ciascuno secondo la sua intelligenza e secondo la perfezione della sua condotta e in modo da far retrocedere ciascuno secondo le sue mancanze. Ciascuno deve ammonire

25 il suo compagno nella ve[ri]tà, con umiltà e amore misericordioso rivolto a ognuno. Nessuno parli a un altro con ira o con maldicenza,

26 con dure[zza o con] cattivo spirito [di gelosia]. Nessuno odi l'altro [nell'incirconcisione del] suo cuore, ma lo ammonisca nel giorno stesso: così non

Colonna VI

1 prenderà la colpa sopra di sé. Inoltre, che nessuno porti un'accusa contro un suo compagno davanti all'Assemblea dei *rabbim*, se questi non è stato (prima) ammonito davanti a testimoni.

2 Ci si deve comportare così in tutti i luoghi in cui si risieda nelle relazioni con i confratelli: l'inferiore deve ubbidire al superiore sia per ciò che riguarda il lavoro, sia per ciò che riguarda problemi economici. Devono mangiare insieme,

3 insieme pronunciare la benedizione e insieme deliberare. In ogni luogo, dove ci siano (almeno) dieci uomini dell'Assemblea della Comunità, che non manchi tra loro

4 un sacerdote. Ognuno sieda davanti a lui secondo il suo grado e così potranno porre problemi su qualsiasi argomento. Quando avranno apparecchiato la tavola per mangiare o per bere

5 vino, il sacerdote stenderà la mano per primo

6 per benedire la primizia del pane o del vino. E non manchi mai nel luogo, dove siano (almeno) dieci, uno che studi la Torah giorno e notte

7 continuamente, a turno vicendevolmente. I *rabbim* veglieranno insieme per un terzo di ogni notte dell'anno, leggendo il Libro, cercando le decisioni (volute da Dio)

8 e benedicendo insieme. Questa è la regola per la riunione dei *rabbim*: ciascun membro (sieda) secondo il suo grado. I sacerdoti siederanno per primi, poi gli anziani e (infine) siederà il resto

9 di tutto il popolo, ciascuno secondo il suo grado. Così potranno porre domande circa la normativa e circa ogni decisione e affare che riguardi i *rabbim*. Ciascuno potrà rispondere secondo la propria conoscenza

10 all'Assemblea della Comunità. Nessuno deve parlare, quando sta parlando un altro, prima che il fratello abbia finito di parlare. Inoltre che nessuno parli prima del suo turno,

11 (cioè) di colui che è iscritto prima di lui. (Anche) chi è interrogato può parlare solo quando è il suo turno. Durante la seduta dei *rabbim* che nessuno dica nulla senza il loro permesso, anche se è

12 il presidente dei *rabbim*. Chiunque abbia qualcosa da dire ai *rabbim* senza trovarsi al turno di chi può interrogare l'Assemblea

13 della Comunità, deve alzarsi in piedi e dire: «Ho qualcosa da dire ai *rabbim*». Se gli si darà il permesso, che parli. In quanto a tutti coloro che si mostrano volenterosi (di separarsi) da Israele

14 per unirsi all'Assemblea della Comunità, il *paqid* che è a capo dei *rabbim* deve esaminare ciascuno circa il suo intelletto e le sue opere. Se (questi) è (trovato) capace di (osservare) la disciplina, (il *paqid*) lo faccia entrare

15 nel Patto, perché si possa convertire al Bene e allontanarsi da tutto il Male; lo deve istruire in tutte le norme della Comunità. Poi, quando (il nuovo adepto) sarà entrato, resterà in piedi davanti a(ll'Assemblea de)i *rabbim* e tutti saranno interrogati

16 riguardo a lui. A seconda di come sarà la decisione dell'Assemblea dei *rabbim*, sarà ammesso o respinto. Tuttavia, anche quando è ammesso all'Assemblea della Comunità, egli non deve toccare la purità

17 degli altri membri, finché non sia stato esaminato riguardo al suo spirito e alle sue opere per un anno intero. Inoltre egli non può mettere i suoi beni in comune coi *rabbim*.

18 Quando avrà passato un anno intero dentro la Comunità, i *rabbim* saranno interrogati sul suo conto riguardo al suo intelletto e alle sue opere nella Torah. Se nei suoi confronti sarà presa la decisione

19 che si può avvicinare all'Assemblea della Comunità, secondo il parere dei sacerdoti e della maggioranza degli uomini del Patto, allora sia ammesso anche il suo patrimonio e il suo lavoro nelle mani

20 del sovrintendente (*mebaqqer*) delle attività dei *rabbim*. (Il nuovo adepto) scriverà il patrimonio di sua mano nel registro, ma non potrà (ancora) usarlo per gli altri membri. Egli non può toccare la bevanda dei *rabbim* fino al

21 compimento del secondo anno in mezzo agli uomini della Comunità. Allo scadere del secondo anno sia esaminato secondo il parere dei *rabbim*. Se per lui

22 la decisione sarà che può essere ammesso nella Comunità, egli dovrà essere iscritto nell'ordine del suo rango in mezzo ai suoi fratelli per quanto riguarda la Torah, la normativa, la purità e la comunanza dei beni. (Da questo momento) il suo consiglio e

23 il suo giudizio appartengono alla Comunità.

Normativa per le punizioni

24 Queste sono le norme, con le quali si giudicherà in un procedimento della Comunità a seconda dei casi. Se fra di essi si trova qualcuno, che mente

25 riguardo al patrimonio e lo fa coscientemente, questo deve essere separato dal mezzo della purità dei *rabbim* per un anno e deve essere punito con (la privazione di) un quarto del suo pane. Colui che risponde

26 a un suo compagno con durezza e gli parla con impazienza, trascurando il fondamento della loro comunione, ribellandosi all'autorità di un compagno che è iscritto in posizione più alta della sua,

27 [...]*šy'h* la sua mano, deve essere punito per u[n] anno [... . Col]ui che pronuncia una parola contro il nome glorioso al di sopra di tutti *h*[...]

COLONNA VII

1 e se bestemmia, perché preso da improvviso timore sia per una difficoltà sia per qualsiasi altro motivo che gli capiti, mentre sta leggendo il Libro o pronunciando una benedizione, deve essere cacciato

2 e non torni più nell'Assemblea della Comunità. Se uno ha parlato con ira contro un sacerdote di quelli iscritti nel libro, deve essere punito per un anno

3 e stia separato dalla purità dei *rabbim*, in solitudine. Ma se ha parlato per inavvertenza, egli deve essere punito per (solo) sei mesi. Colui che mente coscientemente

4 deve essere punito per sei mesi. Colui che offende coscientemente e ingiustamente un compagno deve essere punito per un anno

5 e stia separato. Colui che parla con un suo compagno con arroganza o agisce coscientemente (nei suoi confronti) con rilassatezza, deve essere punito per sei mesi; ma se

6 è (solo) negligente contro il suo compagno, deve essere punito per tre mesi. Se uno si comporta con negligenza nei riguardi del patrimonio della Comunità così da danneggiarlo, deve ripagare il danno

7 di persona.

8 Se poi egli non è in grado di ripagarlo, deve essere punito per sessanta giorni. Colui il quale mantiene rancore contro un compagno senza motivo, deve essere punito per un anno.

9 Lo stesso (vale) per chi si vendica da sé per qualsiasi motivo. Colui il quale pronuncia con la sua bocca un discorso sciocco, (deve essere punito) per tre mesi. Per colui che interrompe le parole di un compagno (*scil.* durante una seduta dell'Assemblea)

10 dieci giorni. Colui il quale si sdraia e si addormenta durante una seduta dei *rabbim*, trenta giorni. Lo stesso per chi si allontana durante una seduta dei *rabbim*

11 senza permesso. Colui che si addormenta (*scil.* senza sdraiarsi) fino a tre volte durante una medesima seduta, deve essere punito per dieci giorni; ma se lo si fa alzare

12 e quello se ne va, deve essere punito per trenta giorni. Colui il quale cammina nudo davanti a un suo compagno, senza essere malato, deve essere punito per sei mesi.

13 Colui il quale sputa in mezzo a una seduta dei *rabbim*, deve essere punito per trenta giorni. Colui il quale fa uscire il suo pene da sotto alla sua veste,

14 o se questa è a brandelli cosicché si veda la sua nudità, deve essere punito per trenta giorni. Colui che ride stupidamente, in modo da essere sentito, deve essere punito per trenta

15 giorni. Colui il quale fa uscire (dalla veste) la sua mano sinistra per appoggiarsi (?) su di essa, deve essere punito per dieci giorni. Colui il quale sparge calunnie contro un suo compagno,

16 deve essere separato per un anno dalla purità dei *rabbim* e punito; ma se egli sparge le calunnie contro i *rabbim*, deve essere espulso da mezzo a loro

17 e non sarà più riammesso. Colui che mormora contro le autorità della Comunità deve essere espulso e non più riammesso; ma se mormora ingiustamente contro un suo compagno

18 deve essere punito (solo) per sei mesi. Colui il cui spirito devia dal fondamento (dottrinale) della Comunità, tradendo la Verità

19 e procedendo nella durezza del suo cuore, se si pentirà, sarà punito per due anni. Durante il primo non deve toccare la purità dei *rabbim*

20 e nel secondo non dovrà toccare la bevanda dei *rabbim*, ma siederà dietro a tutti i membri della Comunità. Quando saranno passati

21 due anni, i *rabbim* saranno interrogati riguardo a lui. Se lo (ri)ammetteranno, sarà iscritto (di nuovo) nel suo rango e poi si potrà richiedere il suo parere.

22 Se uno è stato nell'Assemblea della Comunità per almeno dieci anni,

23 ma (poi) il suo spirito si ritrae, tradendo la Comunità, e abbandona

24 i *rabbim*, procedendo nella durezza del suo cuore, questi non può più essere riammesso nell'Assemblea della Comunità. Se qualcuno dei membri della Comuni[tà che abbia rap]porti

25 con lui riguardo alla purità o al patrimonio, ch[e...] i *rabbim*, questi deve avere la medesima condanna: deve essere e[spulso... .]

Colonna VIII

Norme per vivere nella Comunità santa

1 Nell'Assemblea della Comunità (ci devono essere) dodici laici e tre sacerdoti, perfetti (nell'osservanza) di tutti (i comandamenti) rivelati di tutta

2 la Torah, che osservino la verità, la giustizia, il diritto, l'amore misericordioso, l'umiltà gli uni verso gli altri.

3 Devono osservare la fedeltà (a Dio) nella terra (di Israele) con animo fermo e spirito contrito. Devono espiare la colpa praticando il giusto comportamento

4 e (accettando) terribili sofferenze. Essi devono comportarsi con tutti secondo la misura della Verità e secondo la norma del tempo. Quando queste cose si saranno realizzate in Israele,

5 l'Assemblea della Comunità sarà salda nella Verità, (così da diventare) una pianta eterna, il tempio santo di Israele, il fondamento del Santo

6 dei Santi di Aronne, testimoni della Verità per il (momento) del Giudizio, eletti dal beneplacito (divino) per fare l'espiazione in favore della terra (di Israele) e per dare

7 ai malvagi la giusta retribuzione. Questo sarà il muro provato, la pietra angolare preziosa,

8 i cui fondamenti non vacilleranno, né si muoveranno dal loro posto. Essi saranno il luogo del Santo dei Santi

9 di Aronne, (avranno) la conoscenza del tutto, perché il Patto voluto da Dio sussista e per offrire (in sacrificio a Dio) un profumo soave. (Essi saranno) il tempio perfetto e vero in Israele,

10 per realizzare il Patto secondo i comandamenti eterni. Essi avranno la funzione di fare l'espiazione, secondo il beneplacito (divino), in favore della terra (di Israele) e di emettere il giudizio contro la malvagità. (Allora) non ci sarà più il male. Quando questi (uomini) saranno stati saldi nel fondamento dottrinale della Comunità due anni, giorno per giorno, con condotta perfetta,

11 essi si separeranno come santi in mezzo all'Assemblea degli uomini della Comunità. Tutte le cose nascoste a Israele, ma che saranno scoperte

12 da colui che studia (nei libri sacri), non devono essere tenute nascoste a questi per timore dello spirito di apostasia. Quando questi saranno diventati una Comunità in Israele,

13 devono separarsi dall'Assemblea degli uomini del Male, per andare nel deserto a spianarvi la via della Verità,

14 come sta scritto: «Nel deserto spianate la via del Signore, rendete diritto nella steppa il sentiero al nostro Dio» (Is 40:3).

15 Questo (si riferisce al)lo studio della Torah, c[h]e Egli ha ordinato per mezzo di Mosè, per comportarsi secondo tutto ciò che è stato rivelato di tempo in tempo

16 e come i profeti hanno rivelato per mezzo del Suo spirito santo. Chiunque degli uomini del Patto

17 trasgredisca volontariamente un qualunque comandamento, non deve toccare la purità degli uomini santi

18 e non deve sapere nulla delle loro deliberazioni, finché le sue opere non siano state purificate da ogni male, procedendo sulla via perfetta. (Allora) sarà (ri)ammesso

19 all'Assemblea secondo il parere dei *rabbim* e poi sarà (di nuovo) iscritto nel suo rango. (Ci si comporterà) in questo modo con chiunque si unisca alla Comunità.

20 Queste sono le norme con cui devono comportarsi tra di loro gli uomini della santità perfetta:

21 tutti quelli che entrano nell'Assemblea santa di coloro che procedono nella via perfetta come Egli ha ordinato, - chiunque

22 trasgredisca un qualunque comandamento della Torah di Mosè sia deliberatamente sia per rilassatezza sarà espulso dall'Assemblea della Comunità

23 e non sarà più riammesso. Nessuno degli uomini santi dovrà più avere alcuna relazione con lui per ciò che riguarda sia il suo patrimonio, sia il suo consiglio - senza

24 nessuna eccezione. Ma se agisce per inavvertenza, deve essere (solo) separato dalla purità e dall'Assemblea. Si applichi questa norma:

25 per due anni che non giudichi nessuno e non gli si chieda nessun consiglio. Se la sua condotta sarà perfetta,

26 sarà riammesso nell'abitazione, allo studio e all'Assemblea [secondo il parere dei] *rabbim*, sempre che non abbia più commesso colpe per inavvertenza fino al compimento di due anni

27 giorno per giorno.

COLONNA IX

1 Infatti, per una colpa commessa per inavvertenza uno deve essere punito per due anni, ma in quanto a colui che agisce volontariamente, questi non deve essere più riammesso. Solo colui che ha peccato per inavvertenza

2 deve essere provato per due anni per quanto riguarda la perfezione della sua condotta e delle sue idee - secondo il parere dei *rabbim*; dopo lo si iscriva (di nuovo) al suo posto nella Comunità santa.

3 Quando queste cose si verificheranno in Israele secondo tutti questi ordinamenti, si costituirà il fondamento dello spirito santo nella Verità

4 eterna; (allora) si dovrà fare l'espiazione per il peccato di ribellione e per la trasgressione peccaminosa, (per attirare) la benevolenza (divina) verso la terra (di Israele) senza la carne degli olocausti e senza il grasso dei sacrifici. Ma l'offerta

5 delle labbra, (fatta) secondo le norme (della Comunità), sarà come un profumo di giustizia e la perfezione della condotta sarà offerta spontanea e accetta. In quel tempo gli uomini

6 della Comunità si separeranno (dagli altri ebrei) per formare il tempio santo di Aronne, unendosi (a formare) il Santo dei Santi e il tempio della Comunità di Israele, (cioè) di coloro che si comportano perfettamente.

7 Solo i figli di Aronne avranno autorità per quanto riguarda la normativa e il patrimonio. Sarà presa secondo il loro parere ogni decisione riguardante la posizione degli uomini della Comunità e il patrimonio degli uomini santi, la cui condotta è perfetta. Il loro patrimonio non deve avere rapporti con quello dei lassisti, i quali

9 non hanno purificato la loro condotta, separandosi dal Male e comportandosi perfettamente. Essi non si allontaneranno mai da nessuna deliberazione (presa secondo) la Torah, per comportarsi

10 secondo tutta la durezza del loro cuore. Essi saranno giudicati secondo le prime disposizioni, nelle quali cominciarono ad essere istruiti gli uomini della Comunità,

11 finché non giungano il profeta e i messia di Aronne e di Israele.

12 Questi sono i comandamenti per il *maśkil*, secondo i quali deve comportarsi con ogni essere vivente, secondo la situazione del tempo e secondo l'importanza di ogni uomo.

13 Deve fare la volontà di Dio secondo tutto ciò che è stato rivelato di tempo in tempo. Ma deve (anche) apprendere tutta la sapienza che è stata trovata a seconda dei tempi,

14 (cioè) la norma del tempo. Egli deve separare e valutare i figli della giustizia secondo i loro spiriti. Deve mantenere saldi gli eletti del tempo secondo

15 la Sua volontà, come Egli ha ordinato. Deve valutare ciascuno secondo il suo spirito, ammettendo ciascuno secondo la purezza delle sue azioni

16 e facendolo avanzare secondo il suo intelletto. Così deve essere il suo amore (verso i compagni): maggiore o minore. Egli non deve rimproverare, né avere liti con gli uomini della fossa,

17 ma tenga nascoste le interpretazioni della Torah in mezzo agli uomini del Male. Deve correggere con la vera conoscenza e con giusto giudizio gli eletti

18 (perché percorrano) la via, ciascuno secondo il suo spirito e secondo la situazione. Egli deve guidarli nella conoscenza ed insegnare loro i misteri meravigliosi della Verità in mezzo

19 agli uomini della Comunità, affinché si comportino perfettamente tra di loro secondo tutto ciò che è loro rivelato. Questo è il tempo per spianare la via

20 verso il deserto e per insegnare loro tutto ciò che è stato trovato (e) che bisogna fare in questo tempo, (cioè) separarsi da tutti quelli che non hanno allontanato la loro via

21 da tutto il male. Queste sono le norme di comportamento per il *maśkil* in questi tempi per quanto riguarda il suo amore e il suo odio: un odio incessante

22 verso gli uomini della fossa, in spirito di nascondimento, pronto a lasciare loro il danaro e la fatica delle mani, come uno schiavo col suo padrone, come l'oppresso di fronte

23 al suo oppressore. Deve essere zelante per il comandamento e per il suo tempo in funzione del giorno della vendetta, facendo la volontà (di Dio) in tutto quello che intraprende

24 e in tutto quello che dipende da lui, come Egli ha ordinato. In quanto a tutto ciò che gli capita, in esso troverà gioia spontanea e, al di fuori della volontà di Dio, non si compiacerà di nulla.

25 Si diletterà [di tut]te le parole della Sua bocca e non desidererà nulla che Egli non abbia ordi[nato, ma guarde]rà sempre a ciò che Dio vuole (da lui momento per momento).

26 [… (anche) nella tri]bolazione benedirà il suo creatore e in tutto ciò che può accadere narre[rà i Suoi gesti di misericordia…(e con l'offerta [?] delle)] labbra lo benedirà

COLONNA X

1 secondo i tempi che Egli ha stabilito: all'inizio del dominio della luce, al momento in cui essa si volge e quando si raccoglie nel luogo che le è stato fissato;

2 all'inizio delle vigilie della tenebra, quando Egli apre il suo deposito e la distende sopra (la terra), al momento in cui si volge e quando si raccoglie prima della luce; quando appaiono

3 i luminari dal palazzo santo e quando si raccolgono nel luogo della gloria; all'entrata delle fasi lunari nei giorni della luna nuova, al momento in cui si volgono e quando

4 esse si susseguono rinnovandosi. Un grande giorno per il Santo dei Santi e il segno dell'aprirsi continuo della Sua misericordia è l'inizio

5 delle fasi lunari per ogni tempo futuro, l'inizio dei mesi secondo le loro fasi e secondo i giorni santi nel loro ordine fissato, come memoriale delle loro fasi.

6 (Con) l'offerta delle labbra Lo benedirò secondo il comandamento fissato per sempre: (Lo benedirò) all'inizio degli anni, al momento in cui si volgono le loro stagioni e quando si completa la legge

7 del loro ordinamento, ché ciascun giorno ha la sua norma. C'è il tempo della mietitura nell'estate e il tempo della semina nella stagione dell'erba verde. Ci sono i cicli degli anni secondo le loro settimane

8 e il primo di una settimana di anni è il tempo della liberazione. Durante tutto il tempo della mia vita ci sarà (sempre) un comandamento scolpito nella mia lingua (per dare) un frutto di lode e un dono delle mie labbra.

Inno di lode

9 Voglio cantare con la conoscenza; tutto il mio canto è per la gloria di Dio; le corde della mia cetra (cantano) il Suo santo ordine (cosmico) e suono il flauto delle mie labbra sul ritmo della Sua volontà.

10 Quando arrivano il giorno e la notte, voglio entrare nel Patto di Dio, e, quando se ne vanno la sera e il mattino, voglio recitare i Suoi comandamenti: nel loro essere voglio porre

11 i miei confini, senza distaccarmene. Riconosco il Suo giudizio conforme alle mie iniquità e il mio peccato sta davanti ai miei occhi come un comandamento scolpito. A Dio io dico: «Tu sei la mia giustizia»

12 e all'Altissimo «Tu sei il fondamento del mio bene, la fonte della conoscenza, la sorgente della Santità, Altezza gloriosa, Onnipotenza di splendore eterno». Voglio scegliere ciò che Egli

13 mi insegnerà e sarà mia gioia tutto ciò che Egli mi farà capitare. All'inizio di un'opera delle mie mani o dei miei piedi benedirò il Suo nome; all'inizio dell'uscire e dell'entrare,

14 quando mi siedo e quando mi alzo, e anche quando mi sdraio nel mio letto, esulterò in Lui e Lo benedirò con l'offerta, che esce dalle mie labbra, alla mensa degli uomini,

15 prima di alzare la mia mano per impinguarmi delle delizie del frutto della terra. Quando cominceranno paura e terrore e quando ci saranno angoscia e desolazione,

16 io Lo benedirò per le grandi meraviglie (che Egli ha fatto). Mediterò sulla Sua potenza e mi appoggerò sulla Sua misericordia ogni giorno. (Perché) io so che il governo

17 di ogni essere è nelle Sue mani e che tutte le Sue opere sono verità. Quando si presenterà l'angoscia, io Lo loderò e allo stesso modo esulterò per la Sua salvezza. Non ripagherò nessuno

18 per il male, (ma) lo perseguiterò col bene, perché il giudizio di ogni essere vivente è presso Dio: è Lui che darà a ciascuno la sua retribuzione. Non invidierò con spirito

19 malvagio, né desidererò ricchezza (che sia frutto) di violenza. Nelle controversie degli uomini della fossa io non avrò nessuna parte fino al giorno della vendetta. Ma non

20 metterò da parte la mia ira contro gli uomini del Male; non sarò contento finché non avrà luogo il Giudizio. Non manterrò il rancore verso coloro che si convertono dal peccato, ma non avrò compassione

21 per coloro che hanno smarrito la (giusta) via. Non consolerò gli oppressi, finché non abbiano reso perfetta la loro condotta. Non custodirò Belial nel mio cuore. Non si udiranno dalla mia bocca

22 né sciocchezze, né menzogna iniqua; né inganni, né menzogne si troveranno sulle mie labbra. Ma sulla mia lingua ci sarà il frutto della santità e su di essa

23 non si troveranno abomini. Aprirò la mia bocca con inni di lode e la mia lingua narrerà sempre la giustizia di Dio e la trasgressione degli uomini in attesa che si compia la misura

24 del loro peccato. Terrò lontane dalle mie labbra le cose vane, impurità e perfidie dai pensieri della mia mente. Con consiglio prudente terrò nascosta la conoscenza

25 e con astuzia costruirò [intorno ad essa una] solida siepe, per custodire la verità e una norma stabile (di vita) secondo la giustizia di Dio. [Misur]erò

26 il comandamento secondo la misura dei tempi. [...] giustizia e amore misericordioso verso gli oppressi, incoraggerò gli inde[cisi; insegnerò]

Colonna XI

1 l'intelligenza agli smarriti nello spirito; istruirò coloro che mormorano contro la dottrina, risponderò con umiltà ai superbi e con spirito di completa sottomissione agli uomini

2 del bastone, che puntano il dito, la cui parola è iniquità e il cui (solo) desiderio è il danaro. Ma, quanto a me, la mia sorte appartiene a Dio e nelle Sue mani è la perfezione della mia condotta e la rettitudine del mio cuore.

3 Egli con la Sua giustizia cancella il mio peccato. Perché dalla fonte della Sua conoscenza Egli ha fatto sgorgare la Sua luce, (cosicché) il mio occhio ha contemplato le Sue meraviglie e la luce del mio cuore il mistero

4 del futuro e l'essere eterno. L'appoggio della mia destra è su una roccia solida, (cosicché) la via del mio passo non vacillerà di fronte a nulla, perché la Verità di Dio è

5 la roccia dei miei passi e la Sua forza è l'appoggio della mia destra. Dalla fonte della Sua giustizia (deriva) il mio giudizio, una luce viene nel mio cuore dai Suoi misteri meravigliosi.

6 Il mio occhio contempla l'essere eterno: salvezza che è nascosta all'uomo comune. E' una scienza e una conoscenza acuta (che è nascosta) ai comuni mortali: una fonte di giustizia e un recipiente

7 di forza come anche una fonte di gloria (nascosta) all'Assemblea della carne. A coloro che ha eletto Dio ha dato queste cose come possesso eterno; ha dato loro in eredità la sorte

8 degli angeli. Egli ha unito la loro Assemblea a quella dei figli del cielo, per (formare) l'Assemblea della Comunità e l'Assemblea è una costruzione santa, destinata ad essere una piantagione eterna per tutti

9 i tempi futuri. Quanto a me, io appartengo all'umanità malvagia, all'assemblea della carne del Male. Le mie colpe, peccati e trasgressioni, come anche la perversione del mio cuore appartengono

10 all'Assemblea impura (di) coloro che camminano nella Tenebra. Perché a (ogni) uomo (è assegnata da Dio) la sua via e l'uomo non può stabilire il suo passo, perché è Dio che decide e (solo) dalla Sua mano

11 viene la condotta perfetta. Tutto esiste per mezzo della Sua scienza e ogni essere Egli lo stabilisce per mezzo del Suo pensiero: senza di Lui niente può essere fatto. Quanto a me, se io

12 vacillo, la misericordia di Dio è la mia salvezza per sempre, e se inciampo per la colpa della carne, il mio giudizio si fonda sulla giustizia di Dio, la quale dura per sempre.

13 Se mi fa cadere nell'angoscia, Egli mi trae fuori dalla fossa e pone i miei passi sulla via (giusta). Col Suo amore mi ha fatto avvicinare e con la Sua misericordia Egli farà

14 il mio giudizio. Egli mi giudicherà con la giustizia della Sua Verità e con l'abbondanza della Sua bontà espierà tutte le mie colpe. Per mezzo della Sua giustizia Egli mi purificherà dall'impurità

15 dell'uomo e dal peccato dei figli di Adamo, (cosicché) io loderò Dio per la Sua giustizia e l'Altissimo per la Sua gloria. Benedetto Tu, o mio Dio, che hai aperto alla conoscenza

16 il cuore del Tuo servo. Stabilisci nella giustizia tutte le sue opere e poni(lo) come figlio della Tua Verità, come hai voluto per gli eletti di Adamo, che stiano

17 davanti a Te per sempre. Perché senza di Te la condotta non può essere perfetta e senza la Tua volontà non si può fare nulla. Tu hai insegnato

18 tutta la conoscenza, e tutto ciò che esiste, esiste per la Tua volontà. Non c'è nessuno altro al di fuori di Te, che possa opporsi al Tuo consiglio, o che possa insegnare tutto il pensiero della Tua santità, contemplare la profondità dei Tuoi segreti e comprendere tutte le Tue meraviglie, nonché la forza

20 della Tua potenza. Chi potrebbe comprendere la Tua gloria? E che cosa è, infatti, il figlio dell'uomo in mezzo alle Tue opere meravigliose?

21 E il nato di donna, come può stare di fronte a Te? Lui che è un impasto di polvere e il cui corpo sarà pane dei vermi? Egli è (solo) seme emesso (?),

22 (solo) argilla plasmata e la sua pulsione è verso la polvere. In che cosa può opporsi l'argilla e colui che è formato dalla mano? Il progetto di che cosa potrà capire?

German Translation

Die Gemeinderegel

Kolumne I

Präambel

1 Für den […]*šym* für sein Leben, [(das) Buch der Ordn]ung der Gemeinde. Zu suchen

2 Gott von [ganzem Herzen und mit ganzer Seele], zu tun, was gut und recht ist vor ihm, wie

3 er geboten hat durch Mose und durch alle seine Knechte, die Propheten. Und zu lieben alles,

4 was er erwählt hat, und zu hassen alles, was er verabscheut hat, sich fernzuhalten von allem Bösen

5 und anzuhangen allen guten Taten und zu tun Wahrheit und Gerechtigkeit und Recht

6 auf der Erde und nicht weiterhin zu wandeln in Verstocktheit des schuldigen Herzens und Augen der Unzucht,

7 alles Böse zu tun. Und zu bringen alle, die sich willig erweisen, die Gebote Gottes zu tun,

8 in den Bund der Gnade, vereint zu werden in der Ratsversammlung Gottes und vor ihm vollkommen zu wandeln (entsprechend) allem,

9 was offenbart ist zu den Zeiten ihrer Bezeugungen, und um alle Söhne des Lichts zu lieben, jeden

10 nach seinem Los in der Ratsversammlung Gottes, und zu hassen alle Söhne der Finsternis, jeden entsprechend seiner Verschuldung

11 in der Rache Gottes. Und alle, die sich willig erweisen für seine Wahrheit, sollen bringen all ihre Erkenntnis und ihre Kraft

12 und ihren Besitz in die Gemeinde Gottes: um ihre Erkenntnis zu läutern in der Wahrheit der Gesetze Gottes und ihre Kraft einzusetzen

13 nach der Vollkommenheit seiner Wege und all ihren Besitz nach seinem gerechten Rat und nicht zu übertreten ein einziges

14 von allen Worten Gottes in ihren Zeiten und ihre Zeiten nicht vorzurücken und nicht zurückzubleiben

15 von all ihren Zeiten. Und nicht abzuweichen von den Gesetzen seiner Wahrheit, nach rechts oder links zu gehen.

Eintritt in die Bundesgemeinde

16 Und alle, die in die Ordnung der Gemeinde kommen, sollen eintreten in den Bund vor Gott, zu tun

17 entsprechend allem, was er geboten hat, und nicht abweichen von ihm aus irgendeiner Angst oder Furcht oder Prüfungsläuterung

18 während der Herrschaft Belials. Und wenn sie in den Bund eintreten, sollen die Priester

19 und die Leviten den Gott der Rettungen preisen und alle Werke seiner Wahrheit, und alle,

20 die in den Bund eintreten, sollen nach ihnen sprechen: „Amen, amen."

21 Und die Priester sollen die Gerechtigkeitstaten Gottes zusammen mit seinen mächtigen Taten erzählen

22 und sollen berichten alle barmherzigen Gnadentaten an Israel; und die Leviten sollen erzählen

23 alle Sünden der Söhne Israels und all ihre Frevel der Verschuldung und ihre Sünde(n) während der Herrschaft

24 Belials. [Und al]le, die in den Bund eintreten, sollen nach ihnen folgendermaßen bekennen: „Wir haben uns verfehlt,

25 wir sind [ab]trünnig geworden, wir haben [gesün]digt, wir haben gefrevelt, wir [und] unsere [V]äter vor uns, indem wir wandelten

26 […] der Wahrheit; aber gerec[ht ist der Gott Israels und] sein [Ge]richt an uns und [unsren] Vätern,

Kolumne II

1 aber seine gnädige Barmherzigkeit hat er an uns getan von Ewigkeit zu Ewigkeit." Und die Priester sollen segnen alle

2 Männer des Loses Gottes, die vollkommen wandeln in all seinen Wegen, und sie sollen sprechen: „Er segne dich mit allem

3 Guten, und er behüte dich vor allem Bösen, und er erleuchte dein Herz mit Erkenntnis des Lebens, und er sei dir gnädig mit ewiger Erkenntnis,

4 und er erhebe das Angesicht seiner Gnaden über dich zum ewigen Frieden." Und die Leviten sollen verfluchen alle Männer des

5 Loses Belials und anheben und sprechen: „Verflucht bist du in all den frevlerischen Werken deiner Verschuldung; es gebe dir

6 Gott Schrecken durch alle, die Rache rächen; und er suche dich heim (mit) Vernichtung durch alle, die heimzahlen

7 Vergeltung. Verflucht bist du ohne Erbarmen entsprechend der Finsternis deiner Taten, und verwünscht bist du

8 in der Finsternis ewigen Feuers. Nicht sei dir Gott gnädig, wenn du (zu ihm) rufst, und nicht erbarme er sich, deine Sünden zu sühnen;

9 er erhebe sein zorniges Angesicht zur Rache über dich, und nicht sei dir Friede durch alle, die Fürsprache einlegen."

10 Und alle, die in den Bund eintreten, (sollen) sprechen nach den Segnenden und Verfluchenden: „Amen, amen."

11 Und die Priester und die Leviten sollen fortfahren und sprechen: „Verflucht ist, wenn jemand mit den Götzen seines Herzens, um zu übertreten,

12 in diesen Bund eintritt und den Anstoß seiner Sünde vor sich hinlegt, um dadurch abtrünnig zu werden. Und wenn es geschieht,

13 daß er wenn er diese Worte des Bundes hört, sich in seinem Herzen folgendermaßen segnet: „Friede sei mir,

14 auch wenn ich in der Härtigkeit meines Herzens wandle" — dann werde sein Geist vernichtet, das Trockene mit dem Feuchten, ohne

15 Vergebung. Der Zorn Gottes und der Eifer seiner Gerichte sollen über ihn kommen zu ewiger Vernichtung, und ihm mögen anhaften alle

16 Flüche dieses Bundes, und Gott möge ihn aussondern zum Bösen, und er werde ausgerottet aus der Mitte aller Söhne des Lichts, da er abtrünnig geworden ist

17 von Gott in seinen Götzen und dem Anstoß seiner Sünde. Er erhalte sein Los inmitten der ewig Verfluchten."

18 Und alle, die in den Bund kommen, sollen anheben und nach ihnen sprechen: „Amen, amen."

Bundeserneuerung, Verfluchungen, Sühne

19 So sollen sie tun Jahr um Jahr, alle Tage der Herrschaft Belials. Die Priester sollen

20 zuerst in die Ordnung eintreten entsprechend ihren Geistern, einer nach dem andern. Und die Leviten sollen nach ihnen eintreten,

21 und das ganze Volk soll an dritter Stelle in die Ordnung eintreten, einer nach dem andern, zu Tausender- und Hunderter-

22 und Fünfziger- und Zehnergruppen, damit ein jeder Mann Israels den Ort seines Standes in der Gemeinde Gottes weiß

23 zur ewigen Ratsversammlung. Und nicht soll einer herabsteigen vom Ort seines Standes und nicht soll er hinaufsteigen vom Ort seines Loses,

24 denn die Gesamtheit soll in der Gemeinde sein: Wahrheit und gute Demut und gütige Liebe und gerechtes Denken,

25 ein jeder zu seinem Nächsten im heiligen Rat und Söhne des ewigen Rates. Und jeder, der sich weigert, zu kommen

26 [in den Bund Gottes,] zu wandeln in der Härtigkeit seines Herzens, soll ni[cht ...] [Gemein]schaft seiner Wahrheit, denn verabscheut hat

KOLUMNE III

1 seine Seele die Zurechtweisungen der Erkenntnis, die gerechten Gerichte. Er hat nicht festgehalten an dem, der sein Leben umkehrte, und unter die Rechtschaffenen wird er nicht gerechnet,

2 und seine Erkenntnis und seine Kraft und sein Besitz sollen nicht kommen in den Rat der Gemeinde, denn nach verderblichem Frevel ist sein Streben, und Befleckungen sind

3 an seiner Umkehr. Er wird nicht gerecht, wenn er (in) Herzenshärtigkeit wandelt, und Finsternis sieht er statt Wegen des Lichts <und unter> die Vollkommenen

4 wird er nicht gerechnet. Nicht wird er rein in Sühnungen, und nicht kann er sich reinigen in Reinigungswasser, und nicht kann er sich heiligen in Meeren

5 und Flüssen, und nicht kann er sich reinigen in irgendeinem Reinigungswasser. Unrein, unrein wird er sein alle Tage, da er verachtet die Gesetze

6 Gottes, wenn er sich nicht zurechtweisen läßt in der Gemeinde seines Rates. Denn durch den Geist des Rates der Wahrheit in bezug auf die Wege des Menschen werden gesühnt alle

7 seine Sünden, so daß (er) das Licht des Lebens schauen kann. Und durch den Geist der Heiligkeit für die Gemeindein seiner Wahrheit wird er gereinigt von all

8 seinen Sünden; und durch den Geist der Rechtschaffenheit und Demut wird seine Sünde gesühnt, und durch die Erniedrigung seiner Seele für alle Gesetze Gottes wird gereinigt

9 sein Fleisch, so daß man (ihn) mit Reinigungswasser besprenge und (er) sich heilige mit Reinigungswasser. Dann kann er seine Schritte richten, vollkommen zu wandeln

10 in allen Wegen Gottes, wie er geboten hat zu den Zeiten seiner Bezeugungen, und nicht nach rechts und links abzuweichen und nicht

11 zu übertreten eines von allen seinen Worten. Dann wird er wohlgefällig sein in angenehmen Sühnungen vor Gott, und es wird ihm sein zum

12 Bund der ewigen Gemeinschaft.

Das dualistische Stück

13 Für den Unterweiser, einsichtig zu machen und zu lehren alle Söhne des Lichts in den Herkünften aller Söhne des Menschen

14 hinsichtlich aller Arten ihrer Geister in ihren Kennzeichen für ihre Taten in ihren Geschlechtern und ihrer Heimsuchung mit Plagen mit

15 den Zeiten ihres Friedens. Vom Gott der Erkenntnis ist alles, was ist und sein wird, und bevor sie waren, hat er den ganzen Plan für sie festgelegt,

16 und wenn sie werden zu den für sie festgelegten Zeiten, erfüllen sie ihr Werk entsprechend seinem herrlichen Plan, und er gibt keine Änderung. In seiner Hand

17 sind die Gesetze für alles, und es versorgt sie in allem, wessen sie bedürfen. Und er schuf den Menschen zur Herrschaft über

18 den Erdkreis, und setzte für ihn zwei Geister, in ihnen zu wandeln bis zur Zeit seiner Heimsuchung. Diese sind die Geister

19 der Wahrheit und des Frevels. In der Quelle des Lichts ist die Herkunft der Wahrheit, und aus der Quelle der Finsternis ist die Herkunft des Frevels.

20 In der Hand des Fürsten der Lichter ist die Herrschaft aller Söhne der Gerechtigkeit, auf Wegen des Lichts wandeln sie, und in der Hand des Engels

21 der Finsternis ist alle Herrschaft der Söhne des Frevels, und auf Wegen der Finsternis wandeln sie. Und durch den Engel der Finsternis geschieht die Verführung

22 aller Söhne der Gerechtigkeit, und all ihre Sünde(n) und Übertretungen und ihre Verschuldung und die Frevel ihrer Taten geschehen durch seine Herrschaft

23 entsprechend den Geheimnissen Gottes bis zu seiner Zeit. Und all ihre Plagen und die Zeiten ihrer Bedrängnisse geschehen durch die Herrschaft seiner Feindschaft.

24 Und alle Geister seines Loses (sind darauf aus), die Söhne des Lichts zum Straucheln zu bringen. Aber der Gott Israels und der Engel seiner Wahrheit sind eine Hilfe für alle

25 Söhne des Lichts. Und er hat die Geister des Lichts und der Finsternis geschaffen, und auf sie hat er jedes Werk gegründet

26 l[...]hn jede Tat, und auf ihre Wege [jede ...]wdh. Den einen liebt Gott für alle

KOLUMNE IV

1 ewigen [Zei]ten, und an all seinen Handlungen hat er auf ewig Gefallen; des andern Rat verabscheut er, und all seine Wege haßt er auf ewig.

2 Und dies sind ihre Wege auf dem Erdkreis: das Herz des Menschen zu erleuchten und vor ihm alle Wege der Gerechtigkeit der Wahrheit zu ebnen und sein Herz fürchten zu machen die Gerichte

3 Gottes; und ein Geist der Demut und Langmut und Fülle des Erbarmens und ewige Güte und Einsicht und Verständnis und mächtige Weisheit, die vertraut auf alle

4 Werke Gottes und sich stützt auf die Fülle seiner Gnade; und ein Geist der Erkenntnis in allem Planen der Tat und Eifer für die gerechten Gerichte und

5 heiliges Denken mit festem Sinn und Fülle der Gnade für alle Söhne der Wahrheit und herrliche Reinheit, die alle Götzen der Unreinheit verabscheut, und demütiger Wandel

6 in Klugheit von allem, und zu verbergen für die Wahrheit die Geheimnisse der Erkenntnis. Dies sind die Ratschläge (oder: Grundlagen) des Geistes für die Söhne der Wahrheit auf dem Erdkreis, und die Heimsuchung aller, die darin wandeln, ist zur Heilung

7 und Fülle des Friedens in Länge der Tage und Fruchtbarkeit des Samens mit allen ewigen Segnungen und ewiger Freude im ewigen Leben und Krone der Herrlichkeit

8 mit dem Gewand des Glanzes im ewigen Licht.

Der Geist des Frevels

9 Und dem Geist des Frevels kommt zu: Habgier und Lässigkeit der Hände im Tun der Gerechtigkeit, Frevel und Lüge, Stolz und Hochmut des Herzens, Trug und grausame Täuschung

10 und Fülle der Ruchlosigkeit, Jähzorn und Fülle der Torheit und Eifer des Übermuts, Werke des Greuels im Geist der Hurerei und Wege der Unreinheit im Tun der Unreinheit

11 und Zunge der Lästerung, Blindheit der Augen und Schwere (=Taubheit) des Ohrs, Starrheit des Nackens und Härtigkeit des Herzens, zu wandeln auf allen Wegen der Finsternis, und böswillige Hinterlist; und die Heimsuchung

12 aller, die in ihm wandeln, ist zur Fülle der Plagen durch alle Engel der Nichtigkeit zum ewigen Verderben durch den Zornesgrimm Gottes, Rache zum ewigen Abscheu und

13 ewige Schmach mit endgültiger Vernichtung im Feuer der Finsternisse. Und all ihre Zeiten sind für ihre Generationen in Traurigkeit des Kummers und Unheil der Bitternisse im Verderben der Finsternis bis

14 zu ihrer Vernichtung, ohne Rest und Rettung für sie.

Die beiden Arten der Menschen

15 In diesen (beiden Geistern) ist die Herkunft aller Söhne des Menschen, und an ihren Abteilungen hat ihr ganzes Heer für all ihre Geschlechter Anteil, und in ihren Wegen wandeln sie, und alles Werk

16 ihrer Taten ist in ihren Abteilungen entsprechend dem Erbe eines Menschen, sei es viel oder wenig, für alle ewigen Zeiten. Denn Gott hat sie zu jeweiligen Teilen gesetzt bis zur

17 letzten Zeit, und er hat ewige Feindschaft gesetzt zwischen ihren Abteilungen: Ein Greuel für die Wahrheit sind die Taten des Frevels, und ein Greuel für den Frevel sind alle Werke der Wahrheit, und eifervoller

18 Streit ist über all ihre Bestimmungen. Denn sie wandeln nicht gemeinsam. Und Gott, in den Geheimnissen seiner Erkenntnis und seiner herrlichen Weisheit, hat ein Ende gesetzt für die Existenz des Frevels, und zur Zeit

19 der Heimsuchung wird er ihn für ewig vernichten. Und dann wird für immer die Wahrheit für den Erdkreis hervortreten, denn er hat sich gewälzt auf den Wegen des Frevels unter der Herrschaft der Bosheit bis zur

20 Zeit des festgesetzten Gerichts. Und dann wird Gott durch seine Wahrheit alle Taten des Menschen läutern, er wird sich reinigen den Bau (d.h. Leib) des Menschen (oder: von den Menschensöhnen), um zu vernichter jeden Frevelgeist aus den Gliedern

21 seines Fleisches und um ihn zu reinigen mit heiligem Geist von allen Freveltaten. Und er wird auf ihn den Geist der Wahrheit sprengen wie Reinigungswasser von allen Abscheulichkeiten der Lüge und dem sich Wälzen

22 im Geist der Unreinheit, damit die Rechtschaffenen die Erkenntnis des Höchsten verstehen und die Weisheit der Söhne des Himmels, um zu unterweisen, die vollkommen wandeln. Denn sie hat Gott zum ewigen Bund erwählt,

23 und ihnen kommt die Herrlichkeit Adams zu. Und es wird keinen Frevel geben, und zu Schanden werden alle Werke des Trugs. Bis dahin kämpfen die Geister der Wahrheit und des Frevels im Herzen des Menschen;

24 sie wandeln in Weisheit und Torheit, und entsprechend dem Erbe eines Menschen an der Wahrheit ist er gerecht, und so haßt er den Frevel, und entsprechend seinem Besitz am Los der Bosheit frevelt er dadurch, und so

25 verabscheut er die Wahrheit. Denn je und je hat Gott sie gesetzt bis zur festgesetzten Zeit und der Neumachung (=Neuschöpfung). Und er kennt das Werk ihrer Taten für alle Zeiten,

26 [...]*n* und er gibt sie zum Anteil den Söhnen des Menschen, zu erkennen gut [...und zu wer]fen die Lose für alle Lebewesen entsprechend seinem Geist *b*[... der] Heimsuchung.

KOLUMNE V

Ordnung für das Leben in der Gemeinde

1 Und dies ist die Ordnung für die Männer der Gemeinde, die sich willig erweisen, umzukehren von allem Bösen und festzuhalten an allem, was er nach seinem Willen befohlen hat, sich zu trennen von der Gemeinschaft

2 der Männer des Frevels, daß sie seien zu einer Gemeinde in Tora und Besitz und verantwortlich seien gegenüber den Söhnen Zadoqs, den Priestern, den Bewahrern des Bundes, und gegenüber der Menge der Männer

3 der Gemeinde, die am Bund festhalten. Auf ihr Geheiß hin ergeht die Bestimmung des Loses für jede Sache in bezug auf die Tora und den Besitz und das Recht, zu tun Wahrheit, Gemeinschaft und Demut,

4 Gerechtigkeit und Recht und gütige Liebe und demütigen Wandel in all ihren Wegen, so daß keiner in der Härtigkeit seines Herzens wandle, in die Irre zu gehen nach seinem Herzen

5 und seinen Augen und der Absicht seines Triebes. Vielmehr soll er beschneiden in der Gemeinde die Vorhaut des Triebes und den harten Nacken, zu gründen eine Gründung der Wahrheit für Israel zu einer Gemeinde

6 des ewigen Bundes, zu sühnen für alle, die sich willig erweisen, zu einem Heiligtum in Aaron und einem Haus der Wahrheit in Israel; und die sich ihnen anschließen zu einer Gemeinde und zum Rechtsstreit und zum Gericht,

7 um zu Frevlern zu erklären alle, die das Gebot übertreten. Und diese sind die Festlegung für ihre Wege bezüglich all dieser Gesetze, wenn sie sich versammeln zur Gemeinde: Jeder, der in den Rat der Gemeinde kommt,

8 trete ein in den Bund Gottes vor den Augen aller, die sich willig erweisen. Und er soll auf sich nehmen mit einem bindenden Eid, umzukehren zur Tora Moses entsprechend allem, was er geboten hat, von ganzem

9 Herzen und von ganzer Seele hinsichtlich allem, was offenbart ist daraus den Söhnen Zadoqs, den Priestern, den Bewahrern des Bundes und den nach seinem Willen Forschenden, und der Menge der Männer ihres Bundes,

10 die sich willig erweisen, gemeinsam zu seiner Wahrheit, und zu wandeln nach seinem Willen. Und er soll im Bund auf sich nehmen, sich zu trennen von allen Männern der Bosheit, die wandeln

11 auf dem Weg des Frevels; denn sie werden nicht zu seinem Bund gerechnet. Denn nicht suchen sie und nicht forschen sie nach ihm in seinen Gesetzen, zu erkennen die verborgenen Dinge, in denen sie in die Irre gingen

12 zu ihrer Verschuldung. Und die geoffenbarten Dinge taten sie vorsätzlich, um Zorn zum Gericht zu erregen und zum Rächen der Rache durch die Flüche des Bundes, damit (Gott) an ihnen tue

13 große Gerichte zur ewigen Vernichtung, so daß kein Rest mehr ist. Nicht komme er ins Wasser, die Reinheit der Männer der Heiligkeit zu berühren. Denn sie werden nicht rein,

14 wenn sie nicht umkehren von ihrem Bösen. Denn unrein ist er (zusammen) mit allen, die sein Wort übertreten. Und keiner vereinige sich mit ihm in seiner Arbeit und in seinem Besitz, damit er nicht auf ihn bringt

15 Sünde der Schuld. Denn er soll sich von ihm fernhalten in jener Sache, denn so steht geschrieben: „Von jeder lügnerischen Sache halte dich fern." Und keiner der Männer

16 der Gemeinde soll ihnen gegenüber antworten bezüglich der ganzen Tora und des Rechts. Und er soll von ihrem Besitz nichts essen und nicht trinken, und er nehme auch nicht irgendetwas aus ihrer Hand,

17 das nicht auf Kaufpreis beruht, wie geschrieben steht: „Steht fern vom Menschen, in dessen Nase Hauch ist; denn für was wird er gerechnet?" Denn

18 alle, die nicht zu seinem Bund gerechnet werden, sind abzutrennen, und alles, was ihnen gehört. Und kein Mann der Heiligkeit stütze sich auf irgendeine

19 nichtige Sache; denn nichtig sind alle, die seinen Bund nicht kennen; und alle, die sein Wort verschmähen, wird er vom Erdboden vernichten, und all ihre Taten sind zur Unreinheit

20 vor ihm, und Unreines ist an all ihrem Besitz. Und wenn einer in den Bund eintritt, zu tun entsprechend diesen Gesetzen, sich zu vereinigen zur heiligen Gemeinschaft, dann sollen sie erforschen

21 seinen Geist in der Gemeinde, zwischen dem einzelnen und seinem Nächsten, entsprechend seiner Erkenntnis und seinen Werken in der Tora, auf Anordnung der Söhne Aarons, die sich willig erweisen in der Gemeinde,

22 seinen Bund aufzurichten und zu befolgen alle seine Gesetze, die er zu tun geboten hat, und auf Anordnung der Menge Israels, die sich willig erweisen, umzukehren in der Gemeinde zu seinem Bund.

23 Und man soll sie einschreiben in die Ordnung, einen jeden vor seinem Nächsten entsprechend seiner Erkenntnis und seinen Taten, damit alle gehorsam sind, ein jeder gegenüber seinem Nächsten, der Kleine gegenüber dem Großen. Und sie sollen

24 prüfen ihren Geist und ihre Werke Jahr um Jahr, um jeden aufrücken zu lassen entsprechend seiner Erkenntnis und der Vollkommenheit seines Weges und ihn zurückzustufen entsprechend seiner Verkehrtheit; zurechtzuweisen

25 ein jeder seinen Nächsten in Wa[hr]heit und Demut und gütiger Liebe zu jedem. Er rede zu ihm nicht in Zorn oder Murren

26 oder mit [hartem] Nacken [oder mit eiferndem] Geist des Frevels. Und er hasse ihn nicht [in der Unbeschnittenheit] seines Herzens. Denn am (selben) Tag soll er ihn zurechtweisen, und nicht

KOLUMNE VI

1 lade er seinetwegen Schuld auf sich. Und auch bringe keiner gegen seinen Nächsten eine Sache vor die Vielen, bei der es nicht Zurechtweisung vor Zeugen gab. In diesen (Anordnungen)

2 sollen sie wandeln an all ihren Wohnsitzen, jeder, der vorhanden ist, ein jeder mit seinem Nächsten. Und der Kleine soll dem Großen gehorsam sein bezüglich Arbeit und Geld. Und gemeinsam sollen sie essen,

3 und gemeinsam sollen sie preisen (oder: segnen), und gemeinsam sollen sie beraten. Und an jedem Ort, wo zehn Männer vom Rat der Gemeinschaft sein werden, soll nicht unter ihnen ein

4 Priester fehlen. Und jeder soll entsprechend seiner Rangstufe vor ihm sitzen. Und so sollen sie nach dem Rat für sie fragen hinsichtlich jeder Sache. Und wenn es geschieht, daß sie den Tisch decken, um zu essen, oder den Most,

5 um zu trinken, strecke der Priester seine Hand zuerst aus, um den Erstling des Brotes und des Mostes zu segnen (Dittographie 5b-6a).

6 Und es soll an einem Ort, an dem zehn Männer sein werden, ein Toraforscher nicht fehlen, Tag und Nacht,

7 ständig, im Wechsel, ein jeder mit seinem Nächsten. Und die Vielen sollen gemeinsam ein Drittel aller Nächte des Jahres wachen, um im Buch zu lesen und Recht zu erforschen

8 und gemeinsam zu preisen (oder: segnen). Und dies ist die Ordnung für die Sitzung der Vielen: Jeder in seiner Rangstufe; die Priester sollen an erster Stelle sitzen und die Ältesten an zweiter, und der Rest

9 des ganzen Volkes soll jeder nach seiner Rangstufe sitzen, und so sollen sie nach Recht befragt werden und nach jedem Rat; und bei einer Sache, die vor die Vielen kommt, da soll ein jeder sein Wissen darbieten

10 dem Rat der Gemeinde. Keiner soll in die Worte seines Nächsten hineinsprechen, bevor sein Bruder aufgehört hat zu sprechen. Und auch spreche er nicht vor der Rangstufe dessen, der vor ihm

11 eingeschrieben ist. Der Mann, der gefragt ist, spreche, wenn er an der Reihe ist. Und in der Sitzung der Vielen sage keiner irgendetwas, das nicht nach Billigung der Vielen ist, auch wenn es der

12 Aufseher über die Vielen ist. Und jeder, der eine Sache vor den Vielen vorzubringen hat, der aber nicht im Stand eines Mannes ist, der den Rat

13 der Gemeinde fragen kann, so soll dieser Mann aufstehen auf seine Füße und sagen: „Ich habe etwas vor die Vielen vorzubringen." Und wenn sie es ihm gestatten, rede er. Und jeder, der sich willig erweist aus Israel,

14 sich dem Rat der Gemeinde anzuschließen, den soll der Aufseher, der an der Spitze der Vielen steht, prüfen hinsichtlich seiner Erkenntnis und seiner Taten. Und wenn er Zucht annimmt, sollen sie ihn

15 in den Bund bringen, umzukehren zur Wahrheit und abzuweichen von allem Frevel; er soll ihn belehren in allen Rechtssatzungen der Gemeinde. Und danach, wenn er kommt, um vor den Vielen zu stehen, dann sollen sie alle befragt werden

16 wegen seiner Sachen (=seinetwegen). Und wenn das Los ergeht nach dem Rat der Vielen darf er sich nähern oder muß sich entfernen. Und wenn er sich dem Rat der Gemeinde nähert, berühre er nicht die Reinheit (d.h. die reinen Speisen)

17 der Vielen, bis sie ihn geprüft haben hinsichtlich seines Geistes und seiner Taten, bis er ein volles Jahr vollendet hat. Und auch habe er nicht Anteil am Besitz der Vielen,

18 und wenn er ein Jahr inmitten der Gemeinschaft vollendet hat, dann sollen die Vielen über seine Angelegenheiten bezüglich seiner Einsicht und seiner Werke in der Tora befragt werden. Und wenn ihm das Los ergeht,

19 sich dem Rat der Gemeinde auf Geheiß der Priester und der Menge der Männer ihres Bundes zu nähern, dann sollen sie auch seinen Besitz und seine Arbeit(seinkünfte) herzubringen zu Händen des Mannes, der

20 Aufseher ist über die Einkünfte der Vielen, und sie sollen (es) auf ein Konto durch ihn aufschreiben, aber für die Vielen darf er es nicht ausgeben. Nicht berühre er das Getränk der Vielen, bis

21 er vollendet hat ein zweites Jahr inmitten der Männer der Gemeinde. Und wenn er das zweite Jahr vollendet hat, sollen sie ihn auf Geheiß der Vielen prüfen. Und wenn für ihn

22 das Los ergeht, ihn der Gemeinde nahezubringen, sollen sie ihn in die Ordnung seines Ranges inmitten seiner Brüder einschreiben bezüglich Tora und Recht und Reinheit, und seinen Besitz zu integrieren. Und sein Rat

23 soll der Gemeinde gehören und sein Urteil.

24 Und dies sind die Rechtsordnungen, nach denen sie richten sollen in gemeinsamer Untersuchung aufgrund der Sachverhalte: Wenn unter ihnen ein Mann gefunden wird, der lügt

25 über Besitz, und er wird erkannt (oder: und er weiß es), dann sollen sie ihn für ein Jahr ausschließen aus der Mitte der Reinheit der Vielen, und er soll bestraft werden mit einem Viertel seiner Nahrung. Und wenn einer

26 seinem Nächsten mit Halsstarrigkeit antwortet und im Jähzorn redet, so daß er das Fundament seiner Gemeinschaft zerbricht durch Widerspenstigkeit gegen seinen Nächsten, der vor ihm eingeschrieben ist,

27 dem hat seine Hand [ge]holfen (d.h. der hat Selbsthilfe geübt), und er soll bestraft werden mit ein[em] Jahr [und ausgeschlossen werden. Und w]er etwas erwähnt im Namen dessen, der geehrt ist über alles *h*[… .]

KOLUMNE VII

1 Und wenn er flucht, sei es, weil er überwältigt ist von einer Not oder wegen jeder Sache, die ihn betrifft, (und) er liest im Buch oder preist, dann sollen sie ihn ausschließen,

2 und er komme nicht mehr zurück in den Rat der Gemeinde. Und wenn (jemand) gegen einen der Priester, die aufgeschrieben sind im Buch, im Zorn redet, soll er bestraft werden mit

3 einem Jahr und selbst ausgeschlossen sein von der Reinheit der Vielen. Und wenn er versehentlich geredet hat, dann soll er mit sechs Monaten bestraft werden. Und wer mit Wissen lügt,

4 der wird bestraft mit sechs Monaten. Und der Mann, der ohne Grund seinen Nächsten mit Wissen schmäht, der soll bestraft werden mit einem Jahr

5 und ausgeschlossen werden. Und wer gegen seinen Nächsten in Bitterkeit redet oder mit Wissen trügerisch handelt, der wird mit sechs Monaten bestraft. Und wenn er

6 seinen Nächsten täuscht, wird er bestraft mit drei Monaten. Und wenn er beim Besitz der Gemeinde täuscht, so daß er einen Verlust verursacht, so soll er ihn erstatten

7 in seinem vollen Wert.

8 Und wenn er nicht in der Lage ist, ihn zu erstatten, so soll er mit sechzig Tagen bestraft werden. Und wer seinem Nächsten grollt, und es ist ohne Grund, der soll bestraft werden mit einem Jahr (ursprünglich stand: mit sechs Monaten).

9 Und so für den, der irgendetwas für sich rächt. Und wer mit seinem Mund etwas Törichtes sagt, (soll bestraft werden) mit drei Monaten. Und wer in die Worte seines Nächsten redet:

10 zehn Tage. Und wer sich legt und schläft bei der Sitzung der Vielen: dreißig Tage. Und so dem Mann, der sich entfernt während der Sitzung der Vielen,

11 wenn es ohne Beschluß ist. Und wer einschläft bis zu drei Mal bei einer Sitzung, der soll bestraft werden mit zehn Tagen. Und wenn sie stehen

12 und er entfernt sich, so soll er bestraft werden mit dreißig Tagen. Und wer vor seinem Nächsten nackt geht und nicht gezwungen ist, der soll bestraft werden mit sechs Monaten.

13 Und ein Mann, der spuckt inmitten der Sitzung der Vielen, der soll bestraft werden mit dreißig Tagen. Und wer sein Glied aus seinem Gewand herauskommen läßt und es

14 flattert, so daß seine Blöße gesehen wird, der soll bestraft werden mit dreißig Tagen. Und wer töricht lacht, so daß er seine Stimme hören läßt, der soll bestraft werden mit dreißig

15 Tagen. Und wer seine linke Hand herausstreckt, um darauf niederzusinken (d.h. um sich darauf abzustützen, oder: um zu fuchteln), der soll zehn Tage bestraft werden. Und der Mann, der sich verleumderisch verhält mit seinem Nächsten,

16 den sollen sie für ein Jahr ausschließen von der Reinheit der Vielen, und er soll bestraft werden. Und der Mann, der sich verleumderisch gegen die Vielen verhält, der ist von ihnen wegzuschicken,

17 und er kehre nicht wieder zurück. Und der Mann, der murrt gegen das Fundament der Gemeinde, den sollen sie wegschicken, und er kehre nicht zurück. Und wenn er gegen seinen Nächsten murrt,

18 und es ist ohne Grund, so soll er bestraft werden mit sechs Monaten. Und der Mann, dessen Geist gegenüber der Grundlage der Gemeinde schwankt, so daß er (treulos) die Wahrheit verläßt,

19 um zu wandeln in seiner Herzenshärtigkeit, der soll, wenn er umkehrt, mit zwei Jahren bestraft werden: im ersten soll er nicht die Reinheit der Vielen berühren,

20 und im zweiten soll er nicht das Getränk der Vielen berühren und soll hinter allen Männern der Gemeinde sitzen. Und wenn er vollendet hat

21 zwei Jahre, sollen die Vielen befragt werden über seine Angelegenheiten. Und wenn sie ihn näherkommen lassen, dann soll er eingeschrieben werden in seiner Rangstufe. Und danach kann er befragt werden über das Recht

22 [Text getilgt]. Und jeder Mann, der sich im Rat der Gemeinde bis zur Vollendung von zehn Jahren befindet

23 [Text getilgt] und dessen Geist abweicht, abtrünnig zu werden von der Gemeinschaft, und er geht weg von

24 den Vielen, zu wandeln in seiner Herzenshärtigkeit, der soll nicht wieder in den Rat der Gemeinde zurückkehren. Und ein Mann von den Männern der Gemein[de, d[er sich mit ihm] verbindet

25 in seiner Reinheit oder seinem Besitz, welch[er …]der Vielen. Und sein Urteil soll wie seines sein: (ihn) [aus]zu[schließen … .]

KOLUMNE VIII

Ordnungen für die heilige Gemeinschaft

1 Im Rat der Gemeinde sollen zwölf Männer und drei Priester sein, vollkommen in allem, was offenbart ist aus der ganzen

2 Tora, zu tun Wahrheit und Gerechtigkeit und Recht und gütige Liebe und demütigen Wandel, ein jeder mit seinem Nächsten,

3 um Treue im Lande zu bewahren mit festem Sinn und einem zerbrochenen Geist und um Schuld zu sühnen, indem sie Recht tun,

4 und Not der Läuterung (zu ertragen) und mit allem zu wandeln nach dem Maß der Wahrheit und der Festlegung der Zeit. Wenn dies in Israel geschieht,

5 dann steht der Rat der Gemeinde fest in Wahrheit zu einer ewigen Pflanzung, ein heiliges Haus für Israel und ein allerheiligstes Fundament

6 für Aaron, Zeugen der Wahrheit für das Recht und Auserwählte des Wohlgefallens (Gottes), zu sühnen für das Land und zu vergelten

7 den Frevlern ihre Tat. Dies ist die erprobte Mauer, der kostbare Eckstein,

8 seine Fundamente wanken nicht und weichen nicht von ihrem Platz. Eine allerheiligste Wohnung

9 für Aaron in aller Erkenntnis, zu einem Bund des Rechts, und um darzubringen einen angenehmen Opferduft, und ein Haus der Vollkommenheit und Wahrheit in Israel,

10 um einen Bund zu errichten nach ewigen Gesetzen. Und sie sind zum Wohlgefallen, zu sühnen für das Land und festzusetzen das Gericht über den Frevel; und es wird kein Frevel mehr sein. Wenn diese in den Grundlagen der Gemeinde festgemacht sind, zwei Jahre in vollkommenem Wandel,

11 sollen sie abgetrennt werden als Heiliges inmitten des Rats der Männer der Gemeinde. Und jede Sache, die vor Israel verborgen war und gefunden wurde von einem Mann,

12 der forscht, die soll er vor ihnen nicht verbergen aus Furcht vor einem abtrünnigen Geist. Und wenn diese zur Gemeinde in Israel werden,

13 so sollen sie entsprechend diesen Ordnungen abgesondert werden aus der Mitte der Niederlassung der Männer des Frevels, in die Wüste zu gehen, um dort den Weg des Herrn (?) zu bereiten,

14 wie geschrieben steht: „In der Wüste bereitet den Weg des Herrn, macht eben in der Steppe eine Bahn für unseren Gott."

15 Dies ist das Erforschen der Tora, w[i]e er geboten hat durch Mose, zu tun entsprechend allem, was von Zeit zu Zeit offenbart ist,

16 und wie die Propheten durch seinen heiligen Geist geoffenbart haben. Und jeder Mann von den Männern der Gemeinde, des Bundes

17 der Gemeinde, der von dem ganzen Gebot in einer Sache vorsätzlich abweicht, darf nicht die Reinheit der Männer der Heiligkeit berühren

18 und darf nichts wissen von ihrem ganzen Rat, bis seine Werke rein geworden sind von jedem Frevel, so daß er auf vollkommenem Weg wandelt. Und sie sollen ihn näherbringen

19 in den Rat auf Geheiß der Vielen, und danach soll er eingeschrieben werden nach seiner Rangordnung; und entsprechend diesem Gesetz (ist zu verfahren) für jeden, der sich der Gemeinde anschließt.

20 Und dies sind die Rechtsverordnungen, nach denen die Männer der vollkommenen Heiligkeit wandeln sollen, ein jeder mit seinem Nächsten.

21 Jeder, der in den Rat der Heiligkeit derer kommt, die wandeln auf vollkommenem Weg, wie er befohlen hat, (für ihn gilt): Jeder Mann von ihnen,

22 der ein Wort aus der Tora Moses absichtlich oder nachlässig übertritt, den sollen sie aus dem Rat der Gemeinde ausschließen,

23 und er kehre nicht wieder zurück. Und keiner von den Männern der Heiligkeit soll Gemeinschaft mit ihm haben in seinem Besitz und in seinem Rat bezüglich jeder

24 Sache. Und wenn er versehentlich gehandelt hat, dann soll er von der Reinheit und vom Rat getrennt werden, und sie sollen das Gesetz so auslegen,

25 daß er keinen richten darf und nicht gefragt werden darf bezüglich irgendeines Rates zwei Jahre lang. Wenn sein Wandel vollkommen ist

26-27 in der Sitzung, beim Studium und im Rat [auf Geheiß der] Vielen, (dann soll er zurückkehren) — wenn er nicht wieder irrtümlich handelt bis zwei Jahre vorüber sind —,

KOLUMNE IX

1 denn wegen eines Versehens soll er zwei Jahre bestraft werden. Aber für den, der vorsätzlich handelt, gilt: Er kehre nicht mehr zurück. Nur wer versehentlich handelt,

2 soll zwei Jahre geprüft werden hinsichtlich der Vollkommenheit seines Weges und seines Rates auf Geheiß der Vielen. Und danach soll man (ihn) in seiner Rangstufe zur Gemeinde der Heiligkeit einschreiben.

3 Wenn diese Dinge in Israel geschehen nach all diesen Bestimmungen, zu einem Fundament des heiligen Geistes in

4 ewiger Wahrheit, zu sühnen für Frevelschuld und Abfallsünde und zum Wohlgefallen für das Land, ohne das Fleisch von Brandopfern und ohne das Fett von Schlachtopfern, denn ein Hebopfer

5 der Lippen nach Vorschrift ist wie ein rechtes Beschwichtigungsopfer und ein vollkommener Wandel wie eine freiwillige wohlgefällige Opfergabe. In dieser Zeit sollen die Männer der Gemeinde absondern

6 ein heiliges Haus für Aaron, um sich als ein Allerheiligstes zu vereinen, und ein Haus der Gemeinde für Israel, derer die vollkommen wandeln.

7 Allein die Söhne Aarons sollen herrschen bei der Rechtsprechung und beim Besitz, und auf ihr Geheiß ergeht das Los über alle Festsetzung der Männer der Gemeinde.

8 Und den Besitz der Männer der Heiligkeit, die vollkommen wandeln, — nicht vermische man ihren Besitz und den Besitz der Männer des Trugs, die

9 ihren Wandel nicht gereinigt haben, um sich zu scheiden vom Frevel und zu wandeln auf vollkommenem Weg. Und sie sollen nicht abweichen von irgendeinem Rat der Tora, um zu wandeln

10 in jeder Härtigkeit des Herzens, und sie sollen gerichtet werden nach den früheren Gesetzen, in denen die Männer der Gemeinde angefangen haben, Zucht anzunehmen,

11 bis der Prophet kommt und die Messiasse Aarons und Israels.

12 Dies sind die Gesetze für den Unterweiser, darin zu wandeln mit allen Lebenden entsprechend der Ordnung der jeweiligen Zeit und dem Gewicht eines jeden Mannes,

13 den Willen Gottes zu tun entsprechend allem, was offenbart ist für die jeweilige Zeit, und die ganze Einsicht zu lernen, die entsprechend den Zeiten gefunden wird, und das

14 Gesetz der Zeit, um abzusondern und zu wiegen die Söhne der Gerechtigkeit entsprechend ihrem Geist und festzumachen die Auserwählten der Zeit entsprechend

15 seinem Willen, wie er befohlen hat. Und jedem nach seinem Geist sein Recht zukommen zu lassen, und jeden entsprechend der Reinheit seiner Hände näherzubringen, und entsprechend seiner Einsicht

16 ihn herzutreten zu lassen, und so bei seinem Lieben und seinem Hassen. Und er soll nicht zurechtweisen oder streiten mit den Männern der Grube

17 und soll den Rat der Tora vor den Männern des Frevels verbergen, aber zurechtweisen wahre Erkenntnis und gerechtes Gericht gegenüber den Auserwählten

18 des Wandels, jeden entsprechend seinem Geist nach der Ordnung der Zeit, sie zu leiten in Erkenntnis und sie so zu belehren in den wunderbaren und wahren Geheimnissen inmitten

19 der Männer der Gemeinde, um vollkommen zu wandeln, ein jeder mit seinem Nächsten, in allem, was ihnen geoffenbart ist — das ist die Zeit des Bereitens des Weges

20 in der Wüste — und sie alles zu lehren, was gefunden wird, zu dieser Zeit zu tun. Und sich zu trennen von jedem Menschen und nicht seinen Weg zu ändern

21 wegen irgendeines Bösen. Dies sind die Festsetzungen des Weges für den Unterweiser zu diesen Zeiten in bezug auf sein Lieben und sein Hassen: Ewigen Haß

22 mit den Männern der Grube im Geist des Verbergens, ihnen zu lassen Besitz und Arbeit der Hände, wie ein Sklave gegenüber dem, der über ihn herrscht, und Demut gegenüber

23 seinem Herrn. Und jeder sei ein Eiferer für das Gesetz und bereit für den Tag der Rache, zu tun (Gottes) Willen bei jedem Unternehmen

24 und in seiner ganzen Herrschaft, wie er befohlen hat. Und an allem, was durch ihn getan wird, habe er bereitwillig Gefallen, und außer Gottes Willen soll ihm nichts gefallen,

25 [und an alle]n Worten seines Mundes habe er Gefallen. Und er begehre nichts, was er nicht ge[boten hat,] sondern [nach] Gottes [Geric]ht halte er beständig Ausschau,

26 [... und in Bedrän]gnis preise er seinen Schöpfer, und in allem, was geschieht, erzäh[le] er [seine Gnadentaten] (zusammen mit den Lobopfer) seiner Lippen. Er soll ihn preisen

KOLUMNE X

1 zu den Zeiten, die <Gott> festgesetzt hat: Zu Beginn der Herrschaft des Lichts, bei seiner Wende, und wenn es sich zurückzieht an den ihm festgesetzten Ort, zu Beginn

2 der Wachen der Finsternis, denn er öffnet ihre Kammer und legt sie über (die Erde), und bei ihrer Wende, wenn er sie vor dem Licht zurückzieht. Wenn aufstrahlen

3 Leuchten von der heiligen Wohnung, wenn sie sich zurückziehen zum Ort der Herrlichkeit. Wenn Festzeiten kommen an den Tagen des (Neu)Mondes mit ihrer Wende und

4 ihrer Aufeinanderfolge, einer nach dem andern. Wenn sie sich erneuern, (ist) ein großer Tag für das Allerheiligste und ein Zeichen (?) zur Eröffnung seiner ewigen Gnaden. Bei den Anfängen

5 der Festzeiten zu jeder Zeit, die sein wird, zu Beginn der Monate zu ihren Festzeiten, den heiligen Tagen nach ihrer Festsetzung, zum Gedächtnis in ihren Festzeiten.

6 (Mit) der Hebe der Lippen will ich ihn preisen, es ist wie ein eingegrabenes Gesetz für immer. An den Anfängen der Jahre und der Wende der Festzeiten, wenn sich das Gesetz

7 ihrer Ordnung vollendet, jeder einzelne Tag nach seiner Bestimmung: Zeit der Ernte zum Sommer und Zeit der Aussaat zur Zeit des (frischen) Grüns, die Festzeiten der Jahre zu ihren (Jahr-)Wochen,

8 und zu Beginn ihrer (Jahr-)Wochen zur Zeit der Freilassung. Solange ich bin, ist ein Gesetz auf meiner Zunge eingegraben zur Frucht des Lobpreises und Teil meiner Lippen.

Der Schlußpsalm

9 Ich will singen mit Erkenntnis, und all mein Saitenspiel ist zur Ehre Gottes, und die Saiten meiner Harfe sind entsprechend seiner heiligen Ordnung, und die Flöte meiner Lippen will ich erheben nach der Richtschnur seines Rechts.

10 Wenn Tag und Nacht kommen, will ich eingehen in den Bund Gottes, und wenn Abend und Morgen gehen, will ich seine Gesetze aussprechen. Solange sie sind, will ich errichten

11 meine Grenze, damit ich nicht zurückkehre (d.h. abfalle), und seinem Urteil will ich Recht verschaffen entsprechend meiner Verkehrtheit, und meine Freveltaten sind vor meinen Augen wie ein eingegrabenes Gesetz. Und zu Gott will ich sprechen: Meine Gerechtigkeit,

12 und zum Höchsten: Gründer meines Gutes, Quelle der Erkenntnis und Ort der Heiligkeit, Höhe der Herrlichkeit und Macht von allem zur ewigen Herrlichkeit. Ich will erwählen, was

13 er mich gelehrt hat, und Gefallen haben, wie er mich richtet. Bevor ich meine Hände oder Füße ausstrecke, will ich seinen Namen preisen; wenn ich ausgehe und eingehe,

14 mich setze oder aufstehe, und wenn ich auf meinem Lager liege, will ich ihm zujauchzen. Ich will ihn preisen mit der Hebe dessen, was von meinen Lippen kommt, in der Reihe der Männer.

15 Und bevor ich meine Hand erhebe, um mich zu sättigen von den herrlichen Erträgen des Erdkreises, zu Beginn von Furcht und Schrecken und am Ort der Not und Öde

16 will ich ihn preisen, weil er überaus wunderbar handelt, und über seine Macht will ich nachsinnen und auf seine Gnadentaten will ich mich stützen den ganzen Tag. Denn ich weiß, daß in seiner Hand das Gericht

17 über alle Lebewesen ist und Wahrheit alle seine Taten sind. Und wenn Bedrängnis sich auftut, will ich ihn rühmen, und über seine Rettung will ich ebenso jubeln. Einem Menschen will ich nicht zurückzahlen

18 die böse Tat, mit Gutem will ich den Mann verfolgen. Denn bei Gott ist das Gericht über alle Lebewesen, und er vergilt dem Menschen seine Tat. Ich will nicht eifern mit Geist

19 des Frevels, und nach Besitz der Gewalt begehrt meine Seele nicht, und Streit mit den Männern der Grube will ich nicht aufnehmen bis zum Tag der Rache. Und meinen Zorn will ich nicht

20 abwenden von den Männern des Frevels, und ich will nicht zufrieden sein, bis er Gericht festgesetzt hat. Nicht will ich Zorn bewahren gegenüber denen, die von der Sünde umkehren, aber ich will mich nicht erbarmen

21 über alle, die vom Weg abweichen. Nicht will ich trösten die Zerschlagenen, bis ihr Wandel vollkommen ist, und Belial will ich nicht in meinem Herzen bewahren, und nicht werde aus meinem Mund

22 Torheit gehört, und Trug der Sünde und Täuschungen und Lügen sollen auf meinen Lippen nicht gefunden werden. Aber heilige Frucht sei auf meiner Zunge, und Abscheuliches

23 soll darauf nicht gefunden werden. Mit Lobliedern will ich meinen Mund öffnen, und die Gerechtigkeitstaten Gottes soll meine Zunge ständig erzählen und den Abfall der Menschen bis zum Ende

24 ihrer Sünde. Nichtiges will ich tilgen von meinen Lippen, Unreinheiten und hinterlistige Kämpfe von der Erkenntnis meines Herzens. Im Rat der Einsicht will ich Erkenntnis verkündigen (ursprünglich: verbergen),

25 und mit Klugheit der Erkenntnis will ich sie bewahren, [ein] fester Bereich, um Treue zu bewahren und starkes Recht zur Gerechtigkeit Gottes. [Ich will zut]eilen

26 das Gebot nach der Richtschnur der Zeiten [...], Gerechtigkeit, gütige Liebe gegenüber den Demütigen und starke Hände gegenüber den Furchtsam[en, um zu lehren]

1 die Strauchelnden im Geist Erkenntnis und zu unterweisen die Murrenden in Lehre, (in) Demut zu antworten gegenüber den Hochmütigen und in zerbrochenem Geist den Männern

2 der Bedrückung, die mit dem Finger zeigen, die Sünde reden und Besitz erwerben. Aber was mich betrifft, so ist bei Gott mein Rechttun und in seiner Hand mein vollkommener Wandel zusammen mit der Geradheit meines Herzens.

3 Und durch seine Gerechtigkeitstaten tilgt er meine Sünden. Denn aus der Quelle seiner Erkenntnis hat er ein Licht für mich eröffnet, und auf seine Wunder hat mein Auge geblickt, und das Licht meines Herzens (ist gerichtet) auf das Geheimnis

4 des Seins und ewigen Werdens. Stütze meiner Rechten, auf starkem Fels ist der Weg meiner Schritte, vor nichts wird er wanken. Denn die Wahrheit Gottes, sie ist

5 der Fels meiner Schritte, und seine Macht ist die Stütze meiner Rechten, und aus der Quelle seiner Gerechtigkeit kommt mein Recht. Ein Licht ist in meinem Herzen aus seinen wunderbaren Geheimnissen. Auf das, was ewig ist,

6 hat mein Auge geblickt, (auf) Rettendes, das verborgen ist vor den Menschen, Erkenntnis und kluge Weisheit, (verborgen) vor den Menschenkindern: Quelle der Gerechtigkeit und Born

7 der Kraft zusammen mit dem Brunnen der Herrlichkeit, (verborgen) vor der Versammlung des Fleisches. Denen, die Gott erwählt hat, hat er sie zum ewigen Besitz gegeben, und er hat ihnen Anteil gegeben am Los

8 der Heiligen, und mit den Söhnen des Himmels hat er ihre Gemeinschaft vereint zum Rat der Gemeinde und die Gemeinschaft des heiligen Gebäudes zu einer ewigen Pflanzung für alle

9 Zeit, die kommen wird. Aber ich, (ich gehöre) zur frevlerischen Menschheit, zur Gemeinschaft des sündigen Fleisches. Meine Übertretungen, meine Vergehen, meine Sünden zusammen mit der Verkehrtheit meines Herzens

10 (lassen mich angehören) der Gemeinschaft des Gewürms und derer, die in Finsternis wandeln. Denn (k)ein Mensch bestimmt seinen Weg, und der Mensch lenkt nicht seinen Schritt. Denn Gott kommt das Recht zu, und aus seiner Hand ist

11 der vollkommene Wandel, und durch sein Wissen ist das Sein von allem, und alles, was sein wird, hat er durch sein Planen festgesetzt, und ohne ihn geschieht es nicht. Aber ich, wenn

12 ich wanke, so sind die Gnadenerweise Gottes meine Hilfe für immer. Und wenn ich strauchle durch die Sünde des Fleisches, so ist mein Recht durch die Gerechtigkeit Gottes, die für immer besteht.

13 Und wenn er meine Not eröffnet, dann rettet er meine Seele aus dem Verderben, und er lenkt meinen Schritt auf den Weg. In seinem Erbarmen hat er mich nahegebracht, und durch seine Gnadentaten bringt er

14 mein Recht. Durch die Gerechtigkeit seiner Wahrheit hat er mich gerichtet, und durch die Fülle seiner Güte sühnt er alle meine Sünden, und durch seine Gerechtigkeit hat er mich gereinigt von der Unreinheit

15 des Menschen und der Sünde der Menschenkinder, um Gott für seine Gerechtigkeit zu preisen und den Höchsten für seine Herrlichkeit. Gepriesen seist du, mein Gott, der du zur Erkenntnis öffnest

16 das Herz deines Knechtes. Lenke durch Gerechtigkeit alle seine Taten, und richte den Sohn deiner Wahrheit (oder: deiner Magd?) auf, wie du Wohlgefallen hast an den Erwählten der Menschen, sie hinzustellen

17 vor dir für immer. Denn ohne dich wird kein Wandel vollkommen, und ohne deinen Willen geschieht nichts. Du hast gelehrt

18 alle Erkenntnis, und alles, was ist, geschieht durch deinen Willen. Und es ist keiner außer dir, um auf deinen Rat zu antworten und zu unterweisen

19 in all deinem heiligen Planen, und um zu blicken in die Tiefe deiner Geheimnisse und zu verstehen all deine Wunder zusammen mit der Kraft

20 deiner Macht. Und wer kann deine Herrlichkeit erfassen? Und was ist auch das Menschenkind unter deinen wunderbaren Werken,

21 und der von der Frau Geborene, wie kann er vor dir bestehen? Und er ist (doch) aus Staub geknetet, und Fraß der Würmer sein Aufenthaltsort. Und er ist (doch) abgekniffener

22 Lehm, und nach dem Staub ist sein Begehr (d.h. Geschick, Ziel). Was kann der Lehm antworten und das mit der Hand Gebildete, und wie deinen Rat verstehen?

Spanish Translation

Regla de la Comunidad

Columna I

Introducción

1 Para […]*šym*, por su vida, [libro de la Reg]la de la Comunidad: para buscar

2 a Dios con [todo el corazón y con toda el alma;] para hacer lo bueno y lo recto en su presencia, como

3 ordenó por mano de Moisés y por mano de todos sus siervos los Profetas; para amar todo

4 lo que él escoge y odiar todo lo que él rechaza; para mantenerse alejados de todo mal,

5 y apegarse a todas las obras buenas; para obrar la verdad, la justicia y el derecho

6 en la tierra, y no caminar más en la obstinación de un corazón culpable y de ojos lujuriosos

7 haciendo todo mal; para admitir a todos los que se ofrecen voluntarios a practicar los preceptos de Dios

8 en la alianza de la gracia, a fin de que se unan en el consejo de Dios y marchen perfectamente en su presencia (de acuerdo con) todas

9 las cosas reveladas sobre los tiempos fijados de sus testimonios; para amar a todos los hijos de la luz, cada uno

10 según su lote en el plan de Dios, y odiar a todos los hijos de tinieblas, cada uno según su culpa

11 en la venganza de Dios. Todos los que se ofrecen voluntarios a su verdad traerán todo su conocimiento, su fuerza

12 y su riqueza a la Comunidad de Dios para purificar su conocimiento en la verdad de los preceptos de Dios y ordenar su fuerza

13 según sus caminos perfectos y toda su riqueza según su consejo justo, y para no apartarse de ninguno

14 de todos los mandatos de Dios sobre sus períodos: y para no adelantar sus tiempos, ni retrasar

15 ninguna de sus fiestas; y para no desviarse de sus preceptos verdaderos yendo a la derecha o a la izquierda.

Ceremonia de ingreso en la comunidad

16 Y todos los que entren en la regla de la comunidad establecerán una alianza ante Dios para cumplir

17 todo lo que ordena y para no apartarse de su seguimiento por ningún miedo, terror o aflicción,

18 las pruebas durante el dominio de Belial. Cuando entren en la alianza, los sacerdotes

19 y los levitas bendecirán al Dios de salvación y a todas las obras de su fidelidad, y todos

20 los que entren en la alianza dirán después de ellos: "Amén, Amén".

21 Los sacerdotes contarán los actos justos de Dios en sus obras poderosas,

22 y proclamarán todas sus gracias misericordiosas con Israel. Y los levitas contarán

23 las iniquidades de los hijos de Israel, todas sus transgresiones culpables, y sus pecados durante el dominio de

24 Belial. [Y tod]os los que entran en la alianza confesarán después de ellos diciendo: "Hemos obrado inicuamente,

25 hemos [tra]nsgredido, hemos [peca]do, hemos actuado impíamente, nosotros [y] nuestros [pa]dres antes que nosotros, en cuanto que marchamos

26 [… .]Verdadero y just[o es el Dios de Israel y] su [ju]icio contra nosotros y contra [nuestros] padres,

Columna II

1 pero él ha derramado sobre nosotros su gracia misericordiosa por siempre jamás". Y los sacerdotes bendecirán a todos

2 los hombres del lote de Dios que marchan perfectos en todos sus caminos y dirán: "Que os bendiga con todo

3 bien y que os guarde de todo mal. Que ilumine vuestro corazón con la inteligencia de vida y os agracie con conocimiento eterno.

4 Que eleve sobre vosotros el rostro de su gracia para paz eterna". Y los levitas maldecirán a todos los hombres

5 del lote de Belial. Tomarán la palabra y dirán: "Maldito seas por todas tus impías obras culpables. Que te entregue (Dios)

6 al terror, a manos de los vengadores de venganzas. Que haga caer sobre ti la destrucción por mano de todos los ejecutores de

7 recompensas. Maldito seas, sin misericordia, según las tinieblas de tus obras, y seas condenado

8 en la obscuridad del fuego eterno. Que Dios no tenga misericordia cuando lo invoques, ni te perdone expiando tus culpas.

9 Que él alce el rostro de su ira para vengarse de ti, y no haya paz para ti en la boca de los que se aferran a los padres".

10 Y todos los que entran en la alianza dirán después de los que bendicen y de los que maldicen: "Amén, Amén".

11 Y los sacerdotes y los levitas continuarán diciendo: "Maldito por los ídolos que su corazón venera

12 quien entra en esta alianza y se pone ante sí su tropiezo culpable para caer en él.

13 Cuando escucha las palabras de esta alianza, se felicita en su corazón diciendo: 'Tendré paz,

14 aunque camino en la obstinación de mi corazón'. Pero su espíritu será destruido, lo seco con lo inundado, sin

15 perdón. Que la ira de Dios y la cólera de sus juicios le consuman para destrucción eterna. Que se le peguen todas

16 las maldiciones de esta alianza. Que Dios le separe para el mal, y que sea cortado de en medio de todos los hijos de la luz por su apartarse

17 del seguimiento de Dios a causa de sus ídolos y del tropiezo de su iniquidad. Que ponga su lote entre los malditos por siempre".

18 Y todos los que entran en la alianza tomarán la palabra y dirán después de ellos: "Amén, Amén".

Renovación de la alianza

19 Así harán, año tras año, todos los días del dominio de Belial. Los sacerdotes entrarán

20 en la regla los primeros, según sus espíritus, uno detrás de otro. Y los levitas entrarán detrás de ellos.

21 En tercer lugar entrará todo el pueblo en la regla, uno detrás de otro, por millares, centenas,

22 cincuentenas y decenas, para que cada hombre de Israel conozca su propia posición en la comunidad de Dios

23 según el plan eterno. Y nadie descenderá de su posición ni subirá del puesto de su lote.

24 Pues todos estarán en una comunidad de verdad, de humildad buena, de amor misericordioso y pensamiento justo,

25 unos para con otros en el consejo santo, miembros de una sociedad eterna. Y todo el que rehúse entrar

26 [en la alianza de Dios] para marchar en la obstinación de su corazón, n[o entrará en la comuni]dad de su verdad, pues

COLUMNA III

1 su alma aborrece las disciplinas del conocimiento del juicio justo. No se ha mantenido firme en la conversión de su vida, y no será contado con los rectos.

2 Su conocimiento, su fuerza y su riqueza no entrarán al consejo de la comunidad, porque labra en el cieno de la impiedad y hay manchas

3 en su conversión. No será justificado mientras siga la obstinación de su corazón, pues mira las tinieblas como los caminos de la luz. En la fuente de los perfectos,

4 él no será contado. No quedará limpio por las expiaciones, ni será purificado por las aguas lustrales, ni será santificado por los mares

5 o ríos, ni será purificado por toda el agua de las abluciones. Impuro, impuro será todos los días que rechace los preceptos

6 de Dios, sin dejarse instruir por la comunidad de su consejo. Porque por el espíritu del consejo verdadero sobre los caminos del hombre son expiadas todas

7 sus iniquidades para que pueda contemplar la luz de la vida. Y por el espíritu de santidad que le une a su verdad es purificado de todas

8 sus iniquidades. Y por el espíritu de rectitud y de humildad su pecado es expiado. Y por la sumisión de su alma a todas las leyes de Dios es purificada

9 su carne al ser rociada con aguas lustrales y ser santificada con las aguas de contrición. Que afirme pues sus pasos para caminar perfectamente

10 por todos los caminos de Dios, de acuerdo con lo que ordenó sobre los tiempos fijados de sus decretos, y no se aparte a derecha ni a izquierda, ni

11 quebrante una sola de todas sus palabras. Así será aceptado mediante expiaciones agradables ante Dios, y habrá para él la alianza

12 de una comunidad eterna.

Tratado de los dos espíritus

13 Para el sabio, para que instruya y enseñe a todos los hijos de la luz sobre la historia de todos los hijos de hombre,

14 acerca de todas las clases de sus espíritus, según sus signos, acerca de sus obras en sus generaciones, y acerca de la visita de su castigo y

15 del tiempo de su recompensa. Del Dios de conocimiento proviene todo lo que es y lo que será. Antes que existieran fijó todos sus planes,

16 y cuando existen completan sus obras de acuerdo con sus instrucciones, según su plan glorioso y sin cambiar nada. En su mano están

17 las leyes de todas las cosas, y él las sostiene en todas sus necesidades. El creó al hombre para dominar

18 al mundo, y puso en él dos espíritus, para que marche por ellos hasta el tiempo de su visita: son los espíritus

19 de la verdad y de la falsedad. Del manantial de la luz provienen las generaciones de la verdad, y de la fuente de tinieblas las generaciones de la falsedad.

20 En mano del Príncipe de las luces está el dominio sobre todos los hijos de la justicia; ellos marchan por caminos de luz. Y en mano del ángel

21 de las tinieblas está todo el dominio sobre los hijos de la falsedad; ellos marchan por caminos de tinieblas. A causa del ángel de las tinieblas se extravían

22 todos los hijos de la justicia, y todos sus pecados, sus iniquidades, sus faltas y sus obras rebeldes, están bajo su dominio

23 de acuerdo con los misterios de Dios, hasta su tiempo; y todos sus castigos y sus momentos de aflicción son a causa del dominio de su hostilidad;

24 y todos los espíritus de su lote hacen caer a los hijos de la luz. Pero el Dios de Israel y el ángel de su verdad ayudan a todos

25 los hijos de la luz. El creó a los espíritus de la luz y de las tinieblas, y sobre ellos fundó cada obra,

26 l[…]hn todo trabajo, y sobre sus caminos [todo…]wdh. Dios ama a uno por todos

Columna IV

1 [los tie]mpos eternos, y en todas sus acciones se deleita por siempre; del otro, él abomina su consejo y odia todos sus caminos por siempre.

2 Estos son sus caminos en el mundo: iluminar el corazón del hombre, enderezar ante él todos los caminos de justicia y de verdad, instalar en su corazón el temor de los preceptos

3 de Dios; es un espíritu de humildad, de paciencia, abundante misericordia, bondad eterna, inteligencia, comprensión, sabiduría poderosa que confía en todas

4 la obras de Dios y se apoya en la abundancia de su gracia; un espíritu de conocimiento en todos los planes de acción, de celo por los preceptos de justicia, de planes

5 santos con inclinación firme, de abundante misericordia con todos los hijos de la verdad, de pureza gloriosa que odia todos los ídolos impuros, de conducta modesta

6 con prudencia en todo, de discreción acerca de la verdad de los misterios del conocimiento. Estos son los consejos del espíritu a los hijos de la verdad (en) el mundo. Y la visita de todos los que en él marchan será para curación,

7 paz abundante en una larga vida, fructuosa descendencia con todas las bendiciones perpetuas, gozo eterno con vida sin fin, y una corona de gloria

8 con un vestido de majestad en la luz eterna.

9 Pero al espíritu de falsedad (le corresponde) la avaricia, la debilidad de manos en el servicio de la justicia, la impiedad, la mentira, el orgullo y la altanería de corazón, la falsedad, el engaño, la crueldad,

10 mucha hipocresía, la impaciencia, mucha locura, celo insolente, obras abominables con espíritu de lujuria, caminos inmundos al servicio de la impureza,

11 lengua blasfemadora, ceguera de ojos, dureza de oídos, rigidez de nuca, dureza de corazón para marchar por todos los caminos de tinieblas, y la astucia maligna. Y la visita

12 de todos los que marchan en él será para abundancia de castigos a manos de todos los ángeles de destrucción, para condenación eterna por la ira abrasadora del Dios de la venganza, para error perpetuo y vergüenza

13 sin fin con la ignominia de la destrucción por el fuego de las regiones tenebrosas. Y todos los tiempos de sus generaciones se pasarán en llanto acerbo y amargos males en los abismos de tinieblas hasta

14 su destrucción, sin que haya un resto o un sobreviviente entre ellos.

15 En ellos está la historia de todos los hombres; en sus (dos) divisiones tienen su heredad todos sus ejércitos, por sus generaciones; en sus caminos marchan; toda obra

16 que hacen (cae) en sus divisiones según sea la herencia del hombre, grande o pequeña, por todos los tiempos eternos. Pues Dios los ha dispuesto por partes iguales hasta el tiempo

17 final, y ha puesto un odio eterno entre sus divisiones. Los actos de falsedad son abominación para la verdad, y todos los caminos de verdad son abominación para la falsedad. Hay una feroz

18 disputa sobre todos sus preceptos, pues no caminan juntos. Dios, en los misterios de su conocimiento y en la sabiduría de su gloria, ha fijado un fin a la existencia de la falsedad, y al tiempo

19 de su visita la destruirá por siempre. Entonces la verdad se alzará por siempre (en) el mundo que se ha contaminado en caminos de maldad durante el dominio de la falsedad hasta

20 el momento decretado para el juicio. Entonces purificará Dios con su verdad toda las obras del hombre, y refinará para sí la estructura del hombre arrancando todo espíritu de falsedad de las entrañas

21 de su carne, y purificandolo con el espíritu de santidad de toda acción impía. Rociará sobre él el espíritu de verdad como aguas lustrales (para purificarlo) de todas las abominaciones de falsedad y de la contaminación

22 del espíritu impuro, para que los rectos entiendan el conocimiento del Altísimo, y los perfectos del camino comprendan la sabiduría de los hijos del cielo. Pues a ellos los ha escogido Dios para una alianza eterna,

23 y a ellos pertenecerá toda la gloria de Adán. Y no habrá iniquidad, y todas las obras de engaño serán una vergüenza. Hasta ahora los espíritus de verdad y de falsedad se disputan en el corazón del hombre

24 y ellos marchan en sabiduría o en necedad. De acuerdo con la heredad del hombre en la verdad será él justo, y así odiará él la injusticia; y según su parte en el lote de injusticia obrará impíamente en ella, y así

25 abominará la verdad. Pues Dios los ha dispuesto en partes iguales hasta el final fijado y la renovación. El conoce el resultado de sus obras por todos los tiempos

26 [...]n, y los ha dado en heredad a los hijos de los hombres para que conozcan el bien [..., y para que de]terminen el lote de todo viviente de acuerdo con el espíritu que hay en[... la] visita.

Columna V

Regla de la comunidad

1 Esta es la regla para los hombres de la comunidad que se ofrecen voluntarios para convertirse de todo mal y para mantenerse firmes en todo lo que ordena según su voluntad. Que se separen de la congregación de

2 los hombres de iniquidad para formar una comunidad en la ley y en los bienes, y sometiéndose a la autoridad de los hijos de Zadok, los sacerdotes que guardan la alianza, y a la autoridad de la muchedumbre de los hombres

3 de la comunidad, los que se mantienen firmes en la alianza. Por su autoridad será tomada la decisión del lote en todo asunto que concierne a la ley, a los bienes y al juicio, para obrar juntos la verdad y la humildad,

4 la justicia y el derecho, el amor misericordioso y la conducta modesta en todos sus caminos. Que nadie marche en la obstinación de su corazón para extraviarse tras su corazón

5 y sus ojos y los pensamientos de su inclinación. Sino que circuncide en la comunidad el prepucio de su inclinación y de su dura cerviz, para establecer un fundamento de verdad para Israel, para la comunidad de la alianza

6 eterna. Que expíen por todos los que se ofrecen voluntarios para la santidad en Aarón y para la casa de la verdad en Israel, y por los que se les unen para la comunidad. Que en el proceso y en el juicio

7 declaren culpables a todos los que quebrantan el precepto. Estas son sus normas de conducta según todos estos preceptos cuando son admitidos a la comunidad. Todo el que entra en el consejo de la comunidad

8 entrará en la alianza de Dios en presencia de todos los que se ofrecen voluntarios. Se comprometerá por juramento, bajo pena de muerte, a retornar a la ley de Moisés, con todo lo que prescribe, con todo

9 el corazón y con toda el alma, según todo lo que ha sido revelado de ella a los hijos de Zadok, los sacerdotes que observan la alianza e interpretan su voluntad, y a la muchedumbre de los hombres de su alianza

10 que juntos se ofrecen voluntarios para su verdad y para marchar según su voluntad. Que por la alianza se comprometa por su vida a separarse de todos los hombres de iniquidad que marchan

11 en la senda de la impiedad. Pues ellos no son contados en su alianza, ya que no han buscado ni han investigado sus preceptos para conocer las cosas ocultas en las que erraron

12 por su culpa, e hicieron con insolencia las cosas reveladas, levantando la cólera para el juicio y para infligir venganzas por las maldiciones de la alianza, para ejecutar con ellos juicios

13 grandes de destrucción eterna sin que haya un resto. Que no entre en las aguas para participar en el alimento puro de los hombres de santidad; pues no se han purificado

14 a no ser que se conviertan de su maldad; pues es impuro entre todos los transgresores de su palabra. Y que nadie se junte con él en su trabajo o en sus bienes para que no le cargue

15 de pecado culpable; sino que se mantenga alejado de él en todo asunto, pues así está escrito: "Te mantendrás alejado de toda mentira". Y que ninguno de los hombres

16 de la comunidad se someta a su autoridad en ninguna ley o norma. Que nadie coma de ninguno de sus bienes, ni beba, ni tome nada de sus manos,

17 si no es por su precio, pues está escrito: "Absteneos del hombre, cuyo hálito está en su nariz, pues ¿en cuánto puede ser estimado?" Pues

18 todos aquellos que no son contados en su alianza serán separados, ellos y todo lo que les pertenece. Que ningún hombre santo se apoye en ninguna obra de

19 vanidad, pues son vanidad todos aquellos que no conocen su alianza. Y a todos los que desprecian su palabra los hará desaparecer del orbe; todas sus obras son impureza

20 ante él, y hay impureza en todos sus bienes. Y cuando uno entra en la alianza para obrar de acuerdo con todos estos preceptos uniéndose a la congregación de santidad, examinarán

21 sus espíritus en la comunidad, (distinguiendo) entre uno y su prójimo, según su discernimiento y sus obras en la ley, bajo la autoridad de los hijos de Aarón, los que se ofrecen voluntarios en la comunidad para establecer

22 su alianza y para observar todos los preceptos que ordenó cumplir, y bajo la autoridad de la muchedumbre de Israel, los que se ofrecen voluntarios para retornar en la comunidad a su alianza.

23 Y los inscribirán en la regla, uno delante de su prójimo, según su discernimiento y sus obras, de manera que cada uno obedezca a su prójimo, el pequeño al grande.

24 Y su espíritu y sus obras deberán ser examinados año tras año a fin de promover a cada uno de acuerdo con su discernimiento y la perfección de su camino, o de degradarlo según sus faltas. Que uno reprenda

25 a su prójimo en la ve[rd]ad, en la humildad, y en el amor misericordioso para con el hombre. Que nadie hable a su prójimo (4QS^d; MS: a su hermano ?) con ira o murmurando,

26 o con [dura] cerviz, [o con celoso] espíritu maligno, y que no le odie [en la obstinación] de su corazón, sino que le reprenda en el día para no

Columna VI

1 incurrir en pecado por su culpa. Y además que nadie lleve un asunto contra su prójimo delante de los Numerosos si no es con represión ante testigos. Así

2 se conducirán en todos sus lugares de residencia. Siempre que se encuentre uno con su prójimo, el pequeño obedecerá al grande en el trabajo y en el dinero. Comerán juntos,

3 juntos bendecirán, y juntos tomarán consejo. En todo lugar en el que hay diez hombres del consejo de la comunidad, que no falte entre ellos un

4 sacerdote; cada uno, según su rango, se sentará ante él, y así se les pedirá su consejo en todo asunto. Y cuando preparen la mesa para comer, o el mosto

5 para beber, el sacerdote extenderá su mano el primero para bendecir las primicias del pan

6 y del mosto. Y que no falte en el lugar en el que se encuentran los diez un hombre que interprete la ley día y noche,

7 siempre, substituyendo uno a su prójimo (MS: sobre las obligaciones [?] de uno para con su prójimo). Y los Numerosos velarán juntos un tercio de cada noche del año para leer el libro, interpretar la norma,

8 y bendecir juntos. Esta es la regla para la reunión de los Numerosos. Cada uno según su rango: los sacerdotes se sentarán los primeros, los ancianos los segundos, y el resto de

9 todo el pueblo se sentará cada uno según su rango. Y de igual manera serán interrogados con relación al juicio, y a todo consejo y asunto que se refiere a los Numerosos, para que cada uno aporte su saber

10 al consejo de la comunidad. Que nadie hable en medio del discurso de su prójimo, antes de que su hermano haya terminado de hablar. Y que tampoco hable antes que uno cuyo rango está inscrito

11 antes que el suyo. Aquel que es interrogado, hablará a su turno. Y en la reunión de los numerosos que nadie diga nada sin la aprobación de los Numerosos. Y si aquel

12 que inspecciona a los Numerosos retiene a quien tiene algo que decir a los Numerosos pero no está en posición del que interroga al consejo

13 de la comunidad, que se ponga este hombre de pie y diga: "Yo tengo algo que decir a los Numerosos". Si se lo dicen, que hable. Y a todo el que se ofrece voluntario de Israel

14 para unirse al consejo de la comunidad lo examinará el Instructor que está al frente de los Numerosos en cuanto a su discernimiento y a sus obras. Si es apto para la disciplina, lo introducirá

15 en la alianza para que se vuelva a la verdad y se aparte de toda iniquidad, y lo instruirá en todos los preceptos de la comunidad. Y después, cuando entre para estar ante los Numerosos, serán interrogados

16 todos sobre sus asuntos. Y según resulte el lote en el consejo de los Numerosos será incorporado o alejado. Si es incorporado al consejo de la comunidad, que no toque el alimento puro de

17 los Numerosos mientras lo examinan sobre su espíritu y sobre sus obras hasta que complete un año entero; y que tampoco participe en los bienes de los Numerosos.

18 Cuando haya completado un año al interior de la comunidad, serán interrogados los Numerosos sobre sus asuntos, acerca de su discernimiento y de sus obras con respecto a la ley. Y si le sale el lote

19 de incorporarse a los fundamentos de la comunidad según los sacerdotes y la mayoría de los hombres de la alianza, también sus bienes y sus posesiones serán incorporados en manos del

20 Inspector sobre las posesiones de los Numerosos. Y las inscribirán de su mano en el registro, pero no las emplearán para los Numerosos. Que no toque la bebida de los Numerosos hasta que

21 complete un segundo año en medio de los hombres de la comunidad. Y cuando se complete este segundo año será inspeccionado por autoridad de los Numerosos. Y si le sale

22 el lote de incorporarse a la comunidad, lo inscribirán en la regla de su rango en medio de sus hermanos para la ley, para el juicio, para la pureza y para la puesta en común de sus bienes. Y su consejo será

23 para la comunidad, lo mismo que su juicio.

Código penal

24 Y estas son las normas con las que se juzgará en la investigación de la comunidad según los casos. Si se encuentra entre ellos alguien que ha mentido

25 acerca de los bienes a sabiendas, lo separarán de la comida pura de los Numerosos un año y será castigado a un cuarto de su pan. Y quien replica a

26 su prójimo con obstinación o le habla con impaciencia removiendo el fundamento de su compañero, rebelándose contra la autoridad de su prójimo que está inscrito antes que él,

27 [o se hace jus]ticia con su mano, será castigado u[n] año [... .] Quien pronuncia el nombre venerable por encima de todo *h*[...]

COLUMNA VII

1 bien sea blasfemando, o abrumado por la desgracia, o por cualquier otro asunto, o cuando lee el libro, o bendiciendo, será separado

2 y no volverá de nuevo al consejo de la comunidad. Y si ha hablado con ira contra uno de los sacerdotes inscritos en el libro, será castigado

3 un año y será separado, bajo pena de muerte, del alimento puro de los Numerosos. Pero si habló por inadvertencia, será castigado seis meses. Y quien miente a sabiendas

4 será castigado seis meses. Quien a sabiendas y sin razón insulta a su prójimo, será castigado un año

5 y será separado. Y quien habla a su prójimo con engaño, o a sabiendas lo engaña, será castigado seis meses. Y si

6 es negligente con su prójimo, será castigado tres meses. Pero si es negligente con los bienes de la comunidad causando su pérdida, los completará

7 totalmente.

8 Y si no consigue completarlos, será castigado sesenta días. Y quien guarda rencor a su prójimo sin razón será castigado un año.

9 Y lo mismo, a quien se venga en cualquier asunto. Quien pronuncia con su boca palabras vanas, tres meses; y por hablar en medio de las palabras de su prójimo,

10 diez días. Y quien se acuesta y duerme en la reunión de los Numerosos, treinta días. Y así con quien abandona la reunión de los Numerosos,

11 sin razón, o se duerme hasta tres veces en una reunión, será castigado diez días; pero si está en pie

12 y se aleja, será castigado treinta días. Y quien marcha ante su prójimo desnudo, sin estar obligado, será castigado seis meses.

13 Y aquel que escupe en medio de una reunión de los Numerosos, será castigado treinta días. Y quien saca su 'mano' de debajo de su vestido, o si éste es

14 un andrajo que deja ver su desnudez, será castigado treinta días. Y quien ríe estúpidamente haciendo oír su voz, será castigado treinta

15 días. Y el que saca su mano izquierda para gesticular con ella será castigado diez días. Y quien va difamando a su prójimo,

16 será separado un año de la comida pura de los Numerosos y será castigado; pero aquel que va difamando a los Numerosos, será expulsado de entre ellos

17 y no volverá más. Y a aquel que murmura contra el fundamento de la comunidad lo expulsarán y no volverá; pero si murmura contra su prójimo

18 sin razón, será castigado seis meses. Aquel cuyo espíritu se aparta del fundamento de la comunidad para traicionar a verdad

19 y marchar en la obstinación de su corazón, si vuelve, será castigado dos años; durante el primer año no se acercará al alimento puro de los Numerosos.

20 Y durante el segundo no se acercará a la bebida de los Numerosos, y se sentará detrás de todos hombres de la comunidad. Y cuando se hayan cumplido

21 los días de dos años se interrogará a los Numerosos sobre su asunto; si lo incorporan, que sea inscrito según su rango; y después será interrogado con relación al juicio.

22 Pero todo aquel que ha estado en el consejo de la comunidad durante diez años completos,

23 y cuyo espíritu se vuelve para traicionar a la comunidad y sale de la presencia

24 de los Numerosos para marchar en la obstinación de su corazón, que no vuelva más al consejo de la comunidad. Y aquel de entre los hombres de la comunid[ad que se as]ocia

25 con él en materia de pureza o de bienes, qu[e…]los Numerosos, y su juicio será como el suyo, que sea e[xpulsado… .]

Columna VIII

Proyecto de fundación de la comunidad

1 En el consejo de la comunidad (habrá) doce hombres y tres sacerdotes, perfectos en todo lo que ha sido revelado de toda

2 la ley, para practicar la verdad, la justicia, el juicio, el amor misericordioso y la conducta humilde de uno con su prójimo,

3 para preservar la fidelidad en la tierra con una inclinación firme y con espíritu contrito, para expiar por el pecado practicando el derecho

4 y sufriendo las pruebas, para marchar con todos en la medida de la verdad y en la norma del tiempo. Cuando estas cosas existan en Israel,

5 el consejo de la comunidad será establecido en verdad como una plantación eterna, una casa santa para Israel y un fundamento

6 santísimo para Aarón, testigos verdaderos para el juicio y escogidos de la voluntad (de Dios) para expiar por la tierra y para devolver

7 a los impíos su retribución. Ella será la muralla probada, la piedra de ángulo preciosa

8 cuyos fundamentos no vacilarán y no temblarán en su lugar. Será residencia santísima

9 para Aarón con conocimiento total de la alianza de justicia, y para ofrecer un olor agradable; y será una casa de perfección y verdad en Israel

10 para establecer una alianza según los preceptos eternos. Y ellos serán aceptados para expiar por la tierra y para determinar el juicio de los impíos y no habrá iniquidad. Cuando éstos haya sido establecidos en el fundamento de la comunidad dos años cumplidos entre los de conducta perfecta

11 serán separados (como) santos en medio del consejo de los hombres de la comunidad. Y todo asunto oculto a Israel, pero que ha sido hallado por

12 el Intérprete, que no se los oculte por miedo de un espíritu de apostasía. Y cuando éstos existan como comunidad en Israel

13 según estas disposiciones se separarán de en medio de la residencia de los hombres de iniquidad para marchar al desierto para abrir allí el camino de 'Aquél'.

14 Como está escrito: "En el desierto, preparad el camino de °°°°, enderezad en la estepa una calzada para nuestro Dios".

15 Este es el estudio de la ley, q[u]e ordenó por mano de Moisés, para obrar de acuerdo con todo lo revelado de edad en edad,

16 y según revelaron los profetas por su santo espíritu. Y todo aquel de los hombres de la comunidad, la alianza de

17 la comunidad, que se aparte de cualquier cosa ordenada presuntuosamente, que no se acerque al alimento puro de los hombres de santidad

18 y que no conozca nada de sus consejos, hasta que hayan sido purificadas sus obras de toda iniquidad, marchando con los de conducta perfecta. (Entonces) lo incorporarán

19 al consejo bajo la autoridad de los Numerosos, y después lo inscribirán según su rango. Y (obrarán) según este precepto con todo el que se une a la comunidad.

20 Estos son los preceptos en los que marcharán los hombres de santidad perfecta cada uno con su prójimo.

21 Todo el que entra en el consejo de santidad de quienes marchan en el camino perfecto como ha sido ordenado, cualquiera de ellos

22 que transgreda una palabra de la ley de Moisés presuntuosamente o por negligencia, será expulsado del consejo de la comunidad

23 y no retornará de nuevo; que ninguno de los hombres de santidad se mezcle a sus bienes o a su consejo en ningún

24 asunto. Pero si obró por inadvertencia, que sea separado del alimento puro y del consejo, y que le apliquen la norma:

25 "Que no juzgue a nadie y que no se le pida ningún consejo durante dos años completos". Si su camino es perfecto

26 en ellos, que vuelva (MS: en la reunión) a la interpretación y al consejo [según la autoridad de los] Numerosos, si no ha pecado de nuevo por inadvertencia hasta que se le cumplan los dos años

27 completos.

Columna IX

1 Pues por un pecado de inadvertencia será castigado dos años; pero quien obra presuntuosamente no volverá de nuevo. Solo el que peca por inadvertencia

2 será probado dos años completos en cuanto a la perfección de su conducta y de su consejo según la autoridad de los Numerosos, y después será inscrito según su rango en la comunidad de santidad.

3 Cuando éstos existan en Israel, de acuerdo con estas disposiciones, como fundamento del espíritu de santidad en la verdad

4 eterna, expiarán por la culpa de la transgresión y por la infidelidad del pecado, y por el beneplácito para la tierra sin la carne de los holocaustos y sin las grasas del sacrificio - la ofrenda de

5 los labios según el precepto será como el olor agradable de justicia, y la perfección de la conducta será como la ofrenda voluntaria aceptable - En ese tiempo se separarán los hombres de

6 la comunidad (como) casa santa para Aarón, para unirse al santo de los santos, y (como) una casa de la comunidad para Israel, los que marchan en la perfección.

7 Solo los hijos de Aarón tendrán autoridad en materia de juicio y de bienes, y su palabra determinará la suerte de toda disposición de los hombres de la comunidad

8 y de los bienes de los hombres de santidad que marchan en perfección. Que no se mezclen sus bienes con los bienes de los hombres de falsedad que

9 no han purificado su camino separándose de la iniquidad y marchando en camino perfecto. No se apartarán de ningún consejo de la ley para marchar

10 en toda obstinación de su corazón, sino que serán gobernados por las ordenanzas primeras en las que los hombres de la comunidad comenzaron a ser instruidos,

11 hasta que venga el profeta y los mesías de Aarón e Israel.

12 Estas son las normas para el Instructor, para que marche en ellas con todo viviente, de acuerdo con la disposición de cada tiempo y de acuerdo con el valor de cada hombre:

13 que haga la voluntad de Dios de acuerdo con todo lo revelado para cada tiempo; que aprenda toda la sabiduría que ha sido hallada según los tiempos, y la

14 norma del tiempo; que separe y pese a los hijos de justicia según sus espíritus; que refuerce a los elegidos del tiempo según

15 su voluntad, como ha ordenado; que haga el juicio de cada hombre de acuerdo con su espíritu; que incorpore a cada uno según la pureza de sus manos, y que según su inteligencia

16 lo haga avanzar. Y así será su amor, y así su odio. Que no reprenda ni se dispute con los hombres de la fosa,

17 sino que oculte el consejo de la ley en medio de los hombres de iniquidad. Que reprenda (con) conocimiento verdadero y (con) juicio justo a los que escogen

18 el camino, a cada uno según su espíritu, según la disposición del tiempo. Que les guíe con conocimiento y que así les instruya en los misterios de maravilla y de verdad en medio de

19 los hombres de la comunidad, para que marchen perfectamente, cada uno con su prójimo, en todo lo que les ha sido revelado. Este es el tiempo de preparar el camino

20 al desierto, y él les instruirá en todo lo que ha sido hallado para que lo hagan en este tiempo y para que se separen de todo aquel que no ha apartado su camino

21 de toda iniquidad. Y éstas son las disposiciones de conducta para el Instructor en estos tiempos, sobre su amor y su odio. Odio eterno

22 con los hombres de la fosa en espíritu de secreto. Que les deje los bienes y el producto de las manos como un siervo a su amo y como el oprimido ante

23 quien le domina. Que sea un hombre celoso del precepto y preparado (MS: de su tiempo) para el día de la venganza. Que haga la voluntad (de Dios) en todo lo que emprende su mano

24 y en todo lo que él domina, como él ordenó. Y todo lo que le sucede lo aceptará voluntariamente, y en nada se complacerá fuera de la voluntad de Dios.

25 Se deleitará [en toda]s las palabras de su boca, no deseará nada que él no haya orden[ado, y] vigilará siempre [el precep]to de Dios.

26 [...]*qh* bendecirá a su creador, y en todo lo que sucede con[tará...] de los labios le bendecirá

Columna X

1 durante los períodos que él decretó. Al comienzo del dominio de la luz, durante su circuito, y cuando se recoge en su morada prescrita. Al comienzo

2 de las vigilias de tinieblas, cuando abre su depósito y las extiende por arriba, y en su circuito, y cuando se recogen delante de la luz. Cuando brillan

3 las lumbreras del firmamento santo, cuando se recogen en la morada de gloria. En la entrada de las constelaciones en los días de la luna nueva junto con sus circuitos durante

4 sus posiciones, renovándose unas a otras. Es un gran día para el santo de los santos, y un signo para la abertura de sus gracias eternas, para los comienzos

5 de las constelaciones en cada época futura. Al comienzo de los meses en sus constelaciones, y de los días santos en su orden, como recuerdo en sus constelaciones.

6 (Con) la ofrenda de los labios te bendeciré, según la norma inscrita por siempre. Al comienzo de los años y en los circuitos de sus constelaciones, cuando se cumple la norma

7 de su orden, en el día prescrito, uno tras otro; la constelación de la cosecha hasta el verano, la constelación de la siembra hasta la constelación de la hierba, las constelaciones de los años hasta sus septenarios.

8 Al comienzo de los septenarios hasta el tiempo fijado para la liberación. Y en toda mi existencia estará el precepto grabado en mi lengua como un fruto de alabanza y la porción de mis labios.

Himno de alabanzo

9 Cantaré con conocimiento y para gloria de Dios será toda mi música, el sonido de mi arpa para su orden santo, y el silbo de mis labios lo acordaré a su medida justa.

10 Al llegar el día y la noche entraré en la alianza de Dios, y al salir la tarde y la mañana recitaré sus preceptos; y mientras ellos duren me los pondré

11 como frontera, sin retorno. Su juicio me reprende conforme a mis deslices; están ante mis ojos, como leyes grabadas, mis pecados. Pero a Dios le diré: "Mi justicia",

12 y al Altísimo: "Cimiento de mi bien", "manantial de saber", "fuente de santidad", "cima de gloria", "todo-poderoso de majestad eterna". Escogeré lo que

13 me enseña, me deleitaré en cómo me juzga. Cuando comience a extender mis manos y mis pies bendeciré su nombre; cuando comience a salir y a entrar,

14 a sentarme y a alzarme, y acostado en mi cama, le ensalzaré; le bendeciré con la ofrenda que sale de mis labios entre las filas de hombres,

15 y antes de extender mi mano para engrasarme con los frutos deliciosos de la tierra. Al comienzo del terror y el espanto, en el lugar de angustia y desolación,

16 le bendeciré por (sus) grandes prodigios y meditaré en su poder y me apoyaré en su misericordia todo el día. Reconozco que en su mano está el juicio

17 de todo viviente, y todas sus obras son verdad. Cuando se desate la angustia le alabaré, lo mismo que le cantaré por su salvación. No devolveré a nadie una mala recompensa;

18 con bien perseguiré al varón. Pues (toca) a Dios el juicio de todo ser viviente, y es él quien paga al hombre su soldada. No tendré celos del espíritu

19 impío, y mi alma no deseará bienes violentos. No tendré parte alguna en la disputa de los hombres de la fosa hasta el día de la venganza.

20 Pero no apartaré mi cólera de los hombres inicuos, ni estaré satisfecho, hasta que se cumpla el juicio. No guardaré rencor airado a quien se convierte de la transgresión; pero no tendré piedad

21 con todos los que se apartan del camino. No consolaré a los oprimidos hasta que su camino sea perfecto. No guardaré Belial en mi corazón. No se oirán en mi boca

22 obscenidades ni engaños inicuos; argucias y mentiras, no se hallarán en mis labios. El fruto de santidad estará en mi lengua, pero abominaciones

23 no se hallarán en ella. Con himnos abriré mi boca, y mi lengua contará siempre las justicias de Dios y la infidelidad de los hombres hasta que su transgresión sea completa.

24 Alejaré de mis labios las palabras inútiles, impurezas y maquinaciones del conocimiento de mi corazón. Con consejo sabio contaré el conocimiento,

25 y con prudencia de conocimiento lo cercaré [con una] valla sólida para guardar la fidelidad y el juicio firme con la justicia de Dios. [Distri]buiré

26 el precepto con la cuerda de los tiempos [...] justicia, amor misericordioso con los oprimidos, y reforzar las manos de los ansio[sos, para mostrar]

Columna XI

1 comprensión con los de espíritu extraviado, para instruir en la enseñanza a los que murmuran (MS: los que doblan), para responder (con) humildad al altivo de espíritu, y con espíritu contrito a los hombres

2 del palo, los que extienden el dedo, y hablan iniquidad, y son celosos de la riqueza. En cuanto a mí, en Dios está mi juicio; en su mano está la perfección de mi camino con la rectitud de mi corazón;

3 y por sus justicias borra mi pecado. Pues del manantial de su conocimiento ha abierto mi luz, y mis ojos han contemplado sus maravillas, y la luz de mi corazón el misterio

4 futuro. El que es por siempre es apoyo de mi mano derecha, el camino de mis pasos va sobre roca firme, no vacila ante nada. Pues la verdad de Dios es

5 roca de mis pasos, y su poder el apoyo de mi mano derecha. Del manantial de su justicia es mi juicio, y de su misterio maravilloso la luz en mi corazón.

6 Mis ojos han contemplado al que es por siempre, un saber que ha sido ocultado al ser humano, conocimiento y discreción prudente (ocultados) a los hijos de hombre, manantial de justicia y cisterna

7 de poder con una fuente de gloria (ocultados) a la asamblea de carne. A quienes Dios ha escogido, se las ha dado como posesión eterna; hace que las hereden en el lote

8 de los santos. El une su asamblea a los hijos de los cielos para (formar) el consejo de la comunidad y el fundamento de la construcción de santidad, para ser una plantación eterna durante todos

9 los tiempos futuros. Pero yo (pertenezco) a la humanidad impía, a la asamblea de la carne inicua; mis faltas, mis transgresiones, mis pecados, con las perversiones de mi corazón,

10 (pertenecen) a la asamblea de los gusanos y de quienes marchan en tinieblas. Pues al hombre (no le pertenece) su camino, ni al ser humano el afirmar su paso; puesto que el juicio (le pertenece) a Dios, y de su mano

11 viene la perfección del camino. Por su conocimiento existirá todo, y todo lo que existe es él el que lo asienta con sus cálculos, y nada se hace fuera de él. En cuanto a mí, si

12 yo tropiezo, las misericordias de Dios serán mi salvación por siempre; si yo caigo en pecado de carne, en la justicia de Dios, que permanece eternamente, estará mi juicio.

13 Si comienza mi aflicción él librará mi alma de la fosa y hará firmes mis pasos en el camino; me acercará por sus misericordias, y por sus gracias introducirá

14 mi juicio; me juzgará en la justicia de su verdad, y en la abundancia de su bondad expiará por siempre todos mis pecados; en su justicia me purificará de la impureza

15 del ser humano, y del pecado de los hijos de hombre, para que alabe a Dios por su justicia y al Altísimo por su majestad. ¡Bendito seas, Dios mío, que abres al conocimiento

16 el corazón de tu siervo! Haz firmes en la justicia todas sus obras, y alza al hijo de tu sierva para estar eternamente en tu presencia, como lo has querido para los elegidos de la humanidad.

17 Pues fuera de ti no hay camino perfecto, y sin tu voluntad nada se hace. Tú has enseñado

18 todo conocimiento, y todo lo que existe lo es por tu voluntad. Fuera de ti no hay nadie para oponerse a tu consejo, para comprender

19 ninguno de tus pensamientos santos, para asomarse al abismo de tus misterios, para entender todas tus maravillas o la fuerza

20 de tu poder. ¿Quién puede soportar tu gloria? ¿Qué es, en efecto, el hijo de hombre entre tus obras maravillosas?

21 ¿Por qué será contado el nacido de mujer en tu presencia? Formado ha sido en polvo, comida de gusanos será su residencia; es saliva escupida,

22 arcilla modelada, y al polvo (le lleva) su deseo. ¿Qué responderá la arcilla y el formado a mano? ¿Y qué consejo podrá él comprender?

CONTRIBUTORS

I. J. Borowsky, Founder and Chairman of the American Interfaith Institute, the World Alliance of Interfaith Organizations and the Liberty Museum has edited and published numerous books for the development of understanding among Christians and Jews.

J. H. Charlesworth, George L. Collord Professor of New Testament Language and Literature at Princeton Theological Seminary, is Editor of the PTS Dead Sea Scrolls Project. This project is publishing in ten volumes the critical text and translation of over 400 documents that were written by Jews from approximately the third century B.C.E. to the middle of the first century C.E. Charlesworth helped improve the critical text and prepared the translation to the *Rule of the Community* for the PTS Dead Sea Scrolls Project.

M. T. Davis, adjunct professor at New York Theological Seminary, is a Special Assistant to the Editor for the PTS Dead Sea Scrolls Project. He has contributed to the work related to the previously unpublished fragments of the *Rule of the Community* found in Cave 4.

J. Duhaime, Professor of Bible at the Université de Montréal contributed the text and translation of the *War Scroll* to the PTS Dead Sea Scrolls Project. He has written numerous literary and theological works on the Dead Sea Scrolls.

F. García Martínez, Professor of Intertestamental Literature at the State University in Groningen, The Netherlands, is Director of the Institute for the Dead Sea Scrolls at Groningen. He is Executive Secretary for the International Organization of Qumran Studies.

H. Lichtenberger, Professor of New Testament and Ancient Judaism at the Universität Tübingen, Tübingen, Germany. He is world renowned for his distinguished contributions to the Dead Sea Scrolls. He is contributing the critical text and translation to the *Thanksgiving Hymns* for the PTS Dead Sea Scrolls Project. With Charlesworth he chairs the *SNTS* Seminar on the Dead Sea Scrolls and Christian Origins.

E. Qimron, Professor of Bible at Ben Gurion University of the Negev in Israel, is an internationally renowned scholar who is celebrated for his numerous contributions to a better understanding of the Hebrew language, especially as represented in the Dead Sea Scrolls. He has contributed the critical text of the *Rule of the Community* for the PTS Dead Sea Scrolls Project.

H. W. Leathem Rietz, a doctoral candidate in New Testament and Early Judaism at Princeton Theological Seminary, is the Assistant Editor of the PTS Dead Sea Scrolls Project. He is also adjunct assistant professor at New Brunswick Theological Seminary.

P. Sacchi, Professor of Hebrew and Aramaic at the University of Turin, is the editor of the first complete Italian translation of the so-called Old Testament Pseudepigrapha. He has written extensively on Early Judaism and Christian Origins.

B. A. Strawn, a George S. Green Fellow in Old Testament/Hebrew Bible at Princeton Theological Seminary, is an Assistant to the Editor on the PTS Dead Sea Scrolls Project.

148

PRODUCTION NOTES

Designed by Irvin J. Borowsky
Assisted by Albert Gaspari
Proofread by Dana Lang.

Color separations by Prep Services, Inc.
Printed by Consolidated Drake Press
and bound by Hoster Bindery.

Choice of typeface, page layout and illustrations modified
by Nancy O. Grossman.

Printed on 110 lb. Eloquence,
an acid-free museum reproduction paper by Potlatch.